SHAKESPEARE'S GLOBE
REBUILT

SHAKESPEARE'S GLOBE REBUILT

Edited by
J.R.MULRYNE AND MARGARET SHEWRING

Advisory Editor
ANDREW GURR

CAMBRIDGE
in association with
MULRYNE & SHEWRING

PUBLISHED BY THE PRESS SYNDICATE OF THE UNIVERSITY OF CAMBRIDGE
The Pitt Building, Trumpington Street, Cambridge CB2 1RP, United Kingdom
In Association with MULRYNE AND SHEWRING LTD

CAMBRIDGE UNIVERSITY PRESS
The Edinburgh Building, Cambridge CB2 2RU, United Kingdom
40 West 20TH Street, New York, NY 10011–4211, USA
10 Stamford Street, Oakleigh, Melbourne 3166, Australia

First Published 1997

A catalogue record for this book is available fom the British Library

ISBN 0 521 59019 1 (hardback)
ISBN 0 521 59988 1 (paperback)

Designed, produced and typeset by
A.H. JOLLY (EDITORIAL) LTD
Yelvertoft Manor, Northamptonshire NN6 7LF

Printed in Great Britain by
Clifford Press Ltd. Coventry

Front Cover Illustration: David Spilman
Back Cover Illustration: Pentagram Design

CONTENTS

LIST OF ILLUSTRATIONS

Colour Plates

Figures

ABOVE: Sam Wanamaker CBE (1919–1993) (*Photo: Brian Rybolt*)

LEFT: Theo Crosby (1925–1994), Architect of the Globe (*Photo: Pentagram Design*)

PREFACE

Shakespeare's Globe Rebuilt pays tribute to the many years of research and practical endeavour that have gone into one of the most imaginative projects of recent decades. The initiative that brought the project into being, and sustained it through most of its often difficult years, was that of Sam Wanamaker CBE, a man of vision, integrity and determination. A gifted actor on stage and screen, and a director of rare insight, he brought to the project not only a passionate belief in its rightness and timeliness, but also an understanding and sensitivity possible only to a remarkable man of the theatre. The completion of the project, which this book salutes, came after his death, but it remains his achievement.

Wanamaker's co-worker for many years was Theo Crosby, architect and visionary, who also sadly died just before the work came to fruition. Without Theo's inspiration, skill and generosity of spirit, the project could not have been completed. *Shakespeare's Globe Rebuilt* acknowledges this fact both by way of direct reference, and through the chapters written for it by Crosby's associate and successor as architect to the project, Jon Greenfield. Crosby's firm, Pentagram Design Ltd., has made an incalculable contribution to the success of the Globe rebuilding, and has remained generous in supporting this book.

We have incurred many debts in editing and drawing the book together. We are deeply grateful to Andrew Gurr, our advisory editor, for support and encouragement, and for scholarly advice. John Orrell not only contributed to the book but read it throughout, and saved us from a number of errors. Many of those who work for the International Shakespeare Globe Centre assisted us with practical help, advice and sometimes admonition: Michael Holden, Patrick Spottiswoode, Tiffany Foster, Lucy Beevor, Jane Arrowsmith and Phil Robins. Colleagues at the University of Warwick have been unstinting in coming to our aid when time ran out or scholarship failed: Jane Stevenson, Peter Davidson, Pauline Wilson and Alison Cressey. Siobhan Keenan went far beyond her role as unpaid research assistant, giving very generously of her time and scholarship. Dr Peter Addyman, Director of the York Archaeological Trust, and Dr Nat Alcock of the University of Warwick gave us valued advice on matters associated with timber framing. Our M.A. and doctoral students in the Centre for the Study of the Renaissance were tolerant of the diversion of our energies for too long a period, and helped with suggestions and comments.

We should like to offer especial thanks to those who wrote chapters for the book. All showed resilience and good humour in coping with repeated requests for revision, when time was short and their own commitments pressing. Peter McCurdy, whose knowledge and practical skill made possible one of the chapters, has been most helpful in allowing us to learn something, however limited, about the craft of timber-framing. Simon Blatherwick has taught us about archaeology and John Ronayne about Elizabethan decoration and iconography. Editing the book has been for us a learning experience, both in terms of knowledge gained and in appreciation of the generosity of fellow-scholars in a range of specialisms.

A very great debt is owed to Mr Alec Jolly, who has seen this book through a difficult and necessarily hasty printing process with his usual good humour, interest and skill. In this he has been most ably assisted by Jane Martin. Sarah Stanton at Cambridge University Press has been tolerant, helpful and wonderfully trusting. Our families have endured, once again, a protracted period when the demands of the book have at times taken priority over our other commitments. We should like to thank Eithne, John, James, Richard and Evelyn for their severely tried understanding.

R.M. M.S.
March 1997

NOTE ON THE SPELLING OF ELIZABETHAN NAMES

Elizabethan orthography is notoriously variable, especially in the spelling of proper names. We have chosen to regularise the spelling of Peter Streete, but to permit variations in the spelling of other names such as Wenceslaus or Wenceslas Hollar, and Aernout or Ahrend or Arend van Buchell (or Buchel).

ACKNOWLEDGEMENTS

English Heritage: plates 15, 22
The Folger Shakespeare Library, Washington D.C.: fig. 6
Tiffany Foster: plate 11
Andrew Fulgoni: fig. 10
The Guildhall Library, London: figs 3, 4, 7, 23–25
Richard Kalina: plates 28, 29
Peter McCurdy: plate 4
The Vicar and Churchwardens, St Mary's, Langley Marish: fig. 56, plate 14
Museum of London Archaeology Service (MOLAS): figs 11, 12, 21–26
The National Trust: plates 16, 19, 20
Ordnance Survey, Crown Copyright: figs 21, 22
Pentagram Design: figs 9, 13, 14, 17, 18, 27–49, plates 1–3, 6, 21, 24–27
University of Reading: plates 5, 7–9
Brett Robertson: fig. 63
John Ronayne: figs. 56–58, 60, 61, plates 12–18, 22, 23
Royal Library, Stockholm: figs 19, 20
John Tramper: fig. 64, plates 30, 31
Bibliotheek der Rijksuniversiteit, Utrecht: figs 2, 5
Victoria and Albert Museum, Department of Prints, Drawings and Photographs: figs 50–55, 57–60, plates 12, 17, 18
Roy Waterson for the International Shakespeare Globe Centre: fig. 16
The Provost and Fellows of Worcester College, Oxford: fig. 15
The Yale Center for British Art, Paul Mellon Collection: fig. 8

PART ONE

PAST AND PRESENT

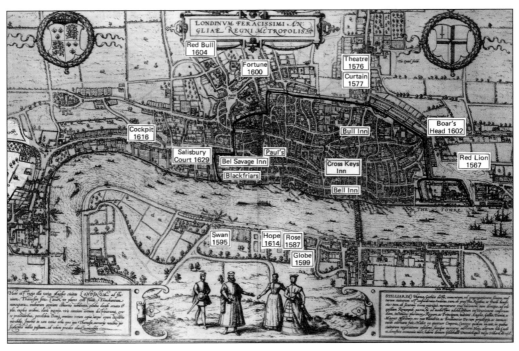

Fig. 1 The location of the London playhouses shown on a contemporary map

❦ I ❦

THE ONCE AND FUTURE GLOBE

Ronnie Mulryne and Margaret Shewring

THE TITLE OF the present book, *Shakespeare's Globe Rebuilt*, is in various ways misleading. The playhouse to which it refers is not *Shakespeare's* Globe. The Elizabethan Shakespeare contributed no more than one element to a collaborative enterprise which took in business interests and performance and organisational skills without which his abounding genius could not have found expression. He was not the owner of the Globe, though he shared in its ownership.[1] His plays were not, all of them, written for the Globe, though from 1599 to 1613, the years of the first playhouse of that name, he had something of the character of resident playwright with the company who performed there. Nor has the original Globe been rebuilt. *Shakespeare's Globe Rebuilt* stands as the title for and expression of an unattainable ideal. As a book it is the record of many years of the most committed academic and practical scholarship which, despite its scruple, knowledge and industry, has had to resort in matters large and small to inference and compromise, in order to ensure the construction of the playhouse which now stands in Southwark. No-one writing here, and no-one associated with the large-scale enterprise that has grown from Sam Wanamaker's passionate advocacy, will contend otherwise.

No doubt the designation of the new playhouse and indeed the whole enterprise it represents and has spawned (including this book) derive from and are dependent upon the cultural authority, the financial leverage and the world-wide currency of Shakespeare's name. In that sense, at least, the building and its activities may truly be labelled Shakespeare's Globe. It is also the case that the Elizabethan Globe depended in large measure for its commercial survival and success on plays of Shakespeare's authorship. Of the twenty-nine extant plays confidently thought to have been written for the Globe up to 1608, fifteen are Shakespeare's, and a further six of those performed there (over and above the twenty-nine) were revivals of Shakespeare pieces written before 1599. Other plays that have not come down to us were certainly performed at the Globe, and the more of these there were, the more Shakespeare's proportionate contribution shrinks. Nevertheless, it must remain an overwhelmingly significant one. In this respect too, therefore, the naming of Shakespeare's Globe is apt. Yet the tension between Shakespeare's role in the Globe's Elizabethan success and his role at the new Globe remains an acute one, even if the tension is concealed by the use of the same name for both. Shakespeare then is not Shakespeare now. Going to the Globe is bound to be for its modern audience an exercise in double vision, present and past.

The Elizabethan theatre-scene to which Shakespeare contributed was a crowded one, even if the City and sometimes the Court attempted through pressure, censorship and legislation to limit its extent and its influence.[2] It has been calculated that, at a conservative estimate, two thousand plays were written and performed in the period between 1590 and 1642.[3] In the absence of other public voices – the pulpit and the book were the only competing media – the playhouse took on the role of shaping and moving people's minds in a way only faintly echoed by theatre today. But the voracious appetite of the playhouses, comparable to that of television now, was stimulated much less by thoughts of political and social influence than by commercial hopes and fears, as documents gathered at the end of this book confirm. Theatre and theatre buildings were business, and politics and creative genius had to make their way through channels opened up by financial success. The playhouses, including the Globe, had to appeal to their audiences and had to accommodate them in a manner likely to attract them to come again. For the modern playgoer, aspects of the rebuilt Globe will seem, certainly at first, *un*attractive. The open air yard at the heart of the building will not strike today's audiences as providing the ideal circumstances for watching theatre, though until very recently football crowds would have thought it odd to watch that particular sport under cover. The analogy is not an idle one, for something of the same blend of commerce and entertainment relates to both activities. The fact that one of the early theatres (the Hope) doubled as a bear-baiting arena only confirms the parallel, at least through the shared practices and habits-of-mind of competitive sport. The *absences* of the rebuilt auditorium will also strike most spectators as odd: no stage lighting, no sound system, no setting (or very little). The decoration of the playhouse, which many will find over-elaborate and even gaudy, accords with Elizabethan taste and visual habits rather than modern, and will be a constant reminder of the cultural otherness of the plays performed within it. Indeed, almost every aspect of the rebuilt playhouse will speak boldly of the distance between today's theatre and the theatre of Elizabethan London. This will be true whether we are talking about the seating arrangements or about the place held by theatre in the communal life of the day. The question to be addressed is whether, despite this distance, the plays performed at the new Globe will make themselves heard in our time. Or, a more ambitious aim, whether they will speak even louder because the circumstances of their performance, in so far as these circumstances can be recreated, accord with the writing practices and performance assumptions of Shakespeare and his contemporaries. It is this latter aim that has implicitly animated the quest for authentic reconstruction, and has driven so much scholarship and so much practical research and experiment towards the goal of the rebuilt Globe.

It is sometimes thought that the Globe typifies the theatre spaces of Shakespeare's England. Recent research has demonstrated what should have been understood as a truism, namely that even among the arena theatre-type to which the Globe belongs there was in reality wide variation in size and structural arrangements. Archaeological investigation of the Rose, the Globe's near neighbour, shows not only that the playhouse was much smaller than we believe the Globe to have been, but that it was adapted in the course of its life in regard both to stage configuration and audience capacity. (*See* the chapter by Simon Blatherwick *below*.) The Swan, another example of the same theatre-type, and the only one for which we have a contemporary sketch of the interior (*see* fig. 5, p. 29) apparently had a quite different 'heavens' (or stage-cover), and possibly different entrance and exit arrangements than we believe was the case at the Globe. Some of the theatres had no stage-cover at all. These are important matters, so far as performance conditions are concerned, and there

FIG. 2 *The View of the Cittye of London from the North towards the Sowth* (>1599), detail showing the Theatre

are others, such as the extent, height and shape of the stage, the position of the stage-pillars – where they existed – and the carpentry and decoration of the *scenae frons* (or scenic wall) that must have differed, perhaps widely, from playhouse to playhouse. The question that arises is the justification for rebuilding the Globe to such exacting standards of accuracy (wherever possible) when other playing places used by Shakespeare and his fellows were different in so many respects. The question is made more acute by evidence that Shakespeare's company, the Chamberlain's Men, would have strongly preferred to move to the indoor Blackfriars theatre when they were forced by opposition from neighbours of the Blackfriars to abandon that plan and make the move across the Thames to the Globe.[4] The Inigo Jones theatre in the current Globe development takes its origin in part from the acknowledgment that an indoor space, built in the seventeenth-century way, also affords playing conditions appropriate to the presentation of Shakespeare's work and that of his contemporaries. Yet the fact is that a major part of the Shakespearean repertory was written for the original Globe, even if through what seems almost an historical accident. The re-creation of its playing conditions, as closely as evidence and modern regulations allow, offers us the only defensible path in the rebuilding experiment. Once swerve from the aim of exactness and authenticity and the result will be compromise, muddle and mish-mash. The Globe was the playhouse for which Shakespeare imagined some of his greatest plays, and its rebuilding affords the opportunity to situate them once more in conditions (spatial, visual and acoustic) akin to those he held in his mind's eye while writing.

The Globe stands at a crucial turning point in the history of Elizabethan playhouse-building. It also sums up in its fabric the past of playhouse construction and forecasts the future. As the successor of the playhouse called the Theatre, making use of timbers from that building, the Globe can be thought of as drawing into itself the essential features of playhouse construction, almost from the first experiments in that building type (fig. 1). As the playhouse that deeply influenced the design of the Fortune, built in 1600 (*see* the chapter by John Orrell below, especially pp. 52–3, and the Fortune contract reprinted among the documents at the end of this book), the Globe can be considered to look equally towards the future. So in this perspective also, the Globe serves as the appropriate playhouse to rebuild as a representative Elizabethan theatre-space. It can in addition serve as the appropriate expression of the success, commercial and artistic, of the playhouses of the period. As 'the symbol of an entire art', in Bernard Beckerman's words, the construction of the Globe 'initiated a glorious decade during which the company achieved a level of stability and a quality of productivity rarely matched in the history of theater.'[5] The years immediately preceding and following its opening, from 1595 to 1604, were marked, as Andrew Gurr has noted, by an oversupply of the type of amphitheatre playhouse to which the Globe belonged.[6] James Burbage had already refurbished the Theatre, and Henslowe enlarged the Rose (in 1592), while new playhouses were now being built (or in the case of the Globe *rebuilt*) in what for the period were remarkable numbers: the Swan (1595), the Globe (1599), the Fortune (1600), the Boar's Head (1599; 1600) and the Red Bull (by 1604). In the competitive circumstances thus created, only the Globe, the Fortune and the downmarket Red Bull were genuine successes. Once again, given the achievement of its greatest playwright, and what we must infer was the excellence of its acting company, the Globe offers itself as the theatre to reconstruct in our time.

A glance at the map of Elizabethan London (fig. 2) shows the amphitheatre playhouses (in contrast to the city inns and the indoor playhouses) distributed around the periphery of the city, outside the city walls. The establishment of the Globe on Bankside, to the south of the river, confirmed the playhouse-builders' recognition that, whatever their wishes might be for social advancement, and for a more socially-elevated locality for their playhouse, current political conditions and public opinion would not easily allow it. The first playhouses were built to the north and east of the city, outside city jurisdiction. The subsequent cluster of amphitheatres on Bankside, also outside the city's writ, reinforced what was already an entertainment ghetto of considerable extent. Animal baiting and other bloodsports joined in this area with brothels to give the place a feisty reputation (fig. 3). As Roy Porter notes, on Bankside, in the borough of Southwark, 'disorderly behaviour, if not exactly licensed, was borne with a certain resignation', though that resignation did not extend to tolerance, since the area hosted no fewer than five prisons.[7] It was also a place of inns and hostelries, being the area where the roads to and from Sussex, Surrey and Kent came together and an area of workshops, tanneries, soapyards, breweries and lumber yards. Altogether, Bankside and Southwark were known as a bustling unfashionable locality, and the site of activities of which modern residents might not be entirely proud. It was also the home of a noteworthy artistic community.[8] While we cannot know in any detail the composition of the Elizabethan Globe's audience, and while some, including many of the socially better elements, will certainly have come from across the Thames – to the profit of the watermen – many of the spectators must have felt that in attending the Globe they were engaging in an activity which if not exactly *risque* was certainly not a manifestation of

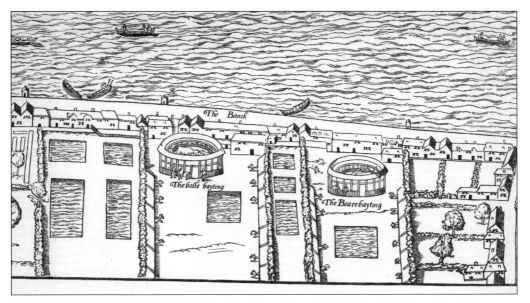

FIG. 3 *Civitas Londinium* (the so-called 'Agas' map), detail of Bankside prior to the building of the Globe

unalloyed high culture, in the way that attendance at mainstream theatre is understood today. Much has recently been made of the topographically marginal placing of Elizabethan playhouses, as an index of their socio-political marginality and potential for subversion, in the minds of London audiences if not more widely. It is an easy matter to exaggerate, and exaggeration has not always been resisted. Yet this is undoubtedly one aspect of the cultural role of the Elizabethan Globe which the rebuilt theatre will not be able to replicate. The new theatre will have attached to it assumptions placing it within educational and tourist agendas at variance with those of its Elizabethan predecessor. Such agendas will have to be embraced, or submerged, by the professional excellence of the performances if the new Globe is to thrive. Perhaps it is some comfort that even today Southwark retains memories of its sturdy unfashionableness, too far along the South Bank from the Festival Hall and the National Theatre to figure as part of London's culture industry. How long it will retain this unprivileged position, given the development of the Bankside Tate, the Thames pedestrian walkway and the proposed footbridge across the river, is a matter for speculation. So far as tourist interest is concerned, a wiredrawn comfort might be that almost all the descriptions we have of Elizabethan playhouses were penned by visiting foreigners. Even in Shakespeare's day the London playhouses figured as a tourist attraction.

The busyness of the Elizabethan theatre spilled over into performance spaces well beyond the amphitheatre playhouses such as the Globe, or indoor playhouses like the Blackfriars. When the earliest amphitheatres (the Red Lion, 1567, and the Theatre, 1576) were brought into use, professional playing was already a long-established craft employing a multiplicity of performance venues. College halls and the communal rooms of great houses, city inns (the Cross Keys and the Bel Savage for example) and the lawyers' Inns of Court (Gray's Inn for instance and the Middle Temple), churches, guildhalls, streets and market places and many more were all pressed into service. After the new amphitheatres were available, the overspill continued, with performances taking place in all of the public venues just summarised (except for the city inns, where playing was stopped after 1595) as well as in more settled circumstances during command performances at Court (a recognition vital to the prestige even more than the financial well-being of the companies), and on tour. It is often forgotten that the Elizabethan companies, including those with which Shakespeare was associated, spent long periods on the road, driven out of their London venues by plague – the theatres were closed when plague deaths reached forty per week – or by restraints on playing of one sort or another. Touring on the European mainland, even, was far from unknown among professional players of the period, including some of the most successful, and involving at least a splinter group from a company as celebrated as the Lord Admiral's.[9] Adaptability to varying performance spaces must have been the hallmark of the Elizabethan actor, and the Elizabethan script. If we are to understand the performance opportunities offered by rebuilding the Globe we must do so while recognising the readiness of the Elizabethan actor to devise ways of turning to account the facilities, and the absences, of the playhouse, in a manner learned from touring to diverse and often highly informal venues. Too strict an accounting of the features of the playhouse will result only in a failure to recognise the actor's improvisational skills, now as well as then. Undoubtedly a performance lexicon responding to the architecture of stage and auditorium must have built up at the original Globe, in the context of the remarkably stable acting company that played it. It may be possible to re-invent the terms of this lexicon, or translate them into other terms, if the rebuilt Globe can attract and retain a company as talented and unchanging as the company for which Shakespeare wrote, and within which he worked.[10] This is not just a matter of company 'style', though the conventions and abbreviations gestured towards in that term are a part of what we mean. This style, together with the recognition of individual actors and individual skills, will play a part in giving solidity to the new venture, as they must have done to the original one, as hints in Shakespeare's scripts and the scripts of other playwrights suggest.

Today's audience will, it is true, make the achievement of such a goal difficult. The expected international and tourist elements of the audience will tell against continuity and recognition, though it may be hoped that a core of playgoers within reasonable travel distance will begin to learn what the Globe and its company have to tell us about early plays (and perhaps more recent). What is less open to dispute is that today's actors are equipped, by experience and inclination, to discover what the distinctive playing conditions of the Globe have to offer in giving voice to the plays performed there. It is more than a hundred years since actors began to experiment with theatre space as an element in the animation of scripts, on the European mainland in Antoine's *Théâtre Libre*, for instance, or in the work of Reinhardt or Jarry, as well as, partly in imitation, in England. Even more, the last forty years have seen in Britain a multitude of explorations of theatre venues from the smallest basement or pub theatre through studios and courtyard playhouses to found spaces and outdoor installations. And all this in addition to the construction of more established venues which have contributed to the overthrow of the proscenium arch, such as the Manchester Royal Exchange or, in a different sense, the Olivier (at the National Theatre) or the Stratford-on-Avon Swan.[11] Actors are nowadays fully accustomed to responding to the language of theatre space as an essential element in their performance vocabulary. It might indeed be argued, without serious overstatement, that today's actors belong to the first generation equipped with the improvisatory skills, in relation to space, of their Elizabethan precursors, even if the dominance of film and television have unfitted some for the outgoing performance-techniques demanded by an auditorium as large as the Globe. The discoveries of the work-shop and prologue seasons in the unfinished playhouse have at least given cause to hope that the rich possibilities of the space will be opened up when a resident company has in due time explored them fully and incorporated them into their playing.

If we were to ask what further potentialities the new Globe will offer for re-discovery, the most evident must be a stage-audience relationship conditioned by both proximity and distance. Referring to the Royal Shakespeare Company's Swan Theatre at Stratford-on-Avon, a three-galleried courtyard-type space constructed predominantly of oak, with a deep thrust stage, the actor Brian Cox spoke of its ability to blend the epic and the intimate.[12] Something of the same sort might be said about the Globe, though the terms need modification to allow for the anti-illusionistic effect of the daylight auditorium. Where the Swan uses the full range of modern stage lighting, on the Globe stage the actor is exposed, not only by his three-dimensional presence within an embracing range of galleries, but as a result of sharing the same visual space with his audience, unmodified by the conditioning effects of illusionistic lighting. The stage at the Globe is high (about five feet), thus clearly separating the actor from the spectator. Yet the stage cannot be said to be a privileged space, except in a limited sense. The results for the player and the audience are numerous. At the most obvious end of the spectrum, interplay between stage and auditorium is encouraged and made easy. The backchat between Launce and the spectators, amusingly abetted by Launce's dog, in the prologue season's *The Two Gentlemen of Verona*, was one of the enlivening elements of the production. No doubt there is a boundary to be learned and observed here, as Shakespeare seems to suggest in Hamlet's remarks to the players, directing the clown to speak no more than is set down for him — remarks that followed the departure from the company of the extemporising Kemp, to be replaced by the more contained Armin. But other more subtle and elusive effects remain to be learned on the Globe stage, such as sharing the same visual space with Macbeth's murderous self-communing — and murderous action — or the tragic loading of Othello's bed. Perhaps it may be said that in the contemporary theatre we have already discovered something of these effects in outdoor productions, or in a studio production such as Trevor Nunn's famous *Macbeth*. Yet there are usually devices of one kind or another even in the most experimental production to separate audience from stage. At the Globe, the separation will be in terms of costume and gesture and sometimes voice, significant elements of performance to be sure, but by no means cancelling the kind of naturalism that goes with proximity and daylight. Yet this intimacy, for all its importance as an element of the experience, is qualified at the rebuilt Globe by the epic scale of the place and the presence (ideally) of a full house of spectators — even if their number in the modern playhouse is no more than 1400, as compared with the 3000 spoken of in early reports. Elizabethan reaction to the playhouses emphasised how sumptuous they seemed, with words such as gorgeous and stately routinely applied to the outdoor amphitheatres. The traveller Thomas Coryat, to take a representative case, derided the Venetian playhouses in a publication of 1611 as 'very beggarly and base in comparison of our stately play-houses in England'.[13] The scale and the sumptuous decoration (a telling matter, this) of the rebuilt

Globe will undoubtedly affect an audience's reading of the stage-spectacle, giving it an aspect, if not of the epic, at least of the imposing and grand. Events taking place before the carved and painted *scenae frons*, between marbled and embellished pillars, and under a lavishly decorated heavens (or stage roof) will be read, in performances of the more serious scripts at any rate, as being of momentous significance. In Shakespeare's case, the characteristically exotic locations of the comedies will also seem aptly continuous with the elaborate decor.

There are other features of watching plays in the rebuilt theatre that will affect the total experience. A member of the audience will be acutely conscious in this daylight playhouse of all the other audience members – not unlike a football crowd again – including those who come to be seen as well as to see, sitting in the Lords' rooms or Gentlemen's rooms. He or she will be caught up in an audience's common reactions, when the alchemy of the occasion successfully draws the watching spectators together. A laugh or a gasp, or for that matter a hoot of derision, runs round an amphitheatre or courtyard theatre with a readiness and vigour that in a proscenium house it does not. We have become accustomed in modern playhouses, from the Edinburgh Traverse or The Other Place at Stratford on Avon to the National Theatre's Cottesloe, to seeing our fellow spectators. At first this induces a degree of self-consciousness, even alienation. Then the sense of common purpose and common enjoyment blots out the discomfort. But not without leaving a residue of detachment, as audience members with quirkish habits or outlandish clothing claim our attention. The Elizabethan spectators, with their experience of theatre firmly grounded in fairground performance or touring fit-ups, were fully accustomed to this kind of fragile attentiveness, no doubt exacerbated for those standing in the playhouse yard by jostling among their fellow groundlings and, perhaps, if report runs true, by commercial and even amatory activity. We are not so accustomed. John Russell Brown has written convincingly of the need for the Elizabethan actor to *take over* his audience by the sheer power of his language and the sheer vigour of his performance.[14] When this was successful the outcome must have been magical. Shakespeare felt bold enough to have his Paulina say to the stage-audience (but equally to the playhouse-audience), as she unveiled the statue of Hermione, (*The Winter's Tale*, V. iii. 21; given at the Globe 15 May 1611) 'I like your silence'. But not infrequently the audience must have been distracted and restless.[15] It will be a fascinating matter to see how actors of the rebuilt Globe learn to play upon the imaginations of their audience. We may well learn a good deal from them not only about the tactics of audience engagement but also about that elusive matter, the rhythms of the Shakespearean script.

Bernard Beckerman has written that the Globe 'was a theater built by actors for actors'.[16] Even if one may quibble with the detail of this (Richard Burbage was an actor, but his brother Cuthbert was not, and their father James, the builder of the original Theatre, became principally an impressario) in spirit it is right. The success or otherwise of the new Globe will depend upon the actors' discovery of how to tune their performance in all its aspects, visual and aural, to the conditions of the rebuilt playhouse. Yet the audience has its part to play too, especially given that actors and audience share at the Globe the same visual space. But here problems that go close to the heart of the enterprise begin to make themselves apparent. The modern actor cannot turn himself into the Elizabethan actor, however adaptable he may be. Even if we knew a great deal more about Elizabethan performance techniques – and we know very little indeed – too much theatre-history, and television and cinema, have come between then and now to make a pastiche of Elizabethan acting tolerable or even accessible. The dead hand of museum culture would strangle the attempt at birth. It is true that the most evident contrast between Elizabethan and modern performance, the Elizabethan use of boys in female roles (and the remarkable plays written for, and the notable success of, the Elizabethan boy companies, with all the roles played by boys) may not be the stumbling-block it has sometimes seemed. The new Globe, in its unfinished state, has already presented Richard Edwards's *Damon and Pythias*, a play of the 1560s written by the Master of the Chapel Royal for his choirboys, using on the modern stage an all-female cast. The result was to throw into relief some of the dislocation between performer and role of which an Elizabethan audience must have been conscious, and with which Shakespeare worked in, for example, *As You Like It*.[17] Yet the modern actor must feel the artificiality of such performances, even when they result in full or modified success. With the audience, the case is even more patent. Today's audience cannot be an Elizabethan audience, for reasons that stretch from cultural knowledge to physical size, and take in, for the Globe, the celebrity and touristic status of the new enterprise and its sponsoring dramatist. Terence Hawkes has written entertainingly on his reservations about the rebuilding of the Globe, giving a wry voice to objections that are shared by many less sophisticated commentators. Hawkes senses a tension between the accuracy aimed at in the rebuilding and the cultural distance that separates modern audiences from Elizabethan. 'The new Globe', he writes, 'can never take on the role of the old one because that culture has irretrievably gone', giving as his compelling instance the proximity to the high culture of the Elizabethan playhouse of the cruelty of the animal-baiting arena a few yards away on Bankside. The erroneous labelling of the Globe as 'Beere bayting' in the Hollar engraving merely gives fortuitous expression, he argues, to the similar physical frame and the shared frame of reference of the two structures (*see* fig. 7, p. 37). 'We have to accept,' Hawkes asserts, 'that the audience which responded intelligently and with sensitivity to, say, *A Midsummer Night's Dream*, or *Hamlet* or *King Lear*, and thus made those creations possible, was also an audience which liked to see a blind and screaming Harry Hunks [the bear] whipped until he bled.' Hawkes protests that the claimed 'universality' and timelessness of Shakespeare are not universal at all, but on the contrary 'clearly derive from and are responsive to a particular time and place'. He is sceptical, in fact, that Shakespeare's Elizabethan sensibility can speak across the intervening divide to modern spectators, much less to the international audience the new Globe confidently expects.[18]

Hawkes is, at least in part, right. There is a tension between the attempted, if modified, accuracy of the playhouse reconstruction, and the acknowledged distance between Shakespeare's world and ours. Yet the analysis is a superficial one. Every performance of a classic play represents a negotiation between now and then, and the creation of an always imperfect liaison between our sensibility (in so far as that can be thought of as uniform) and theirs. Jonathan Miller's *Subsequent Performances*[19] valuably explores the 'after-life' of a play, its record of re-enactments in different playhouses, at different historical periods and by different actors, as constituting an authenticity of performance that is always varying and never complete. Theatre performances, we might say, represent (re)discoveries of potential meanings encoded in a given script, in response to cultural conditions accessible to us only because they are points in a history that is also ours. Every performance records continuity as well as distance. Playing *King Lear* offers a recollection of our past as well as an acknowledgment of our present – a past in which it would be unsurprising to discover, in that play especially, remnants of the cruelties suffered by Harry Hunks. To play *King Lear* at a rebuilt Globe is to call to an audience's mind, by spatial and visual means as well as verbal, a world now gone but nevertheless, even if changed, also accessible through the scripts of its plays. The reminder of the past is especially strong at the Globe, in comparison to auditoria that have sprung from more recent architectural and theatrical conventions. Yet reminiscence, if the performances are sufficiently strong, will not swamp currency, but rather provide the circumstances for a richer history in which both terms participate. This book offers a record of the endeavours of specialist scholars who have sought over many years to make the liaison between the two terms as firmly grounded and fruitful as evidence and regulations allow.

It was Sir Peter Hall who wrote in his diary in May 1975, on visiting the ancient Greek theatre at Epidaurus:

> My first introduction to the great theatre at Epidaurus. I was overwhelmed by it. The whole day was unforgettable. It's exactly as if someone had said to me, 'The Globe has after all been preserved on the South Bank, come over and have a look at it, then you might understand something about staging Shakespeare'.[20]

That opportunity now exists, as authentically as scholarship and craftsmanship can contrive. We may hope the outcome for the staging of Shakespeare will be as fruitful as Hall desired.

Notes to Chapter One

1   Andrew Gurr, *The Shakespearean Stage* (3rd., ed., Cambridge, 1992), pp. 44, 45.

2   *See*, e.g., Janet Clare, '*Art made tongue-tied by authority*' *Elizabethan and Jacobean Dramatic Censorship* (Manchester, 1990), Richard Dutton, *Mastering the Revels: The Regulation and Censorship of English Renaissance Drama* (London, 1991) and Peter Thomson *Shakespeare's Theatre* (London, 1983), p. 3.

3   G.E. Bentley, quoted in Peter Thomson, *op. cit.*, p. 56.

4   *See* Glynne Wickham, *Early English Stages* II (London, 1963) pt.i, p. 157: 'however surprising it may seem ... the professional acting companies had a marked preference throughout the whole hundred-year period for indoor performance'.

5   Bernard Beckerman, *Shakespeare at the Globe, 1599–1609* (New York, 1962), p. ix.

6   Gurr, *Shakespearean Stage*, p. 120.

7   Roy Porter, *London, a Social History* (London, 1994), p. 56.

8   Jean Wilson, 'This Grave shall have a living monument: Shakespeare's Globe and the Southwark Sculptors' in *Around the Globe: the Magazine of the International Shakespeare Globe Centre*, Winter 1996, p. 14, suggests that 'Southwark was also Elizabethan London's equivalent of Paris's Left Bank, not only in its sleaziness, but in providing a home for many artists, often of foreign origin; the atmosphere must not only have been louche but cosmopolitan and intellectual'.

9   *See* Jerzy Limon, *Gentlemen of a Company: English Players in Central and Eastern Europe 1590–1660* (Cambridge, 1985), *passim*.

10 One notable implicit feature of Shakespeare's scripts is that he was able to cast in depth, in contrast for example to the Admiral's Men when they were presenting Marlowe, where the scripts require high-level performance from two or three actors only.

11 *See* J.R. Mulryne and Margaret Shewring, *This Golden Round* (Stratford-on-Avon, 1989) and *Making Space for Theatre: British Architecture and Theatre since 1958* (Stratford-on-Avon, 1996).

12 *See This Golden Round*, p. 117.

13 Quoted in C.Walter Hodges, *The Globe Restored* (2nd. ed., Oxford, 1968), p. 67.

14 John Russell Brown, *Free Shakespeare* (London, 1974), p. 51

15 Brown, *op. cit.*, p. 48.

16 Beckerman, *op. cit.* in note 5, p. ix.

17 *See* Rosalind King, 'A Chain of True Friendship' in *Around the Globe*, Winter, 1996, p. 8.

18 Terence Hawkes, 'Harry Hunks, Superstar' in *Around the Globe*, Autumn 1996, pp. 12–13.

19 London, 1986, *passim*.

20 John Goodwin, ed., *Peter Hall's Diaries* (London, 1983), entry for 19 May 1975.

FIG. 4 Detail from an engraving of London published by Claes Jan Visscher in Amsterdam in 1616.

❧ 2 ❧

SHAKESPEARE'S GLOBE

A HISTORY OF RECONSTRUCTIONS AND
SOME REASONS FOR TRYING

Andrew Gurr

A Brief History of Attempts to Reconstruct a Globe

Ever since people began to realise how different the open-air Shakespearean theatres were from modern theatres attempts have been made to reconstruct them. Most reconstructions only lived on paper. Through the last two hundred years, though, more than twenty physical reconstructions have been launched. Today we have ten or more versions of the Globe and the Fortune around the world, done with varying degrees of faithfulness. Five are in the USA, two in Japan, one in Germany, one in Australia, and at last one is in the UK.

Edmond Malone started the long voyage in quest of what the Globe was like in 1790. In the first substantial account of the original conditions for which Shakespeare wrote his plays, he identified the Globe as a tall circuit of galleries, probably six-sided, capable of holding over a thousand spectators. Malone was the first scholar to get access to Edward Alleyn's papers about his and his father-in-law Philip Henslowe's work at Shakespeare's neighbour theatres the Rose and the Fortune. They were archived at Alleyn's foundation, Dulwich College, and came to light just as Malone was launching his edition of Shakespeare and his first set of studies into the early theatres.

What exactly led Malone to his idea of the six-sided shape, besides Cornelius Visscher's engraving of 1616 which showed the Globe as a tall octagon, we cannot be sure. But he was an eminently respected antiquarian, whose work appeared at the height of scholarly enthusiasm for rediscovering the material details of English history. A supreme and on the whole only moderately irritable reacher after historical fact and reason, he made theatre history and serious study of the lost traditions not only a respectable scholarly activity but a practicable one. The marriage between antiquarian study of old manuscripts and the magic of Shakespeare's plays in modern theatres proved to be a fertile union. We are its direct descendants.

The idea that a reconstruction of the original design might be useful to both historians and actors of Shakespeare did not take long to emerge once Malone set out his stall. First with the idea was the German scholar and translator of Shakespeare Ludwig Tieck. He saw Malone's books and the Henslowe papers when he visited London in 1817. In the 1830s he proposed to use the specifications found in the original builder's contract for the Fortune, surviving in the Henslowe papers, for a theatre he wanted to build in Dresden. (*See* pp. 180–2 *below*.) Tieck and his great colleague Schlegel were then busy completing their unique translations of the Shakespeare *oeuvre*. It seemed a logical extension of this work of translation to re-create one of the original theatres for which the plays were written. Plans were made, based on the dimensions provided in the Henslowe contract, to a design by the architect of the new Dresden Opera House, Gottfried Semper.

Like most subsequent visions of this kind, Tieck's scheme did not secure much financial backing, and never went beyond the drawing-board. But the fact that the idea of making a tangible replica of Shakespeare's peculiar kind of theatre took root so quickly shows the firm hold that Shakespeare as an artist of the theatre had already taken on people's imaginations. For Tieck and others, gripped by the plays and the story of Shakespeare's time that Malone had put together, the desire to reconstruct versions of his original theatre had several justifications. Plain worship of the master's *opus* was one, but the real drive to reconstruct his theatre came more from a sense of its strangeness, its remoteness from the modern experience of urban life and theatre-going. This introduced the urge to discover more about the peculiar circumstances that helped to generate those amazing plays. The things we like we normally seek to know better. Once the work of Malone and other scholars had made it clear how alien Shakespeare's theatre world was from those available in the nineteenth century, attempts to return to that lost world were bound to follow.

It was largely a romantic, and a Romantic, quest. In England, once the exotic joys of the alien in eighteenth-century Gothic fantasies were transformed into Victorian delight in the medieval, the concept of Elizabeth I's 'Merrie England' grew until it became a vision of the good life, a pre-industrial culture of peace, prosperity and village community. William Morris and the Arts and Crafts movement celebrated the virtues of the homespun and of traditional craft-trades as a reaction against the impersonality of the culture that developed with industrialisation and mass production. Shakespeare's England became a vision of the Victorian nation's Utopia, its most significant Other, a vision of a better England. By the end of the nineteenth century, when national pride began to demand that there must be a national theatre to celebrate the plays that formed such a large part of the national heritage, it was inevitable that it should at first be thought of as a new theatre for Shakespeare. The first serious planning to design an actual building in London to be called a national theatre immediately became entangled in the idea of making it a replica of Shakespeare's Globe.

By that time, however, some new developments had followed from the work of the Malone generation of scholars. In 1888 Karl Theodore Gaedertz, a Berlin librarian and scholar, found a manuscript notebook in the library of the University of Utrecht. It contained copies of a drawing of the interior of the Swan theatre and an account in Latin of the four theatres of Shakespeare's London that existed in 1596. (*See* p. 189 *below*, and fig. 5 on p. 29.) For the first time students of the early theatre had Johannes de Witt's image of a platform stage and its surrounding galleries, now so familiar to us, to fix their imaginations on. It argued for a wholly fresh approach to Shakespearean staging, and proved that the staging of Shakespeare so familiar in Victorian theatres was very far from the original. With actor-impresarios like Kemble and his successors, and especially the greatly acclaimed stagings of the history plays by Charles Kean in the 1850s, Shakespeare's plays became quite literally spectacular narratives, pageant-like showpieces on picture-frame stages. Kean's sets for court scenes faithfully reproduced what the picture-books from Tudor times showed. Even the College of Heralds praised his historical fidelity. The Swan's plain platform was clearly antithetical to the proscenium-arch pictorial staging that Victorian theatre gave to London theatregoers in the years up to the 1890s.

FIG. 5 The copy by Arendt van Buchell of his friend Johannes de Witt's drawing of the Swan playhouse, done in 1596.

By the end of the century some devotees were decidedly disenchanted with Kean's pre-cinematic scenic Shakespeare. Studying the Swan drawing, Henslowe's records and the few other relics of Shakespearean staging that survived, William Poel produced his own version of the Arts and Crafts movement in his scrupulously minimal productions of the Shakespeare plays. Using the Fortune contract to reconstruct his own idea of a Shakespearean playhouse, he staged the plays with no scenery and hardly any props, using black-clad platform stages and putting the emphasis on speech rather than the visual and spectacular. In effect Poel was the first student of Shakespeare to attempt a serious reconstruction of the original performance conditions. An essential part of that attempt was, inevitably, a renewed interest in the original Globe as a design worth reconstructing.

Poel signalled his principles by setting up the 'Elizabethan Stage Society'. This was not just another Shakespeare Society, a reading club of the kind that flourished in every major town in England, but a new kind of group, aiming to renew the conditions of performance of Shakespeare's own time and stage. His productions were antithetical to the current West End style of playing, verbal rather than visual displays. It was a revolutionary Shakespeare that attracted some potent support. George Bernard Shaw was one eminent critic who upheld the principles of Poel and the Elizabethan Stage Society against its inevitable enemies in the theatre establishment. As a drama critic and playwright, by the turn of the century Shaw had become convinced that Shakespeare should be given on platform stages where the play's 'real' values could be brought home to the audience. In his essay 'Shakespeare on the Modern Stage', published in *The Times* on 25 October 1905, he went so far as to declare that the only Shakespeare performances that had ever moved him were 'those of the Elizabethan Stage Society'.

Shaw's was a powerful voice, and inevitably he met powerful opposition. The idea of constructing a new Globe became a shuttlecock between different groups of fiercely battling antagonists. The chief trouble was that the shuttlecock got caught in an even bigger net. The long story of the plans to build a national theatre in London in its early years became substantially the story of the campaign by the Elizabethan Stage Society's supporters to design it in Shakespeare's, or rather his Globe's, own image. Each idea had its own justification, but neither of them could be fitted easily into the other. Poel's idea of a theatre for Shakespeare could never have been married comfortably with a theatre designed to show the whole of England's stage resources, ancient and modern alike. The idea of a reconstructed Globe as the new national theatre became a minor extravagance trapped in a tangle of surprisingly savage intrigue. Personal reputations were staked on it.[1] In the end, practical and financial calculations were bound to weigh against the untenable principle that Shakespeare, being the only great English playwright, must dictate what would be provided for all others.

Some of London's Establishment did take the idea seriously enough to try it out in 1912. For the Earl's Court show of that year the colourful and eccentric architect Edward Lutyens designed a half-size Globe, and visitors witnessed on its stage a simulacrum of the Poel concept of Shakespeare in performance. Opinion was divided, and the division was enough to sink the idea of a new Globe becoming the national theatre. It struggled on hopefully for some time, but there was never anything like enough unanimity to generate the single-minded determination such a scheme needed.

In the 1930s, as Britain slowly came to terms with the fearful effects of the great Depression, the idea resurfaced. Its inspiration grew, as so often in this history, from the grassroots of enthusiasm for Shakespeare. This time the impetus came from F. C. Owlett, a journalist, who conceived the 'Mermaid Shakespeare Society'. He enlisted support from the great and the good in the form of, for instance, Joseph P. Kennedy, then US ambassador in London, Lord Bessborough, and the three leading English Shakespeare scholars of the time. Their plans were based on Cornelius Visscher's octagonal structure depicted in his engraving of 1616, then thought to be the only valid illustration of the first Globe.

The 'Mermaid' factor was to be a pub, based on the myth that Shakespeare and Jonson spent their evenings drinking at the tavern of that name celebrated by Francis Beaumont in his famous poem to Jonson. Writing from his family estate in Leicestershire, Beaumont mourned what he was missing in London.

> ... in this warme shine
> I lie and dreame of your full Mermaid wine ...
> Methinks the little wit I had is lost
> Since I saw you, for a wit is like a rest,
> Held up at tennis, which men do the best
> With the best gamesters: what things have we seen
> Done at the Mermaid? Hard words that have been
> So nimble, and so full of subtill flame,
> As if that every one from whence they came
> Had meant to put his whole wit in a jest,
> And had resolv'd to live a foole the rest
> Of his dull life ...

This was a merry and witty England, with all of England's most famous wits drinking together in the one place. The mythologisers soon attached Shakespeare to this merry gang, so the Globe to be reconstructed in the thirties was to combine a theatre with a tavern, plus a library for the solitary scholar, thus catering for all the familiar varieties of Shakespeare-worship.

The Mermaid link was a nice story, but a complete fiction. I. A. Shapiro, a sharply sceptical scholar, demolished the case for Shakespeare as a member of the 'Mermaid Club' in 1950.[2] Two years previously he had also demolished the case for basing a reconstruction on Visscher's engraving. Despite Shapiro's work, however, the Visscher view, assumed to be the only clear-cut picture of the first Globe, ruled thinking about the design for several more decades. All too often it recurs as the standard image of the Globe, usually in a nicely-coloured nineteenth-century redrawing, in ill-informed items about Shakespeare's theatre. Even the Folger Shakespeare Library in Washington DC, possessor of the greatest stock of early books from the period and of one-third of all the surviving copies of the First Folio, still sells pictures of the Globe based on Visscher.

In effect, the 'Mermaid Tavern' side of the 1930s project on Bankside was a Shakespeare theme-park concept for the thirties. Perhaps wisely, the proposed site was pre-empted for the massive brick functionality of the Bankside Power Station. The war that started in 1939 put an end to any further plans for that first Southwark-based project. Meanwhile John Cranford Adams in the USA went ahead with his octagonal Visscher-based replica, which became the model for the theatre constructed in Washington DC as part of the Folger

Shakespeare Library. Adams's plans of the Globe were barely completed and published in 1948 when Shapiro's demolition of the idea that any plan could be based on the octagonal Visscher came out. It was time to draw breath. Not until twenty years later, at the beginning of the 1970s, did the focus return to London with C. Walter Hodges, and still more with Sam Wanamaker.

Sam Wanamaker's Globe

By his own account Wanamaker 'took up the torch' that Poel and succeeding generations of academics and theatre people had been carrying since the beginning of the century for a number of reasons. One was his own first experience of Shakespeare. It is a story he retold many times in different forms, but one of the best versions survives in the recording of an interview by Studs Terkel made when Wanamaker revisited Chicago in 1980. Partly inspired by the Mermaid Shakespeare Society, the British Pavilion at the 'Century of Progress' exhibition in Chicago in 1934 had rather paradoxically (given the exhibition's theme) set up a mock Globe theatre. Designed by Thomas Wood Stevens, to a plan not unlike the model used by Olivier ten years later for his film of *Henry V*, it was subsequently rebuilt in San Diego as the 'Old Globe Theatre'. At Chicago Ben Iden Payne, director of the Shakespeare Memorial Theatre in Stratford upon Avon, performed cut-down versions of the plays with a small company, giving one forty-minute version every hour on the hour.[3] The young Wanamaker was so taken with these, his first experience of Shakespeare, that he auditioned for the company, and joined it to play at the Great Lakes Festival, while the Globe was being moved to other places on the way to San Diego.

He went on to train as an actor in the 'Method' school, but as he told Terkel, the 'mumble' school does not do much for poetry, and he never forgot his first encounter with Shakespeare on stage. His own Shakespeare started with the radicalised Stratford traditions that Iden Payne brought to the USA. He loved the verse and its power, as much as the intimate psychology he found in the stories.

But other factors came to weigh strongly with him too. As he argued in an earlier interview, live theatre needs the unfamiliar, the frightening. People go to the theatre to be comfortably reassured, but reassurance is not what ought to happen. There must be an element of danger, of uncertainty, or the audience will sleep. More, extra invention, was needed. Hearing a tape of this interview replayed sixteen years later he identified his plan to reconstruct the original theatre as a novel way to make the old new, and to give the classics back their frightening novelty by renewing the original stage and staging. By 1980, with the Globe project reactivated, he felt he was now in a position to combine the theatre's need to constantly renew the classics in forms that created this frightening novelty with the dream of the 'academics and theatre people' who, ever since Poel, had wanted an 'authentically reconstructed, honestly researched original theatre for Shakespeare'. A new and disturbing Shakespeare would be created by taking the plays back to their original theatre.

Wanamaker related this dream of renewing Shakespeare to the widespread rejection in the 1930s of picture-frame staging and the return to thrust stages, not quite in the round but three-quarter round, as he put it. He linked his dream to the theatre's own rediscovered urge to take acting back into the audiences whence picture-frame staging had for centuries removed it, in the long retreat into its own scenic realm behind the footlights. While cinema made its audiences passive, theatre should dynamise. Such theatre would be new and old at the same time. He could see Brecht and modern plays written for the new stages such as *Rosencrantz and Guildenstern are Dead* fitting easily into the new Globe. It would be international, a gift to the whole English-speaking world. Asked mischievously by Terkel, offering himself as devil's advocate, why it should be him and not Gielgud or Olivier promoting a rebuilt Globe in London, why it should be an American inspiration and not a British one, he noted tactfully but correctly that their principal concern in London was with the National Theatre, a concept which had rightly separated itself off from the dream of a national theatre for Shakespeare. He was taking up an old British torch because its former holders were now carrying another one. And, he noted, the time was especially ripe for its development in the borough of Southwark.

Wanamaker knew at first hand how depressed the Bankside had become. Its shipping activities had died as the new container trade kept the former barge-trade far downstream at the new docks. Southwark was a derelict wasteland looking for a new role. The Greater London Development Plan was seeking to turn it away from its former trades to new things, and Wanamaker saw a new Globe near its original site as an integral part of that renewal. Everything converged: his dream of a new kind of Shakespeare which would supplant the old picture-frame traditions, his understanding of what a rebuilt Globe could do for scholars and students of Shakespeare, and his concern to help regenerate a depressed section of London which had a wonderful history, now lost in its shabby miles of decaying buildings. It was radical, it was visionary, and it ran against the traditions of London's theatre that he had been bumping into from his own very first appearances on the Stratford and London stages. The fact that the National Theatre had taken over, or been taken over by, the Establishment left him free to work his own innovation.

The principle that ruled all his choices, from the earliest discussions with scholars like C. Walter Hodges, Glynne Wickham and Theodore Spencer, was 'authenticity'. The new Globe had to be as faithful a copy as scholarship and theatre historians could get it of Shakespeare's original theatre. That may have seemed a simple principle, but its plain surface concealed some large trapdoors. His insistence that what was built must be a working theatre brought him from very early on into the argument that modern audiences are inescapably different from the Tudors, and that compromises must be made to cater for modern needs.

From the first Wanamaker faced arguments about the value of including, for instance, a plastic or glass roof over the auditorium to protect the audience from London's rain. On my first meeting with him, late in 1981, at Theo Crosby's office at Pentagram,[4] which then overlooked the rail yard at Paddington Station, a sharp image of modern industrial London, I put that question to him to test what his concept of the proposed theatre and its uses really was. I made the point that while a roof would make the theatre more kindly for modern visitors, it would compromise not just the acoustics but the feeling of the place. I did not bother to suggest that it would be a step along a flowery path of compromises and slippage into modern theatre forms (not least that supreme convenience, modern plumbing for the toilets, of which even then I was sure the original Globe had no provision). In a gathering of twenty or more academics, theatre practitioners and architects, he listened to the arguments for both sides, summed them up with the concise clarity that was one of the clearest marks of his real intellectual strength, and concluded, finger in the air, 'No compromise!'

There were many arguments in subsequent years about how to finesse the design so as to meet modern needs. Some demands had to be met. The design would certainly never secure a licence for use as a theatre, for instance, unless the demands of the London Fire Brigade for insulated cladding and more ample exit doors could be met. But many other demands, including plumbing for toilets and the provision of green rooms for players long accustomed to much more space than the narrow tiring house behind the Globe's stage, had to be met by providing facilities outside the building itself. Sam Wanamaker never wavered in his principle of maximum authenticity. It would not be a new and honest experience unless it was a faithful replica of the old building.

Faith is not often free from compromise, and there were ideas about compromises in plenty. One obvious problem was the sheer bulk of modern audiences compared with the underfed Elizabethans. In the early 1980s calculations based on the measurement of skeletons from plague burial sites suggested that the average Elizabethan was 10% smaller than the modern adult. The sufferings of modern visitors who crashed their heads on the ceiling beams and lintels inside Anne Hathaway's Cottage argued for enlargement to match modern sizes. Muriel Bradbrook, herself of a fairly Elizabethan size, mischievously suggested that if the new Globe was not scaled up by 10% it would become an accurate historical experience only for schoolchildren and the older generation of Japanese. It became almost a philosophical question: do we start from the original building, and squeeze in, uncomfortably aware of the incongruity, or do we start with the fact that we are catering for modern audiences, and match the replica to what the Globe would have been if it were built from scratch in 1980? If the intention was to build a working theatre, Shakespeare's factory, to see how his plays were originally intended to work, would we have to go the whole hog and only employ the smallest actors playing to school parties?

Such questions flew around freely in the early stages. Always, though, Wanamaker's own principle of 'authenticity' in the end caught and caged the participants in his own basic requirement: that the theatre should be a working theatre built like the original Globe to the most accurate calculations and materials that the evidence could supply. Subject only to the demands of fire safety, it had to be the nearest that modern scholarship could get to identifying what that structure was, in every component.

That was the theory. From early on practice laid down demands that led the project architect, Theo Crosby, to make compromises in several areas. Toilets we could do without, assuming that we could build some modern facilities next to the Globe, but if the theatre was to get a licence for performance, a vital need if it was to tell us anything about how it worked, the District Surveyor's demands for safety had to be met. It was not enough to point out that the original Globe had been full of nearly three thousand customers when it caught fire, and that everyone had succeeded in escaping unharmed then. The same rules that govern audience safety in modern theatres had to be applied to the new Globe.

Using the original materials, especially lime plaster and thatch, created special hazards. Some of the old materials came out well from the fire tests. A wall made of lath and lime plaster was subjected to a direct flame at 1,000 degrees centigrade to see how long it would last before catching fire, and it exceeded the Building Regulations' requirement that it should stand for an hour nearly threefold. (*See* the chapter by Theo Crosby's successor, Jon Greenfield, pp. 81–96 *below.*) In other aspects of the design, modern technology did give some help. For a long time we expected to have to follow the fire restrictions and imitate the second Globe by roofing the galleries not with thatch but with tiles, the most obvious precaution since it was the thatching that helped the original building to burn down in 1613. Then in 1989 I read a piece in the property pages of the *Financial Times* about insurance for thatched cottages. It said that a new fire-retardant spray had been invented which most insurance companies would now accept, thus bringing the previously uninsurable into the fold. I told Theo Crosby about it, but he was sceptical (his bent being towards the baroque and the decorated, he was quite happy with tiles: they looked prettier than thatch). Later, though, Wanamaker's first principle plus new science coming to the aid of old building technology made sure that suitably treated thatch together with sparge pipes to sprinkle the ridges were agreed for the new Globe.

The full story of the Bankside Globe's design is a long-running saga, with many battles and some sudden deaths. Some of it has been told in various forms and with various agendas already. What has not yet been given much emphasis is the probity of the 'best guess' technique that necessarily became the standard method of working, and the uniquely wide range and variety of expertise that was drawn together to work on it. That was a Wanamaker creation. Most of his sixteen-hour working days were spent seeking out every expert and every form of expertise he could. His insistence on 'authenticity' kept the design work on a strict and narrow path. Without his untiring constancy to drive it the project would certainly have run into the sands, or have become a commercial theme park decades ago, instead of the educational charity that he always insisted it should be.

The Wanamaker Reconstruction: authenticity and the convergence of expertise

The evidence about the original design of the Globe comes from various sources, and much of it is still elusive. Adjectives like 'various' and 'elusive' sound like camouflage for the extent to which the design has evolved through nothing much more specific than the 'best guess' technique. The work has not, though, been nearly as uncertain in its conclusions as that phrase implies. Sam Wanamaker's energy and singlemindedness brought together a unique combination of scholars and practitioners of Shakespeare's theatre, and historians from a range of disciplines who had never previously joined in this kind of analysis and reconstruction. The collective endeavour that resulted augmented the scholars' analysis of the documentary evidence with the fragmentary but tangible evidence of such specialists as archaeologists, historians of traditional building techniques, historians of the Tudor decorative arts, set in frame by the theoretical and practical expertise of craftsmen, architects and engineers. Evaluating the quality of each piece of evidence and expertise has been a complex and long-running process. We had to piece all the different ideas together, cemented with expert advice from all the recent scholarship into what can be deduced from the range of available information, from the evidence for the original staging in the plays themselves and from the surviving buildings that testify to Tudor building techniques. The long labours that have created the new Globe are a unique monument to the range of technical skills available at the end of the millennium.

Piecing the fragments of evidence together is not unlike trying to make up a jigsaw puzzle when you do not know what the finished picture is. You need confidence that you have the right pieces in the right general places, but sometimes sections you thought settled have to be turned upside down to fit into what gradually emerges as the larger picture. Understanding grows slowly, and with it grows confidence in the rightness of the nearly-finished picture. The trick is to reconcile so far as possible all the different bodies of evidence. The problem is that the whole of the original design was an integral structure, and changing any one aspect has a knock-on effect on every other aspect. The level of confidence about the rightness of each element is inevitably variable. Confidence in the final design comes above all from the consistency with which the concept of authenticity is maintained.

The chief reason for that confidence needs to be emphasised. I find, for once, no difficulty, none of the scholar's habitual need to make cautious qualifications, in declaring that the greatest single achievement of the Globe project has been the way it has brought together the best expertise in a uniquely wide range of special skills to address the questions raised in the design process. No previous project has done anything like so much work as this one on questions about the building. They range from the character of Tudor brickwork and traditional carpentry and thatching techniques, or the ironwork that made the Tudor locks and hinges, and how they worked, down to the methods used by Tudor surveyors and illustrators for setting out building sites. No previous age has had such a range of expertise in historical methods of construction available to it. No previous age has sifted the paper evidence with such care and scepticism, and, of course, no previous age has had the benefit of the recent archaeological discoveries. For the first time, once the Rose was exposed in February 1989, we had some of the actual Tudor materials used to make a Tudor theatre for analysis to add to the other work already done on the Globe.

Simplifying drastically, I would identify five main fields of knowledge, fields where what might be called 'primary' evidence was found. It is from these that we have reaped our main information about the Globe's design. They are, in order of their arrival on the Shakespeare scene and onto the architect's table, (1) scholarly analysis of the pictorial evidence; (2) scholarly analysis of the evidence offered by the plays themselves, in stage directions and the like, and any descriptive comments from the time; (3) the archaeological evidence; (4) the evidence of traditional building techniques provided by surviving Tudor timber-frame structures across the country; and (5) the work of art historians on Tudor iconography and decoration. A sixth, the practical experience of modern actors as they use the reconstructed Globe stage, will in time add its own substantial contribution to this assembly of evidence.

The first and oldest of the five is the pictorial, the panoramas of London made in Shakespeare's time. Verbal accounts of the Globe from Shakespeare's own time did not help much, because they called it a round, a cockpit, a wooden O, when we knew that Tudor carpenters did not bend oak, and therefore we deduced that it must really have been a polygon, probably with enough sides to it to make it look round. Some of the early panoramas showed a polygonal shape, but normally of only six or eight sides. For many years, from Malone in 1790 till Cranford Adams in 1946, the Visscher panorama of 1616, which shows a tall, inward-sloping octagon, was assumed to be the only surviving picture of the first Globe. We still see it reproduced all too often as the original Globe (fig. 4). De Witt's drawing of the Swan, the only picture in existence of the interior of an open amphitheatre, complicated that assumption because it seemed to show a many-sided polygon (fig. 5). But its draughtsmanship is shaky, and it has always been a loose cannon in these gunfights. John

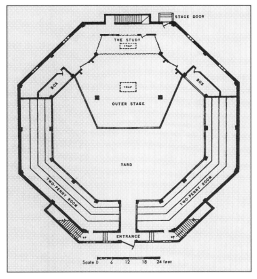

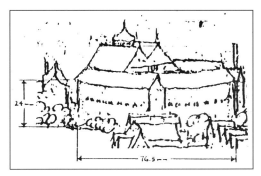

FIG. 6 (LEFT) A plan of a putative Globe prepared in the 1940s by John Cranford Adams of Hofstra College.

FIG. 8 (ABOVE) Hollar's drawing of the second Globe, made from the tower of Southwark Cathedral. The original is less than one inch in diameter.

FIG. 7 A detail from Wenceslas Hollar's 'Long View' of London, published in 1647 from drawings made in the 1630s. The names of the two theatres, the Globe and the bear-baiting house, were accidentally transposed during the engraving process.

Cranford Adams in the 1940s designed his Globe in accordance with Visscher on an octagonal frame (fig. 6).

But in 1948, in the first issue of *Shakespeare Survey*, I. A. Shapiro published a study of the Bankside engravings which cast serious doubt on Visscher's panorama.[5] He showed that Visscher had based his depiction of London on an old copperplate of 1572, made before any of the theatres were built, and had added features that seem to have been based on hearsay, since, Shapiro concluded, he never visited London himself. Other depictions, by Meriam, Hondius, Delaram, and others, Shapiro showed to be derivative from Visscher and therefore equally useless. The only views of Bankside that are of any value, he concluded, are John Norden's tiny inset in his *Civitas Londini*, which offers only a tiny thatch-roofed circular shape at a junction of Maiden Lane (*see* fig. 19, p. 58), and more particularly Wenceslas Hollar's engraving, the famous 'Long View' of London taken from the tower of Southwark Cathedral in the 1630s (fig. 7).

So much for Cranford Adams. The fact that Hollar's engraving shows the second Globe, not the first, was a major disappointment. Even when the pencil original from which Hollar made his engraving turned up (fig. 8) (it is now in the Yale Center for the Study of British Art) that did not alter the drastic limitation for would-be rebuilders that we did not have any detailed or reliable picture of the first Globe.

Matters rested there for some time. In the 1970s Walter Hodges diverged from Sam Wanamaker by planning to use Hollar's evidence to build not a first but a second Globe, on the grounds that Hollar's was the only reliable information we have. Wanamaker insisted that only the first, the one Shakespeare actually paid for and used, would do. This meant that if anything was to be built, 'best guessing' on perilously little evidence, almost none of it pictorial, would have to prevail. A survey of 1634 states that the second Globe was built on the foundations of the first, so that the outline of Hollar's pencilwork might be thought to show the actual size at least of the first Globe's groundplan. Pressure to milk the limited evidence for more facts built up. Then in 1983 John Orrell's *The Quest for Shakespeare's Globe* appeared. I had read it for the publisher early in 1981, some time before I was drawn to work for the Wanamaker project, and it convinced me that Hollar provided a sufficient basis for a reconstruction.

Essentially Orrell laid Hollar's panorama onto a modern Ordnance Survey map, to test Hollar's positioning of some of the London buildings that survive from Hollar's time, and therefore appear on the modern map. Hollar turned out to be remarkably accurate, to within ± 2%. (*See* the chapter by John Orrell, *esp*. pp. 53–4 *below*.) As Orrell went on to show, Hollar evidently made his drawing as a precise tracing on a 'perspective glass'. This technology was sufficiently accurate to indicate that a calculation of the size of the Globe on the basis of his pencil drawing would produce a remarkably good measurement for the second Globe, and so for the foundations of the first too. That, give or take a lot of refinements, was the basis for the first exact plan for the new Globe that Theo Crosby produced in 1984: a twenty-four sided polygon measuring 101 feet in outside diameter (fig. 9).

The second body of evidence, what could be found in the plays and other written texts from the time, gave very little direct help about the design of the whole theatre and auditorium. Its main helps were with the stage and its features and furnishings. For that Hollar, showing only the exterior of the second Globe, was nearly useless. De Witt's drawing of

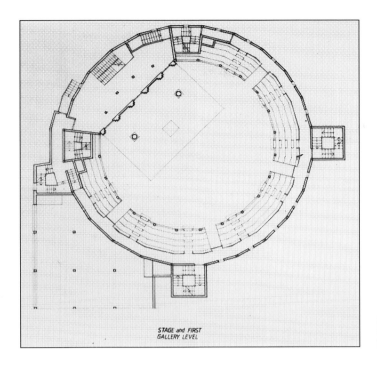

STAGE and FIRST
GALLERY LEVEL

FIG. 9 An early plan for a twenty-four sided Globe, drawn in 1984 by Theo Crosby.

the Swan is tempting but too contentious for comfort, and in any case only one of the plays known to have been staged there has survived. It is a testimony to De Witt's complexity as evidence that nobody has ever tried to reconstruct his vision of the Swan. Apart from his drawing, and the account of London's four playhouses in 1596 that accompanied it (*see* p. 189 *below*), the contemporary comments about either the stage or the auditorium are sparse. Elizabethans knew their playhouses too well to bother describing them in detail. The comments do include a few references to 'twopenny galleries' and the like, which helped to define different sections of the auditorium, and there were snippets like the account of the fire in 1613 and how everyone escaped by 'two small dores' which said something about the auditorium exits. (*See* p. 187 *below*.)

In the end, for the design of the Globe at large, the panoramas and written comments were to prove less directly useful than figures in documents. The trouble was that Hollar, and later the archaeology, gave evidence only about the groundplan, and said almost nothing about what stood on it. For that we turned to the Henslowe archive, and the contract that it contains ordering Peter Streete, who had just built the Globe, to build the Fortune in 1600. (*See* pp. 180–2 *below*.) In many ways it is a frustrating document. For 150 years attempts have been made to use it to make reconstructions, for instance in Dresden in the 1830s, in Tokyo in the 1930s, and in Perth in Australia in the 1970s. Too often it tells Streete to repeat what he had just done at the Globe. But it does specify dimensions, and even though the Fortune was designed as a square structure to contrast with the Globe's nearly-round polygon, it gave the height for each gallery level and several other details which fitted the Globe. So the circuit of timber-framed galleries, each level jutting or jettying over the one below, a merger of Hollar with Henslowe, became a key part of the design.

39

FIG. 10 A bird's-eye view photograph of the Rose's foundations, taken by Andrew Fulgoni in April 1989. The round concrete pillars in the foundations are the remains of Southbridge House, pulled down in 1988.

FIG. 11 A Museum of London Archaeology Service photograph of the Globe's remains that were uncovered behind Anchor Terrace in Park Street in October 1989.

The third body of evidence was the archaeology. (For a discussion of the archaeological evaluation of the site *see* the chapter by Simon Blatherwick pp. 67–80 *below.*) In the course of 1989 the Museum of London's teams of diggers first uncovered 60% of the Rose, and later the 9 or 10% of the Globe accessible behind Anchor Terrace (figs 10 and 11). These two sites in Park Street, so close to the then concrete swimming-pool on top of which Wanamaker's new Globe was to stand, gave us marvellously tangible evidence about building techniques and materials. We learned that the foundations were made first with a trench, then an infill of limestone and clunch pebbles, then a polygon of bricks that provided the basis for the first timbers, the groundsills. Amongst the debris found in the Rose's yard there was a lot of humus, which on analysis proved to be Norfolk reed (the common water reed, not necessarily brought from Norfolk itself), used for the Rose's thatching and thrown down into the yard when it was demolished. There was a mass of lath and plaster, much of it in front of the stage area, where it had been dumped and then swept off into the yard when the stage itself was demolished. And there was the yard surface.

At Pentagram we had discussed various possibilities for the composition of the Globe's yard with the architect. Possibly it should be a little higher in the centre, sloping down slightly towards the galleries, drained from the outside edges by pipes under the gallery walls. Or it could be drained from the centre, using a longer piece of piping but with the advantage of being only one length, compared with the number required for drainage from the periphery. We had opted for the central piping, on the grounds that the yard ought to

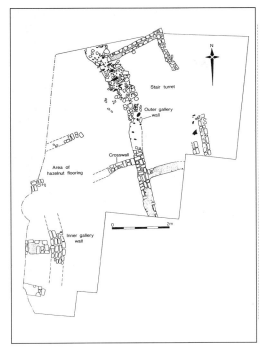

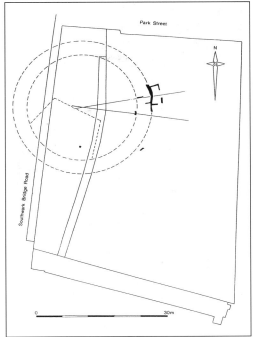

FIG. 12 A Museum of London Archaeology Service interpretative diagram of the remains shown in fig. 11.

FIG. 13 An extrapolation from the Globe's remains, showing the most likely relation between the uncovered section and the full ground plan.

have had if anything an inclination inwards to the stage. We chose to pave it with brick, the most durable kind of outside surface cladding that we knew was commonly used in Tudor times.

This turned out to be less than perfect guesswork. The Rose's yard had been surfaced in strong mortar, to allow drainage down to a kind of sump at the centre, what seems to have been a buried barrel-head just in front of the stage's foundation wall. The mortar had a one-in-ten incline, a rake from the gallery walls down to the centre. On top of this mortar surface was a massive weight of black debris, over a foot thick, probably laid when the Rose was rebuilt in a new shape in 1592 and the new yard had to be resurfaced. The composition of this surface debris excited a lot of comment because it included masses of crushed hazel-nut shells. The archaeologists insisted on calling it industrial waste, a peculiarly modern term. That did not please Sam Wanamaker, who was quoted in the press as calling the nut-shells the remains of Elizabethan popcorn, since playgoers were well known to crack nuts during the performance. Sadly for that idea, John Orrell soon found a book of 1594 which described the by-products of soap factories as an excellent and widely-used road-surfacing material. The useable by-product was a mixture of the ash and clinker from the fires used to boil the lye for the soap with the remains from the hazel-nuts that were crushed to make the oil for the soap. Though I might add that when we had a sample of the industrial waste analysed in 1993 to see how porous it was, as a precedent for the Globe yard's surface, the analysts found not only the nutshells but five cherry stones and a plum stone. Elizabethan popcorn was there. Yard audiences were not all that tidy in 1599.

The digs at the two playhouse sites in 1989 also resolved the question where in the polygonal circuit of bays the stages stood. Where the stage might be in the yard, to the north facing the sun or with its back turned in the south, had been much debated. The Pentagram debates had given the victory to Hollar's south-west location on the grounds of his superior accuracy. For the Globe this proved exactly right, but the Rose dig gave a striking validation to John Norden, who, while showing the fourteen-sided Rose as a hexagon, had placed its stage cover on its northern flank, precisely where the archaeologists found it. He showed a projecting ridge of thatch set out from the northern gallery roofing, ending in a gable front. That seemed to confirm John Orrell's supposition that like the Rose the first Globe's stage cover had been a single gable-fronted ridge, but set like the second Globe's to the south-west, and that its stage was therefore permanently shaded from any sunlight. (*See* the discussion by John Orrell, and figs 17 to 20, pp. 55–8 *below.*)

Many similar by-products of the quest for the Globe came from the archaeological digs. By far the most potent was the analysis of the ten per cent of the Globe's foundations. Now we had something that could be set against the calculations about the dimensions that we had gained from Hollar's picture. First we had to settle that the section dug up was a single set of foundations. This appeared to be the case, validating the evidence from the legal documents that the second Globe was built on the foundations of the first. Then we had to work out which sections of the Globe they were that had been dug up. There were problems in that, particularly in reconciling what the remains appeared to be with Hollar's drawing. For one thing, if as they appeared to they included the foundations of a stair turret, they seemed to stand between eleven and fourteen degrees out of line with Hollar. For another, the turret (fig. 12) was of a different kind from Hollar's picture. Do you believe the hard remains, whatever they are, or do you keep faith with Orrell's calculation of Hollar's accuracy?

This is an argument that will have to stand in suspense until more of the original Globe can be dug up. The best explanation of the various wall sections we found still is that they constitute fragments of the inner and outer gallery walls in two bays of the frame, plus an extruded section which is most likely the foundation for a lobby and stair turret. The lobby foundations are not very substantial if they were designed to carry the tall uprights of a stair turret, but they were built to wrap halfway round each of two adjacent bays. That would mean that the central post linking the two bays on the angle, a huge oak post thirty-two feet high, twelve inches in section, and weighing over two tons, could have served as the newell post at the centre of a narrow staircase. It seems that the remains are of sections of two adjacent bays, separated by crosswalls at the angle, with other crosswalls in one forming a passage from the lobby into the yard (more hazel-nut shells were found at the yard end of this passageway). Two other walls extrude at right angles from the middle of each outer wall of the two bays and turn inwards at right angles to make the lobby. A six-foot opening in the centre on the angle provided the entryway from Maiden Lane, where deposits of stone and pebbles were found. (*See* figs 11 and 12 *above.*)

This wrap-around lobby makes good sense in its bifold structure. The wide opening could admit people in large numbers. They would immediately have to choose to go left or right. In this lobby the left-hand section, occupying half of one bay, took people through the passageway into the yard. The right-hand section would have launched people up the stairs. The other lobby would have been set symmetrically on the other flank of the play-

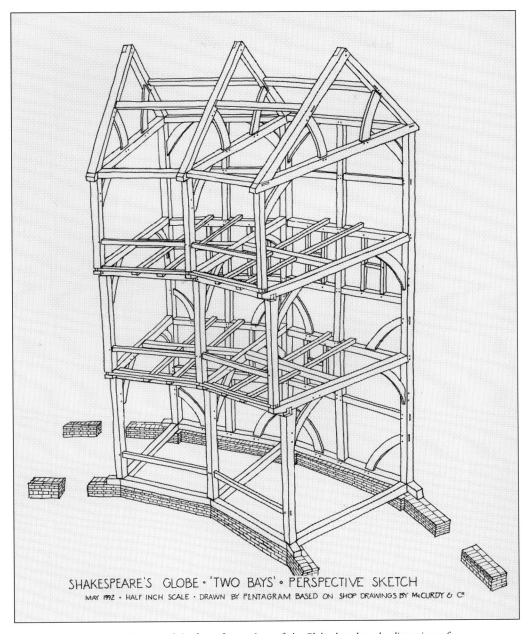

SHAKESPEARE'S GLOBE · 'TWO BAYS' · PERSPECTIVE SKETCH
MAY 1992 · HALF INCH SCALE · DRAWN BY PENTAGRAM BASED ON SHOP DRAWINGS BY McCURDY & Cᵒ

FIG. 14 A drawing of the frame for two bays of the Globe, based on the dimensions of
the two bays uncovered in 1989.

house, offering the yard to those who went in to the right.

The most intriguing consequence of this identification for the remains is the Euclidean
geometry it invites (fig. 13). If you subtend a line from the lobby wall foundations that run
out from the two bays and carry it inwards to the centre of the shape, and subtend others
bisecting the two gallery wall angles, all the lines come close to meeting at just over forty-

nine feet in from the outer wall. That would make the outside diameter ninety-nine feet, very close to the Hollar diameter. And it argues a distinct symmetry, not just in the positioning of the stair turret, but in the size of each bay. The distance between inner and outer wall, centre to centre, at approximately twelve feet six inches, makes a remarkably close match with the same measurements at the Rose and at the Fortune. And the angles allow us to determine the number of bays: twenty at the Globe, which matches the twenty at the Fortune, and fourteen at the smaller Rose. In respect of those dimensions, if in no other, the archaeologists' findings were reassuring. They offset the surprise and discomfort we had in registering how different was the fourteen-sided and tulip-shaped second Rose from the polygonal Globe, and how different both were from the square Fortune. That also had a pay-off in discrediting to some extent the long run of arguments by analogy from De Witt's drawing of the Swan as it might relate to the Globe.

It was on the Euclidean analysis, or best guess, together with the clear plan-form that the dig provided for the two adjacent bay foundations, that in 1991 we constructed two bays in frame, and thatched them, to see what they looked like, in the hope that they might serve as a possible one-tenth section of the Globe's complete frame (fig. 14). By this time we were well into the fourth body of evidence, the knowledge and experience of Tudor techniques possessed by the Society of Construction Historians and the practitioners who had begun to do serious research into the restoration of ancient buildings. Richard Harris, curator of the Downland Museum of ancient buildings, other experts in Tudor building design, brickwork and ironwork, and above all Peter McCurdy, had been deeply involved with the architects in details of the design for years before this, but now came the real test. The two bays were designed and built by Peter McCurdy to the archaeological ground plan (as interpreted by John Orrell and myself), using the Fortune contract to determine the heights and jutties of each level. Traditional Tudor building practices were invoked to decide on such essential features as the use of fresh green oak, the mortice and tenon joints, the dowel pegging, the question of using crucks to make the roofing for the thatch, and the other components that made the two bays an efficient and historically plausible structure. (*See* the detailed discussion by Jon Greenfield, pp. 97–117 *below*.)

The bays stood weathering for nearly a year on what was then self-mockingly called the swimming-pool floor, forty feet below river level, at the Globe site, while engineers, carpentry historians, architects and scholars studied them. Then, as the concreting of the piazza on which the Globe was to stand went ahead they were dismantled and incorporated into the first four bays of the final Globe. They are still visible in the lath-and-plastered frame, looking distinctly more grey than the most recent of the oak beams to go in (plates 1 and 5). They have suffered rather more from surface cracking, but they are fixed firmly and efficiently into place by the locking processes that the wooden jointing system entails. Tudor wood-framing is a building system with tremendous structural strength. We have learned a lot about it, and about other elements in the design of the Globe, from the practical work of designing and making the carpentry of the frame.

The fifth area of expertise, invoked to determine how the Globe's interior might have been painted, and the scheme that best rationalises the design of the stage's iconographic and sculptural decoration, is of equal status with the other evidence. Little is known about the iconography except for the legend about Hercules cited as the Globe's motto. We know

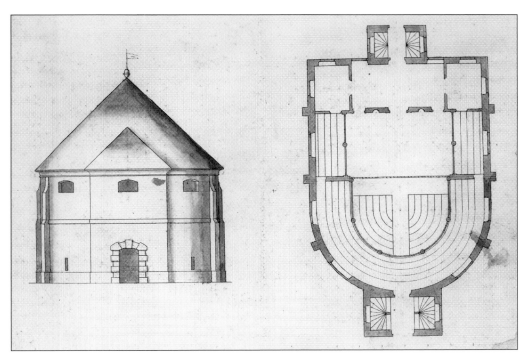

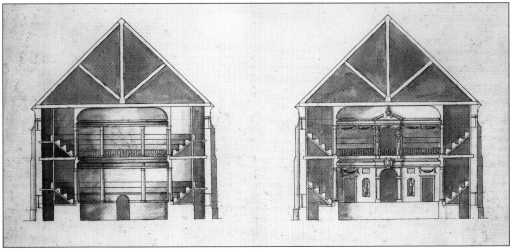

FIG. 15 Inigo Jones's plans for a roofed theatre, possibly the Cockpit in Drury Lane, preserved at Worcester College, Oxford. The basis for the Inigo Jones theatre in the Globe development.

that the stage was painted, and at the Fortune was adorned with satyrs and other carvings 'wrought pilaster-wise', but the precise scheme has to be done by using what we know of Tudor decorative practices to guess the most likely one used for the Globe. We chose a three-tier scheme, with heroes like Hercules himself standing at stage level, and the gods in the heavens, mediated by the Muses at the middle level. The colourful painting used for the stage in the 1996 Prologue season shocked people who expected a Victorian version of black-and-white Tudor half-timbering. The design chosen for the final stage decoration is different, though equally colourful. Its scheme incorporates the images of Hercules and Adonis depicted on the stage hangings made for the Globe by the New Zealand Shakespeare Society (fig. 63). The whole effect, the building's plain exterior unfolding into a brilliantly garish interior scene, conforms to the best information we have about Tudor ideas of decoration. (*See* the chapter by John Ronayne, pp. 121–46 *below*.)

This unique conjunction of so many different areas of expertise, all directed at the same target, has been a revelation. Looking back on the earlier attempts to design a new Globe, I admire the enthusiasm but deplore the lack of knowledge the earlier practitioners brought to the task. You can see why in such a project architects alone are not enough. What Sam Wanamaker did was, first, by insisting that the original location was the only place for it, to give this project an automatic priority over any other reconstruction (to say the least, we had the original weather as an element in our design). Secondly, by his insistence on 'authenticity' (a concept which even now, or perhaps especially now, I have to quarantine in quotation marks), he brought in so many experts in different fields whose knowledge had never before been called on in the thinking about the Globe's design. The location was important because it gave the project a place even when nobody really believed that it would ever be built. The expertise was the guarantee that whatever we ended up with, it would not be another Lutyens fantasy, a Shakespeare Disneyland, but the very best guess, the most faithful reconstruction, that all the leading experts working side by side could come up with.

That was the essential pre-requisite for the giant learning process that the Globe's reconstruction has entailed. The actual requisite, making a single design that would work and would best satisfy the demands of the variable evidence, was what brought the different kinds of expertise together. Each learned from the others. Construction historians learned that it is not always possible to rely on known precedents when no answer to a particular design problem has survived. Archaeologists learned that Tudor remains are a very different kind of challenge from Roman remains, especially when they are as rare, even unique, as were the Elizabethan playhouses. And scholars learned from the architects that it is not enough to retire with a 'not proven' verdict when practical design solutions have to be found.

In the wake of that learning process, some of us tend to hug ourselves in secret delight over one of the hidden bonuses that the project contains, the Inigo Jones theatre. That secondary resource was never going to be a serious fund-raiser, but it is vital to the project, at least as the scholars see it (fig. 15). Whether or not Jones's plans were drawn up for the first theatre built to rival Shakespeare's Blackfriars, the Cockpit of 1616 in Drury Lane, they do stand as the only set of architect's plans from the time that were made for a real working public theatre. Building from these plans removes all of the guesswork that the Globe project has been dogged by. It carries the absolute assurance that, whether built as Jones intended or not, it does represent what he, the Surveyor-Royal, thought a hall theatre like the Blackfriars should resemble. On the site, its Jacobean elegance contrasts wonderfully with the Tudor vernacular of the Globe.

Having a second playhouse that closely resembles the Blackfriars is vital to our understanding of how the Globe worked as a theatre in its own time. James Burbage's first hall playhouse was built three years before the Globe, as an innovatory replacement for the old Theatre, and if Shakespeare's company had been allowed to use it in 1596 the Globe would never have been needed. So it represents what the company's impresario thought in 1596 that the company needed for its future. When they did finally manage to start using it, in 1609, they found that they had so enjoyed their ten years at the Globe that they decided to continue there, making one house the summer theatre and using the other for winter. That tells us a lot about theatres as they ran in London at that time. The radical difference in size between the two stages will make the transfer of plays from the Globe to the Inigo Jones a fascinating test for the players' mobility, their flexibility, and their adaptability. We know how mobile and versatile the Elizabethan players had to be. A similar versatility will have to be developed at the new complex. What other effects that might have on the performances we can at present only guess. Having both playhouses will enable us to copy the Shake-speare company procedures more faithfully than we could if we only had the Globe. And we know that the Inigo Jones plans as a design for an early seventeenth-century theatre are not a flight of the imagination, likely to need modification whenever any new information turns up.

But that is a side-benefit. What the Cockpit or Inigo Jones theatre cannot give us is the same convergence of so many different kinds of expertise that the idea of rebuilding the Globe has produced.

Notes to Chapter Two

1   The debate drew in most of the major names in theatre and Shakespeare studies of the time, including Granville Barker, Gordon Craig, E.K. Chambers, Sidney Lee, and not least Beerbohm Tree. The debate is summarised in Cary Mazer, *Shakespeare Refashioned: Elizabethan Plays on Edwardian Stages*, Ann Arbor, 1981. Poel's ideas are described by Robert Speaight, *William Poel and the Elizabethan Revival*, London, 1954.

2   In a note in *Modern Language Review* 45, 1950, pp. 6–17. It was also Shapiro who demolished the case for the Visscher engraving of the first Globe. Further information about this and other Globe-building projects can be found in this book's predecessor, *Rebuilding Shakespeare's Globe*, by Andrew Gurr with John Orrell, London and New York, 1989.

3   Ben Iden Payne, *A Life in a Wooden O. Memoirs of the Theatre*, New Haven, 1977, p. 187. Iden Payne says that the San Diego Globe was built from the timbers of the Chicago Globe. It has recently been rebuilt after an arsonist burned it down.

4   Wanamaker asked Theo Crosby to become the Globe project's architect in 1978. His work sustained and enhanced the project from then until his death in 1994.

5   'The Bankside Theatres: Early Engravings', *Shakespeare Survey* 1 (1948), 25–37.

PART TWO

VARIETIES OF RESEARCH

FIG. 16 Model of the First Globe 1599–1613 by Roy Waterson
from the designs of Richard Hosley

3

DESIGNING THE GLOBE
READING THE DOCUMENTS

John Orrell

I N 1979 Sam Wanamaker asked me to serve as the principal historical adviser to the architect of the Globe project, Theo Crosby. I leaped at the chance, partly because of my admiration for Theo, one of the leading post-Modern theorists in London, and perhaps even more because the attempt to reconstruct the original Globe looked like being the most exciting thing to happen in Shakespeare studies in my time.

In one sense there was a simple job to do: find out what the original Globe was like, and formulate a description of it that would help Theo Crosby draw up his designs. Most historians of the Globe, faced with a similar task, had accordingly narrowed the field of their research as much as possible. They sought, in a focused way, to discover how big the theatre was, what was its shape, how its stage roof was managed. So did I, at first. But in truth nobody really knew what the first Globe was like in any detail, and repeated searches of the archives by generations of far wilier scholars than I was ever likely to become had failed to discover any impressive new body of evidence.

One thing we can be quite sure of about history is that it is nothing new. Every history is a rewriting of a previous one, and the best historian for our time is merely the one who tells us the most persuasive story about the past. Part of the persuasiveness may lie in the introduction of new facts, or old facts newly interpreted, or simply old facts rearranged. But even a 'fact' is a questionable entity: there are, I suppose, even now an almost infinite number of 'facts' about the year 1599 still in existence in archives all over the world, in the soil beneath the fields and streets, in vibrations (could it be?) locked deep within ancient stones or etched within the irregularities of antique glass. The historian of 1599 (already defined by his task as an artificial construct) selects a handful from the enormous pile, the great world-wide fact-mountain, and from this small sample strings together a formal narrative, which is itself merely a revision of its predecessors. If the story is persuasive it will stand; but it will last only until the next, more timely, revision displaces it with one that is more persuasive still.

In 1979, when I accepted Sam Wanamaker's invitation, the precedent history of the first Globe was enshrined in a beautiful model based on the research of Richard Hosley, who in turn owed something to the work of Richard Southern and C. Walter Hodges (fig. 16). It accepted some fundamental ideas about Elizabethan public theatres in general that were common knowledge. The Globe was a timber-frame structure, 'round' (or more likely polygonal) in plan, with three storeys of galleries giving onto a central yard, at least part of which was open to the weather. Everyone could agree on such matters, but the model went into detail, where agreement was less likely. The prime documents – the 'facts' – that in-formed Hosley's work were a picture of the first Globe that appeared in an engraving of London by C.J. Visscher, published in Amsterdam in 1616 (fig. 4, p. 26); the drawing of the Swan playhouse interior, made by Aernout (or Arendt) van Buchel after a lost original by a Dutch visitor to the theatre in about 1596, Johannes De Witt (fig. 5, p. 29); and the builder's contract for the Fortune playhouse, erected in 1600 by Peter Streete, who is thought to have built the Globe (*see* Documents pp. 180–2). In addition Hosley determined the size of the Globe by reference to a fourth document, the very convincing view of the second Globe made by Hollar in *c.* 1638 (fig. 7, p. 37). Of course there are hundreds, perhaps thousands, of other documents which inform any reading even of these few (one thinks, for example, of the court records that describe some rum goings-on at the Theatre in Shoreditch, or Henslowe's so-called Diary with its fund of information about the Rose playhouse). But most discus-sion of the design of the Globe comes in the end to turn on the small body of evidence so carefully analysed by Hosley.

Only one of these four prime documents actually alludes to the first Globe; the other three describe other playhouses that might have been similar to the Globe, and so were of analogical value. But each of these collections of facts looked more and more problematic the more one gazed at them. There is scant evidence that Visscher ever visited London, and W. W. Braines and I. A. Shapiro showed long ago that his panorama of Bankside was concocted from various other published maps and map-views dating back decades before his time. It bore no independent authority whatever, and had now to be set aside, despite its seductive detail. The Swan drawing was certainly valuable, but didn't show the Globe: without some more certain link, who could say that its evidence was directly useful? In addition its ill-managed perspective made it ambiguous in many parts where one looked for certainty. But Hollar's picture of the second Globe came closer to providing firm informa-tion, not only because of its assured perspective composition, but also because current building regulations and a reliable government survey both told us that the second Globe was built directly on the foundations of the first. It was a fair conclusion, then, that Globe 2 was the same diameter overall as Globe 1, and Hollar seemed to give good information on that score.

But before we come to that there is the Fortune contract to be considered (*see* pp. 180–2 *below*). It is the most potent but also the most tantalizing of the four documents, with many direct references to the first Globe itself. In general it required Peter Streete to make the Fortune just like the Globe, only square in plan where the model was some other shape ('round,' according to several literary allusions). The size of the Fortune's main timber frame was specified as 80 ft each way, with an internal yard 55 ft across so that the storeys of galleries were each 12 ft 6 in. deep at ground floor level. There was to be a tiring house and stage set up 'within' the frame, the stage 43 ft wide, extending to the middle of the yard, and covered by a 'shadow' or stage roof of a kind not further specified. The Fortune's principal posts facing forwards (into the yard) were to be square in section, shaped like pilasters with a carved satyr on each one. In almost every other detail, Streete was merely to follow the example of the Globe, set up on Bankside the year before (presumably by Streete himself though no evidence has come to light telling us so directly). Thus although the Fortune contract says little about the first Globe, it is, in its exasperating and repeated allusions to that theatre as the model Streete was to follow, a formidably persuasive document for the historian of Shakespeare's theatre. It must be taken very seriously indeed.

In particular, the details the contract gives of the overall dimensions surely have some bearing on those of the first Globe. It may be, of course, that the Fortune contract gave particular details only – or mostly – where the model of the Globe was to be departed from. That would seem to be the case in the matter of its square plan. Some people argued that, if the Fortune was 80 ft across, its model – the Globe – must have been the same measure in diameter. But a circle (or many-sided polygon) 80 ft in diameter covers a much smaller area than a square 80 ft across. If the Fortune merely re-used the 80 ft dimension in this way its whole area would have been considerably larger than the Globe's. The model would have been radically superseded, and in a most telling way, offering an altogether larger, more heroic acting space.

Some other way of following the Fortune's dimensions seemed to be necessary, and Hosley found a very attractive one. The theatre's storey heights were specified in the contract, and it is a reasonable bet – though only a bet – that they would not vary much from one playhouse to another. They were not enormously different from large-scale domestic standards to be found in use throughout London, and were probably not very different from the dimensions of the Globe. At the Fortune there was to be a brick plinth at ground level, one foot high, supporting the timber frame of the galleries. These were 12 ft high at the lower level, 11 ft at the middle level and 9 ft at the top, so that the whole height to the wall plates was 33 ft. So perhaps, went Hosley's argument, the first Globe was 33 ft high also. He claimed that the aspect ratio of the second Globe as shown by Hollar was 3 :1, or a width just three times the height to the plates; he therefore calculated that the whole frame was about 100 ft across (3 x 33 = 99). And since after the fire of 1613 the first Globe left the foundations that were reused for the second, it too was 100 ft in diameter.

The argument was clear, simple and persuasive. Until one checked Hollar again, and found that the aspect ratio of width to height was more like 3.3 :1 than 3 :1. Using Hosley's argument, therefore, one should conclude that the Globe was actually about 33 x 3.3 ft = 109 ft in diameter, not 100 ft. Hosley's figure already challenged belief: no-one had supposed before that the Globe could have been as large as he said it was. 109 ft seemed altogether too wide, and prompted a long reappraisal of Hollar's wonderfully precise drawing.

Hollar's sketch of the 'West part o[f] Southwarke,' in which the picture of the Globe and Hope playhouses appeared, was not quite what it seemed (fig. 8, p. 37 *above*). Because they were looking for specific details about a particular building, scholars had tended to read the visual evidence of the prints and drawings at face value, without enquiring closely enough into their mode of production. Visscher's engraving was worthless as independent evidence, because of the way it was made. What about Hollar? I needed to know how he had made his drawing. It contained, I soon discovered, precise pencil marks in positions that could have been produced only if he had used some kind of drawing frame to assist his eye. The view was certainly made from the top of the church tower of St Saviour's, now Southwark cathedral. One can still climb up to the spot where the artist worked, and see the main sweep of the river across the view, much as he saw it in the seventeenth century. In the background of the drawing he sketched in several landmarks to the north of the Thames whose positions can now be located on a modern Ordnance Survey map, with some allowance made of course for the accidents of history between Hollar's time and ours. The gable at the east end of Old St Paul's, for instance, which Hollar marked very exactly on his sheet, is the gable of a building now long gone. But its position is known, and can be traced on the modern map. Hollar also marked the tower of St Martin's, Ludgate; the water tower built by Bevis Bulmer in 1598; the tower of St Bride's church, Fleet Street; and the river front of the Savoy Hospital. All these buildings have now gone, though most have left some remains; all can be accurately located. Once that is done, Hollar's sightlines from his position on the tower can be projected on the map. I now needed to discover whether there was any precise correlation between the surveyed landscape represented by the map, and the scene registered on Hollar's sheet. I took a copy of the sketch marked with the intervals between the landmarks, laid it across the diagram of sightlines, and found that it would fit quite precisely when oriented at about 25° east of true north. The proportions of the intervals between the landmarks in the drawing are not simply those that would be seen by the unassisted eye: they are consistent only with a plane intersection of the visual pyramid of the sightlines, necessarily the product of an optical device that set up a 'picture plane' between the observer and the landscape. The topographical glass is such a device.

A sketch made faithfully at the drawing frame or topographical glass will be a perfect linear perspective, rather like a photograph taken through the undistorting 'lens' of a pinhole camera. Provided one can accurately fix the position of the observer in relation to the view, it can be analysed trigonometrically and each component within it can be measured. Hollar's position on the church tower was known, and his drawing could therefore be subjected to mathematical analysis. I found that large checkable intervals like those between buildings in the background, and small intervals like the width of Winchester House close to, were accurate within plus or minus 2%. The width of the Globe thus deduced was 102.35 ft, and its height to the eaves 31.97 ft, both measurements plus or minus 2%. A known margin also had to be allowed for imprecision in measuring from the drawing, with the result that the whole possible range for the diameter was between 99.34 ft at the minimum and 105.39 ft at the very most. After all the fuss, Hosley's inspired guess was substantially confirmed, though it could now be placed on a firmer theoretical foundation.

The model of the Globe was shaped as a polygon of 24 sides. Hosley had argued that a reasonable bay width at the Fortune was about 11 ft, so that the 55 ft yard at that theatre was surrounded by four ranges of five bays each, with a further bay on each corner, for a total of 24. And the Swan drawing seemed to show half of the round of that theatre, the stage and tiring house masking an estimated 5 bays, with 3 more visible to the left and 4 to the right, making a total of 12 bays for the half of the theatre shown, or 24 altogether. Lacking any other indication of the shape of the first Globe, I found the consistency here persuasive, and decided – mistakenly, as it turned out – to stick with the 24-sided plan.

There was in any case a more difficult matter to contend with. The model was a portable object, about a metre across and consisting of the Globe alone, with no indication of its setting. It contained no theory, therefore, of the theatre's orientation on the site. Theo Crosby's earliest drawings set the stage to the south, to take advantage of service access along Skin Market Place. But Hollar quite clearly placed the stage roof of the second Globe in the south-west, and because of the drawing's rigorous method it was possible to deduce that the Globe actually faced somewhere close to 48° east of true north, the azimuth, as it

FIG. 17 Sunlight penetration of the Globe's galleries at 3.00 p.m. on 11 June, looking west

FIG. 18 Sunlight penetration of the Globe's galleries at 3.00 p.m. on 11 June, looking south

turned out, of the midsummer sunrise. At first Crosby was reluctant to turn the theatre round to this orientation, so we set up an experiment, placing the model of the first Globe on an improvised heliodon and noting the play of direct sunlight and shadow through its structure as we tilted and turned it in the powerful beam of a theatrical profile spot. Our aim was to simulate the insolation of the building during the afternoon performance hours at various seasons and on various alternative orientations. What we found was surprising: on the historical orientation of 48° the stage was always in the shade, and whatever sunlight penetrated the building shone into the galleries rather than on the players (figs 17 and 18). This was precisely the opposite of what most modern people expect; artists' impressions of the Globe commonly show its stage bathed in sunlight and its auditorium conveniently cast in the shade. The effect was so radical and complete that Crosby was convinced, and went to a great deal of trouble to redesign the project to accommodate a Globe facing in the direction Hollar so fortunately recorded.

Crosby was at this time (the early 1980s) still enough of the modernist to use the metric system, converting the Elizabethan figures – like those of the Fortune contract – to convenient metric approximations. In a scheme of January 1981, for example, the Globe appeared as 31m (101 ft 9 in.) in diameter, its yard was 23m across (75 ft 6 in.), and its height to the wall plates was 11m (36 ft 1 in.). If we were to build truly in the Elizabethan way it was clear that these metric niceties would have to be banished. A new subject therefore opened up: recovering the Globe was not a matter merely of finding a detailed technical design, but of understanding how such a design might originally have come into being. We had to know as much as we could discover about Elizabethan building practices, and about the intellectual climate in which men like Peter Streete and his employers moved. From theatre history, then, one had to move to the history of architecture.

Later, when the master carpenter Peter McCurdy joined the project, it would become possible to hand over responsibility for the historical building procedures to him. But for the moment I had to work on my own. Previous reconstructors of the Elizabethan playhouses had very little to say on such matters, though Irwin Smith did include a brief study of jointing practices in his book *Shakespeare's Globe Playhouse*. No theatre historian, it seemed, had understood even the most basic fact about Elizabethan timber-frame building: that it was essentially a method of prefabrication, in which the timbers were carefully prepared in some convenient 'framing place' usually remote from the actual building site, and then transported to the site and erected fairly rapidly. With this procedure in mind I looked again at the Fortune contract and a large body of similar documents, mostly in the Public Record Office and the British Library. It became clear that there were distinct phases to the building operation, each of which was generally marked on completion by the payment of a determined part of the total agreed cost. The timbers were first *made* (hewn, squared and jointed); then, having been transported to the site, they were *erected* or raised; after that the frame was *set up* with joists, rafters and the like; finally it was *finished* perhaps with lath and plaster, or perhaps with joiner's work. Some contracts envisaged payments due at each of these phases, but the Fortune agreement divided the process into two: one payment of half the total to be made after the erection, and the other on completion of the finishing. It seemed fitting that we should follow a similar pattern at the new Globe, and accordingly when Peter McCurdy joined the project he did so on a contract drawn up using these Elizabethan terms.

Written on the back of the Fortune contract are notes showing the progress of the building operations day by day, from the beginning of January until July 1600. The simple two-phase terms of payment were more complicated in practice, Philip Henslowe doling out smaller amounts on behalf of the owner Edward Alleyn (who put up all the capital) as advances against the major sums. From these acquittance accounts we learn that Streete was in the country from January until April with a large team of workmen, purchasing, preparing and jointing the timbers. These prefabricated parts were then barged down the river, possibly to Streete's own wharf at Bridewell. In May the foundations were built on the site in Golden Lane, and immediately afterwards the frame was erected, with the help of some extra carpenters brought in from Windsor. Next came the setting up, and Henslowe left an incomplete account for the purchase of dimensioned lumber which went into the joists, the floorboards and other secondary parts of the structure; he also dined with Streete and some of the workmen almost every week, on paydays, and left a record of that too.

Searching through these rather technical accounts, one develops a sense of the scale of Streete's enterprise at the Fortune. It must have been similar at the Globe, though here of course the timbers were not newly prepared, but simply the dismantled frame of the old Theatre in Shoreditch, carried over the river and reused for the Globe on Bankside. The phases of erection, setting-up and finishing would all have been gone through at the Globe: only the initial 'making' of the timbers was avoided. Those timbers had been prepared long before, in 1576, when the Theatre was originally built, but their cutting and jointing will have been carried out in just the same way as later on at the Fortune.

Most Elizabethan building contracts define their dimensions in feet and inches, sometimes measured between centres but more often taking one surface of the timbers as a plane of reference. Thus a bay might be 11 ft wide, right side to right side of the posts. In trying to make sense of the particular dimensions of the Fortune, however, I found that the yard and its surrounding galleries were related as 1 is to $\sqrt{2}$ if measured at the centres. Assuming for the moment that the groundsills (the horizontal timbers that were mounted directly on the brick plinth) were 11 inches square in section, the centre-to-centre width of the yard would be 55 ft 11 in., and that of the external wall 79 ft 1 in. These two figures are related in the *ad quadratum* proportion: $55.917 \times \sqrt{2} = 79.079$. The demonstration is exact, and suggested that the ancient *ad quadratum* method may have been used to proportion the frame overall to its interior yard, in such fashion that the diagonal of the yard precisely equalled the length of the side of the theatre. And the surface to surface measurement of the yard appeared to be related to the unit of the rod (at 16 ft 6 in. a statute measure in Streete's time, the standard by which running brickwork was estimated, and of course the unit favoured by land surveyors). The yard was 3⅓ rods each way (55 ft), and the frame was 2 rods high to the plates (33 ft). Here, it seemed, was the basic unit we needed for the measurement of the Globe. A standard surveyor's line was three or four rods long, and a polygon whose radius was exactly three rods would make a theatre 99 ft in diameter, or about 100 ft overall if the rod measurement were taken to the centres. Such a figure agreed with Hosley's estimate, and with the more soundly-based deduction I had been able to make from Hollar's drawing, which also showed that the yard of the second Globe was proportioned to the whole width of the frame as 1: $\sqrt{2}$.

Theo Crosby, for so long wedded to a metric approximation to Elizabethan measurements, now produced a delightful *ad quadratum* setting-out diagram for the Globe, based on the three-rod radius (fig. 36, p. 98 *below*). Certainly there have been changes in the plan since then, but the principle remains: the new Globe is a centrally designed structure whose fundamental unit of measure is the statute rod of 16 ft 6 in., and whose proportions (now only at the level of the top storey rather than the sills) are determined in the medieval *ad quadratum* way. (*See* the discussion by Jon Greenfield, pp. 97–100 *below*.)

All this devoted attention to the very grain of the historical documents lifted the theatre from its tenuous metrical moorings in computer-generated drawings, and settled it once more in something like authentic Bankside mud. We were defining the conditions for a reconstruction that would, so far as possible, be governed by traditions of design and craftsmanship like those that had produced the original. But the matter was wider than that. The people who built the Theatre in 1576, and those who built the Rose of 1587, the Swan of c.1595, the Globe of 1599 and the Fortune of 1600 had friends who were involved in a theatrical world that included the smallest, most remote moot-hall in the provinces, and the great well-financed court theatres of Whitehall. There was, that is to say, an intellectual climate that shaped the body of buildings among which the first Globe took its place. There has long been an unfortunate tendency among theatre historians to isolate the playhouses for special study, removed from the main design preoccupations of the day. But Peter Streete personally knew many of the carpenters and other craftsmen who were to build the Jacobean Banqueting House at Whitehall, beginning in 1606. He made a contribution to it himself, lending special equipment for boring out the vast classically-carved columns that supported the interior. We may not know much about Streete's own aesthetic habits, but quite a bit is on record concerning those of Robert Stickells, say, who designed the elevations of the Banqueting House. Stickells left a group of theoretical memoranda in which he discussed the relative claims of medieval *ad quadratum* design and the commensurate proportions of the ancients, as known particularly in Vitruvius. He also designed a geometrical roof derived from Serlio's *Architettura* for Sir Thomas Tresham at Lyveden; a similar geometrical roof was drawn up – by a mathematician called Anderson – for the Banqueting House. Such anglicizings of the European Renaissance tradition were everywhere about Streete while he built the Globe: outside the theatre door, in Southwark, lay the workshops of the Southwark school of funerary sculptors, whose sophisticated polychrome work in

FIG. 19 John Norden, *Civitas Londini* (1600), detail of inset map of London, showing the Globe and Rose theatres

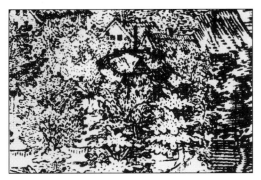

FIG. 20 John Norden, *Civitas Londini* (1600), detail of panorama showing the Globe

marble carried a refined classicism deep into the parishes of England in a series of tombs like those of the Earls of Rutland at Bottesford. (*See* the discussion pp. 128–9 *below*.) So neither Streete nor those for whom he built lived in a design vacuum; their milieu is largely discoverable, and a necessary part of the Globe reconstruction project.

Following the particular evidence of Visscher, which he found partly confirmed in the Swan drawing, Hosley had agreed with Richard Southern and C. Walter Hodges that the 'Heavens' at the Globe covered only part of the stage, leaving the front section open to the weather, and supporting a thing they called a 'hut' whose chief purpose was to house a descent machine. This structure perched crazily at the top of the theatre, and didn't seem to me to be registered in the drawing of the Swan, no matter how ambiguous the Dutch draftsmen had been. Little attention had been paid to a fifth document, the view of London made in 1600 by the local surveyor, John Norden (figs 19 and 20). It contained a bird's-eye view of the Globe, in which the roof over the stage was integral with the roof of the main frame, and presented a gable end towards the centre of the yard (fig. 20). In its essentials this simple, even elegant, scheme was identical with the grander one described in greater detail by Hollar at the second Globe, and since it is improbable that Norden would capriciously have invented something that would later turn out to be built, I found his evidence more pertinent than that of the discredited Visscher or the Swan drawing. Theo Crosby accordingly drew up a scheme for what we called the 'Norden' roof which was then officially adopted (*see* fig. 32, p. 91).

In 1989 the documentary basis of the more focused, specific part of the enquiry was transformed by the discovery of the remains, first of the Rose and later of the Globe itself. The digs are the subject of another chapter in this book (*see* pp. 67–80 *below*), but their evidence immediately established a standard against which to judge one's previous conclusions. It is perhaps too easy to accept the initial findings of the archaeologists at face value; their work, like that of anyone else in historical matters, has to be rightly interpreted if it is to prove useful. The small part of the Globe's foundations revealed beneath the car-park off Park Street was just extensive enough to tempt one towards calculating the overall size of the theatre. The Museum of London, under whose auspices the dig was carried out, made the mystifying claim that a computer showed the diameter to be 80 ft, though what instructions the computer had been fed was never made clear. Simon Blatherwick and Andrew Gurr mercifully also made a guess, based on a rather intuive reading of the evidence, that the figure was more like the 100 ft of Hosley's original estimate. I was able to offer a more methodical analysis which led to the same conclusion: Hollar's drawing of the second Globe was vindicated, and so was Hosley's estimate.

Hosley was also vindicated in another very basic matter. I had argued from the proportions of Hollar's sketch that the plan of the second Globe (and therefore of the first, which provided the foundations) was laid out *ad quadratum* on the ground, so that the outer wall described a diameter of 99 ft, and the internal yard was 70 ft across (70 x $\sqrt{2}$ = 99). With that plan, which had formed the basis of our design since Crosby's *ad quadratum* setting-out diagram had removed the whole thing from its metric strait-jacket, the galleries at ground-floor level were 14 ft 6 in. deep, measured radially. What the two theatre digs made clear was that the galleries at both the Rose and the Globe were, like those of the Fortune contract, 12 ft 6 in. deep measured straight across (about 12 ft 8 in. radially in the case of the polygonal playhouses). Hosley had taken the Fortune as his standard here, and now was proved right. The difference in the depth of the galleries between ground level and the level of the plates (where Hollar showed it to be greater) could be accounted for by forward jetties in each of the two upper storeys: if Hollar's proportioning of the frame of the second Globe spoke also for the first its *ad quadratum* proportioning was true only at the top level.

But the shape of the theatres revealed in the two digs was something of a surprise to everyone. The Rose was originally built (in 1587) as a more-or-less regular polygon of 14 sides, a number no-one had thought likely. And the single bay discovered at the Globe was evidently part of a 20-sided polygon, an almost equally improbable figure. The Elizabethan theatre builders were a good deal more inventive in their geometry than I at least had thought likely, and it was useful to have confirmation that the building was neither 6-sided, 8-sided nor truly round, as scholars had at various times supposed. With hindsight it is now possible to see that there must have been 20 bays at the Fortune, too. Hosley's 'corner' bays, which boosted the total to 24, were a structural impossibility because the jetties could only be accommodated by diagonal framing in the corners (what carpenters called 'dragon beams'): the Fortune probably had only 20 bays in all, just like the Globe.

Some of the findings at the digs strengthened notions that before had seemed mere hints in the documentary evidence. At the Fortune, for example, Streete was contracted to supply strong iron 'pikes' all around the yard, presumably defences to keep the groundlings from climbing into the more expensive lower gallery. No reconstruction of an Elizabethan theatre that I had seen actually showed these murderous devices in position, though spikes of a similar sort were common in English theatres at least until the 1860s, lined across the orchestra partition, along the fronts of the stage boxes and often high in the gallery where it abutted the slips to either side of the house. They represent a kind of outdoor street furniture applied to the interior of a theatre, rendering the public place ambiguous in this respect. No such spikes turned up at the digs, but the surface of the yard of the second Rose (after the reconstruction of 1592) consisted of industrial slag used as a paving material, in precisely the same way as soap-ashes had been used in Southwark and other London boroughs to pave roads and bowling alleys. Similar material was found at the Globe: these two theatres, it seems, combined the roughness of the street with more refined work in their interiors.

That refined work – some part of the finishing phase of construction, and some of a kind excluded by the terms of Streete's contract at the Fortune, and to be undertaken by someone else – is unfortunately the least documented part of the Globe. It was largely a matter of paintwork, and will have followed the fashions of 1599, not the original specifications of the Theatre in 1576. The documents almost persuade us that the tiring-house front (whence the actors entered onto the stage) was left plain, to be adorned only with figured hangings. It's certainly very plain in the Swan drawing, and tricked out with little more elaborate than hangings in the two or three small pictures we have of the interiors of unspecified (and probably imaginary) London theatres in the earlier 17th century. On the other hand we have two *frons* designs by Inigo Jones, both intended for the use of professional acting companies, that enliven their symmetries with terms, urns, statues and busts. There were carved satyrs over the stage at the Fortune, and turned columns at the Hope in 1613. (*See* the contract for the Hope, pp. 183–4 *below.*) While these tiny pieces of information are no more than hints, it is difficult to believe that late Elizabethan craftsmen could leave so obvious a feature as the tiring house unadorned.

One can turn to the triumphal arches erected by the City of London for James I's entry in 1604 for evidence of the style: like the Swan, they were of wood painted to look like colourful stone, and they were informed by a vigorous classicism whose complexities we are only now beginning to understand (*see* figs 50–5, pp. 125–7). The same is true of the work undertaken at the royal palaces and extensively documented in the Works accounts. This too was often painted 'stone colour,' or 'rance like jasper,' or veined black like touch. A third source lay nearby in the sculptors of the Southwark school, men like Gerard Jonson or Richard Stevens, whose magnificent tombs showed what the real stone looked like, with their vocabulary of coloured marbles, obelisks and fine canonical detail. (For more detailed discussion *see* chapter 7, pp. 121–46 *below.*)

There was a tendency, natural enough in the circumstances, to make each succeeding theatre more lovely (and sometimes larger) than its predecessor: the Second Globe was 'far fairer' than the first, and when the Fortune burned in 1621 it was rebuilt both larger and more beautiful. It is likely, then, that the Globe improved on the decor of the Theatre, and although we know nothing directly about what taste guided the painters we do at least know what fashions were currently being cultivated at Court. The Sergeant Painter from 1598 to 1605 was Leonard Fryer, who was something of a specialist at making cheap wood look like expensive stone. The Works accounts give details of the effects he achieved, and John Ronayne has added these to his extensive knowledge of contemporary pigments, media and painting practices to produce a reliable approach to the decorative methods most likely to have been used at the original Globe.

The decorative scheme was shaped most fundamentally by the proportions of the building itself. Many of the documents I have mentioned so far have been discrete objects, the kind that can be reproduced in the illustrations or Part Four of this book. But there is a further 'document,' of a quite different order: the internal logic of the theatre's frame, as we have reconstructed it, exerts its own powerful and usually benign influence on the design of its parts, including the surface decoration. Occasionally there's a hitch, and it shows. Beneath the paint the new Globe's face bears marks of the strain that went into its design.

The tiring house front, the *frons*, is the ground against which the actors are seen, the structure from which they emerge to play their parts and into which they return when they have done. It puts its spin on their work, and finely colours the audience's experience of the play. The design we have arrived at, after a decade and more of discussion and revision, is richly decorated, but just out of sight lies a heavy oak frame whose main timbers define the placing of the doors, pilasters, balustrades and other architectural features. Both in height and in width these rigidly-placed, unforgiving, members have had to be accommodated. Elsewhere in this volume Jon Greenfield describes some of the constraints on their placing, of which two especially influenced the architectural decoration: the height of the lower storey, and the implications of the positioning of the great stage columns that support the Heavens.

The first-floor balcony in the *frons* is principally a place for the most expensive audience seating, but it is also quite often used, in plays written for the first Globe, for small-scale parts of the performance: Brabantio, Desdemona's father, looks out from there, as from an upper-storey window overlooking the street. On very rare occasions – at most only twice in the extant first-Globe plays – it is necessary for an actor to climb from the stage to the balcony, or make the descent, in full view of the audience. At one of the Pentagram seminars the assembled scholars, setting this question of accessibility perhaps too firmly in the foreground of their thoughts, decided to limit the height of the balcony above the stage, if possible to 9 ft, so that Romeo – in a pre-Globe play – could climb down from his Juliet. Theo Crosby responded by lowering the balcony from the height he had previously thought reasonable – thirteen feet – to nine. The result, visually, was disastrous: the upper storeys of the *frons* looked overstated, pompously tall and imposing, while the main floor – the one that the actors normally used – was cramped to the point of meanness. This effect was seen very clearly when one compared Crosby's new drawing with the two Jones *frons* schemes mentioned above (p. 60) both are scaled, and were meant for much smaller buildings than the Globe. Yet both pitch the stage balcony higher than our nine feet: one sets it at 10 ft, and the other at 10 ft 6 in.

Nevertheless our decision had been made, and Crosby set about using a set of design strategies to obviate its worst implications. At first he strengthened the pilasters of the lower order to give the bottom storey the air of a sturdy basement or podium on which the rest of the structure was mounted. But this had the effect of making the ground floor look still more compressed, and it sat ill with the use of hangings, a necessary provision in many plays. And in any case the stage itself was already a podium, as seen from the auditorium. Frustrated in that direction, Crosby chose another: he could extend the order of the ground floor's architecture through to the rail of the balcony balustrade, thus restoring the apparent height of the lower order to his original 13 ft. This imaginative solution worked well enough, but there were difficulties in making it convincing. In effect the balustrade became the entablature of the lower order, a role for which it was rather overscaled. The balcony parapet in the Swan drawing is rendered as part of the lower storey in just this way (fig. 5, p. 29), but is not articulated as part of an architectural order.

In a stream of alternative schemes that flowed from Crosby's pen during his final illness he fought with this difficulty, sometimes letting the balustrade express itself, sometimes hiding it as an entablature. The last drawing, intended for the exhibition at Bankside, made a wonderful compromise, setting figures of the Muses as caryatides on piers rising powerfully through the balcony balustrade: it was a triumphant response to the challenge of the cramped lower storey, even if it meant doing away with the entablature altogether (plate 24).

All this while Crosby had also been developing the decorative grammar of the *frons*, leaving the cool Palladianism with which he began for something much hotter, what he called the 'vernacular' style, owing much to buildings nearly contemporary with the first Globe, including those described in the Works accounts. But it would be Jon Greenfield who was left, sadly, to follow this path to its conclusion. (*See* plates 25, 26.)

Greenfield also had to deal, as he reports later in this volume, with some last-minute changes to the whole stage area, changes that radically reshaped the design of the *frons*. Experiments with a mocked-up steel-and-plywood version of Crosby's design led to demands that the positions of the stage posts and doors of entrance be altered, specifically that the posts be moved back toward the *frons*, and inward from the sides of the stage, and that the doors of entrance be more widely separated. All these things had been placed hitherto where structural considerations dictated: the stage roof, or Heavens, was required to cover the whole of the stage, and the posts that supported it had therefore to be rather widely spaced, and placed as close as possible to the front of the stage. But to set them exactly at the very corners of the stage would have made it impossible for actors to walk round them, or indeed to do much with them at all. So the columns were moved inward from the corners, but only as far as Elizabethan building practices suggested that the roof could project beyond them. Crosby in 1992 thought that half a rod (8 ft 3 in.) was the maximum likely projection, and placed the columns accordingly; later, convinced that so large an oversail was improbable, he reduced the figure to one-third of a rod (5 ft 6 in.) thus still leaving enough room for actors to circle the columns if they had a mind to. Now, late in 1995, came the demand to place the columns even further inboard than the old 8 ft 3 in. After a series of agonizing meetings, and a tremendous burst of activity from Jon Greenfield as he carefully drew out the implications of numerous alternatives, we decided to return substantially to Crosby's earlier scheme, and to place the columns half a rod inboard. That had important implications for the framing of the roof (*see below*, pp. 94–6), but it also meant that the structure of the frame behind the *frons* – the bone structure of the Globe's face – had to be altered too. As the great stage columns were moved closer together so the beams they supported had to be moved with them; and if these massive horizontal timbers were shifted, it also became necessary to relocate the posts that supported them in the plane of the *frons*. Our revision – which did not go as far as the actors, led by Sir Peter Hall and the designer Bill Dudley, would have liked – reduced the span between the stage columns from two rods (33 ft) to one and two-thirds (27 ft 6 in.), and narrowed the interval between the main structural posts of the *frons* accordingly. The three-bay *frons* with which Crosby had been working was now no longer practicable, and Jon Greenfield had to reshape it entirely, taking into account the actors' firm requirement that the doors of entrance should be as widely spaced as possible, and perceptibly outside the span of the columns.

The rejig was no easy matter. The central bay housed the so-called 'discovery space,' or opening large enough to contain a bed and/or several actors, and the doors of entrance had to be ample enough to permit armies (of two or three soldiers) to march on, as they do in *Julius Caesar*. Greenfield determined that nothing less than the two-thirds of a rod (11 ft) bay size with which he had been working hitherto would do for the discovery space; but that left bays of only half a rod (8 ft 3 in.) to flank it on either side between the unbudgeable posts that responded to the span of the stage columns, a total of 27 ft 6 in. apart. Noting that the ratio between the centre bay and those that flanked it was 4 : 3, Greenfield adopted what Alberti called a 'harmonic' proportion, giving the next bays further out – the ones that housed the doors of entrance – the same relation to their predecessors, so that they measured 6 ft 2¼ in., or three-eighths of a rod. The method of 'generating' one measure from another by means of fractions is characteristic of sixteenth-century craftsmanship, and the sequence represented a satisfactory marriage of utility and custom. But the *frons* design that resulted was oddly broken-backed: the diminishing proportions of the bays as they receded from the centre made it appear to weaken towards the extremes. I suggested that it might be strengthened by means of doubling (and coupling) the columns at the ends, left and right, thus providing a sense of closure there. But Greenfield had anticipated this objection, and already had a coupled-column design up his sleevePart Three.

In developing the new *frons* the architect also followed design models that were close to the date and milieu of the first Globe. Peter Streete's 1606 contract for the Beargarden gatehouse shows that he used obelisks as well as carved satyrs there: might he not have used them at the Globe too? Obelisks are characteristic of the contemporary work at the royal households, and appear on most of the 1604 city arches, where they are expressed as free-standing elements rising from a detached order erected in front of the plane of the arch itself. (*See* figs 50–5, pp. 125–7 *below*.) The Southwark school also employed them in this way, as for example in Richard Stevens' Hatton tomb of 1592 in Old St Paul's. Their use in the latest – and, in my view, most successful – *frons* design for the new Globe steadies the composition at either end, so countervailing its lateral weakness. But the obelisks are vertical elements, piercing heavenwards and so lifting the weight from the too-wide, too-low ground floor. Their verticality counteracts the tendency of the framed design to appear to sink in on itself. In short, they are good Elizabethan cosmetics.

Decoration on such a scale is likely to be governed by a scheme, or programme. The vertical hierarchy from the human business of the platform stage to the star-fretted Heavens above is nicely conventional, and when Peter Davidson and Siobhan Keenan were asked for their advice they argued that the planets might appear in the attic storey of the *frons*, a mediating level between the two. Earlier I had advised Theo Crosby to include statues of the dramatic muses, Melpomene and Thalia, to flank the central part of the balcony. There is an English tradition, traceable at least as far back as 1629, and extending to the twentieth century, for these two figures to appear on our stages, often free-standing on substantial pedestals located amongst the actors. There is no direct evidence for them at the Globe, but if its *frons* ran to carved decoration, as at the Fortune, they were the likeliest candidates. They help too with another aspect of the decorative programme, for they are opposites. The later tradition places Tragedy stage right, and Comedy stage left, a sideways tug that enlivens the symmetry of the *frons* and echoes the opposition of the (now) widely-separated doors of entrance. Davidson and Keenan reinforced this polarity by suggesting that the figures of Mercury and Apollo should appear at either end of the stage, two teachers of very different kinds of divine mystery.

The most interesting part of the design project may well therefore have nothing to do with the theatre documents at all. It consists of an attempt to discover, and then live within, the technical and aesthetic tastes of a late Elizabethan builder and his clients. Yet if the scope of the story is thus broadened to include contemporary building practices, design traditions and influences in general, it is also narrowed because the broad view brings with it a new understanding of the few small pieces of precise evidence that we have. One of them will make a fitting close to this brief outline of the process of the new Globe's design. The Fortune contract, it now appears, may offer a very precisely articulated version of the Globe itself. Just why Edward Alleyn's new theatre was built square, where its model was 'round' or polygonal, we shall probably never know. But in clause after clause the contract asserts that the Fortune should follow the precedent of the Globe, so it is particularly interesting to note that it specifies the depth of the ground-floor galleries as 12 ft 6 in., the same interval that one could take a tape to and measure at the archaeological dig on the Globe site. The archaeologists don't like speculating about the whole ground plan of the Globe when all they have to go on is the small patch of foundations they have managed to reveal (*see* Simon Blatherwick's chapter *below*). Those of us charged with the job of suggesting how the theatre was built can't afford the luxury of such scientific restraint: we have no choice but to make the attempt, no matter how tenuous the results of our enquiry may be. So we look for reassurance, and it may be that this shadow of the Fortune in the mud of the Globe site is capable of providing it. If our interpretation is right, the single bay whose dimensions may, at a pinch, be read in the chalk and brick remains was planned as a trapezoid, about 11 ft 6 in. wide at the front (where the gallery overlooked the yard), and 15 ft 6 in. wide at the back (i.e. the exterior of the circumference wall). Since, like the galleries at the Fortune, it was 12 ft 6 in. deep overall, its area was about 168.75 square feet. Its proportions suggest that it was one segment of a regular polygon of twenty sides, and although the Globe itself probably modified this basic shape in some way, as our reconstruction does in the part occupied by the tiring house, we may take it as representing a *schema* of the whole. The notional area of the gallery foundations in this *schema* is 20 x 168.75 = 3375 square feet.

Now consider the Fortune, as described in the contract. It is 80 ft square, with a yard centrally-placed within, 55 ft square, so that the ranges of galleries are all 12 ft 6 in. deep at ground level. The Fortune's yard was therefore quite a bit smaller than the Globe's, if our deductions are correct: 3025 square feet as against 4195 square feet at the Globe. Of course this gross calculation should be altered to take account of the area covered by the stage, and by any intrusion of the tiring house into the yard. But the overall comparison is instructive: the space for the groundlings – the popular, cheap part of the theatre – was probably much larger at the Globe than at the Fortune. But what of the galleries? These are where most of the revenue was raised, and Alleyn, the star actor for whom the Fortune was built, had good reason to want this part of his house to be as large as possible, always within the practical constraints of theatrical effectiveness. The area of the 'footprint' of the galleries is easily calculated, on the same *schema* basis as we have used for the Globe. One simply subtracts the area of the yard from the area overall. 6400 – 3025 = 3375 square feet, just the same figure as we have found to be true of the Globe as interpreted from the data provided by the dig. If those calculations are correct, it appears that Alleyn instructed his builder to make the galleries of the new house hold exactly the same number of people as in the model; and the Fortune was nothing but the round Globe squared.

Bibliographical Note

This essay was not meant to carry footnotes, but a few bibliographical pointers may be useful. Richard Hosley, whose scholarship is my beginning, distilled his work in a chapter on 'The Playhouses' in *The 'Revels' History of Drama in English*, Vol. III *1576–1613*, ed. J. Leeds Barroll and others (London, 1975) pp. 119–235 (the passage on the Globe is on pp. 175–96, and there is a valuable bibliography down to 1975). Photographs of the model appear in plates 2 and 3 of John Orrell, 'Sunlight at the Globe' *Theatre Notebook 38* (1984), pp. 69–76, which also describes the orientation experiment. The visual evidence may best be studied in R.A. Foakes, *Illustrations of the English Stage 1580–1642* (London, 1985). The Fortune contract and its endorsements are printed in *Henslowe's Diary*, ed. R.A. Foakes and R.T. Rickert (Cambridge, 1960) and *below* pp. 180–2. The topographical glass and its use in Hollar's sketch of West Southwark are described in my book, *The Quest for Shakespeare's Globe* (Cambridge, 1983), which includes also a discussion of *ad quadratum* theory. My article, 'Building the Fortune,' *Shakespeare Quarterly* 44.2 (Summer 1993), pp. 1–10 traces the phases of an Elizabethan carpenter's contract. Deductions from the archaeological digs of 1989 are most conveniently described in John Orrell and Andrew Gurr, 'The Rose Playhouse,' *Antiquity* 63 (1989), pp. 421–29; Simon Blatherwick and Andrew Gurr, 'Shakespeare's Factory: Archaeological Evaluation on the Site of the Globe Theatre at 1/15 Anchor Terrace, Southwark Bridge Road, Southwark,' *Antiquity* 66 (1992), pp. 315–29; and John Orrell, 'Spanning the Globe,' *Antiquity* 66 (1992), pp. 329–33, the last two of which are reprinted in Andrew Gurr, Ronnie Mulryne and Margaret Shewring, eds., *The Design of the Globe*, International Shakespeare Globe Centre, 1993, pp. 20–43 and 44–52. The present discussion of the style of the Globe's architecture and decoration is deeply indebted to Sir John Summerson's account of Court practices in *The History of the King's Works*, Vol. IV *1485–1660* (Part ii), gen. ed. H.M. Colvin (London, 1982), pp. 1–364. For the Southwark school *see* Katharine A. Esdaile, *English Monumental Sculpture since the Renaissance* (London, 1927) and – for the lovely illustrations more than the text – Timothy Mowl, *Elizabethan & Jacobean Style* (London, 1993). An important drawing of the Hatton tomb, wrongly attributed to Maximilian Colt, is reproduced in James Lees-Milne, *Tudor Renaissance* (London, 1951), plate 81. The fullest account of the artistic milieu from which the Globe sprang is to be found in *Albion's Classicism: The Visual Arts in Britain, 1550–1660*, ed. Lucy Gent (New Haven, 1995). Finally, the most persuasive influence on our design of the tiring house front at the Globe has been the series of engraved plates in Stephen Harrison, *The Arch's of Triumph* (London, 1604), conveniently reproduced in David M. Bergeron, *English Civic Pageantry 1558–1642* (London 1971), plates 2–8, and, with one exception, in the present volume, figs 50–5.

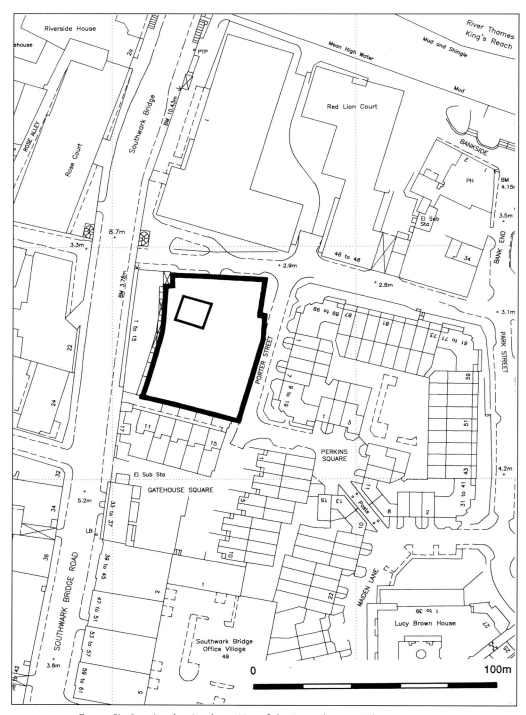

FIG. 21 Site Location showing the position of the site on the 1991 Ordnance Survey map
and the indicative location of the remains shown in illustration fig. 11, p. 40.

4

THE ARCHAEOLOGICAL EVALUATION OF THE GLOBE PLAYHOUSE

Simon Blatherwick

A RCHAEOLOGICAL EVALUATIONS on the Anchor Terrace car park site have confirmed the location of the site of the Globe playhouse, but the nature of the work undertaken means that many questions still remain to be answered about the structure of the theatre. The remains that do exist on the site are preserved *in situ* (in line with current best practice) for future generations. Documentary research has indicated the nature and scale of activity on the site since the construction of the first Globe in 1599 and suggests that the survival of any archaeological remains on the site (related to the Globe and its estate) is largely fortuitous – although further remains appear to survive beneath the standing Anchor Terrace building. The remains recorded during the 1989 evaluation are such that questions relating to such matters as the diameter of the theatre, the type of construction, and the location of the stage cannot be answered with certainty. Despite glimpses of the original remains, historians and scholars will still have to rely on the available documentary evidence to argue their corner on these and other issues.

Archaeological practice and historic sites

Despite the results of over two hundred years of scholarship and research it is only since the late 1980s that the physical remains of London's Tudor and Stuart theatres have been revealed by controlled archaeological excavation. While the results of the archaeological work are far from conclusive they begin to provide answers to questions. Yet, at the same time, the excavation and evaluation of the sites of the Rose and the Globe have posed more questions than archaeologists, architects, academics, building historians and dramatists had begun to think about less than a decade ago.

Before beginning to describe the results of the archaeological work that has taken place on Bankside in the last ten years it is worth describing the processes involved in archaeological excavation and evaluation and describing how archaeology now fits into the planning process. While close connection with the planning system now protects the country's archaeological resource it also provides a commitment to preserve the archaeological resource *in situ* (wherever possible) for future generations of archaeologists and scholars who should possess superior skills and techniques. As archaeology is a developing science and skill, constantly utilising new technologies and drawing upon the experience of new disciplines, there is no reason to believe that this will not be the case.

The process of archaeological excavation is essentially one of the physical destruction of the remains in the ground whilst at the same time undertaking a record of that which is being destroyed/excavated – a process known as 'preservation by record'. To provide a full and accurate picture of a site's archaeology the process of excavation involves the reverse stratigraphic removal of deposits (i.e. the removal of the latest deposit followed by the removal of the immediately preceding deposit) until excavation is complete. Deposits can vary in size, nature and significance. For example, they could consist of the fill of a cesspit, a chalk wall foundation or a brick floor surface. Each deposit (called a context in the archaeological process) is given a unique, individual number, thus identifying it as different from any other context. It is recorded on a special form known as a context sheet, by a drawn plan at a reduced scale (with the plan being located to a specific site grid or to the Ordnance Survey grid) and possibly by photograph, depending on the significance of the deposit. Along with the retained paper record a context may also provide information in terms of the finds or environmental evidence it contains. By undertaking controlled stratigraphic excavation, and by careful recording of contexts and the retrieval of artefacts from those contexts, an archaeologist can begin to build up a picture of the activities and depositional processes that have taken place on a particular site.

With a philosophical shift towards the idea of the preservation of archaeological remains *in situ* and the introduction of Planning Policy Guidance 16,[1] large scale archaeological excavation is not as commonplace as it was. Its place has been taken by a process known as archaeological evaluation which involves an assessment of the surviving archaeological remains (usually by an initial 'desk-top' survey followed by field evaluation) so that informed decisions can be taken about the remains on a site, dependent upon their scale and significance, while also taking into account the threat that is posed by any proposed development. Where significant archaeological remains are recorded during a site evaluation, local planning authorities may require that the site's archaeology is preserved *in situ* and impose conditions on developers which dictate the location of the proposed development or the style of foundations they are allowed to insert into the ground. While this process is intended to prevent a rapidly dwindling archaeological resource being totally lost to future generations, the process of archaeological evaluation is not without its difficulties.

Most archaeological evaluations are undertaken to a 'brief' which requires an assessment of the surviving archaeological deposits, in order to define the character and extent of those remains and at the same time to clarify the nature of intrusions into archaeological deposits. A brief will require the evaluation of all archaeological deposits on the site but not at the expense of other archaeological features which might reasonably be considered to merit preservation *in situ* and where preservation of remains may be a viable option. This can present archaeologists with a dilemma in the need to look at earlier (and therefore almost inevitably deeper) archaeological deposits without destroying or excavating later deposits which may (when and if their significance and merit are understood) be deemed worthy of preservation *in situ*. As it was an evaluation rather than an excavation that took place on the site of the Globe, it is worth bearing in mind that what was undertaken was an assessment of the deposits on the site without those deposits being excavated, analysed and fully understood. It goes without saying, therefore, that what has been written and said about the Globe, while based on available evidence and comparison with the site of the Rose, cannot be irrefutably proven. The complete nature and character of the deposits recorded in 1989 cannot be properly understood although the extent of their horizontal survival is.

Before we begin to consider the remains of the Globe as recorded in the 1989 evaluation it is worth remembering the requirement in an archaeological brief to look at the nature and extent of intrusions into an archaeological site. One must bear in mind that there is never a time in the history of the development of any site when the site is sealed in aspic. From geological, prehistoric and historic times sites and land are constantly subject to changes whether through natural erosion or human activity. The site of the Globe is no different from any other piece of land in London (although we may wish that it had been) and so it too has been subject to constant change.

What I hope to do is to describe the background to the site and the archaeological remains in relation to that background. The significance of those remains for the reconstructed Globe is discussed elsewhere in this book.

Topography and location of the site

The site on which the evaluation of the Globe theatre took place is situated in the London Borough of Southwark to the rear (east) of the building known as Anchor Terrace, Nos. 1/15 Southwark Bridge Road, London SE1, in an area known as Bankside (fig. 21). The site, within its modern property boundaries, covers an area of some 2200 square metres and is bounded to the north by Park Street (previously known as Maid or Maiden Lane), to the west by Anchor Terrace (a Grade 2 Listed Building) to the east by Porter Street and to the south by Gatehouse Square. The Globe Estate, located by W. W. Braines in 1924, falls partially within the boundaries of the modern site. Due to its recent usage the site is referred to as the Anchor Terrace car park site.

The site is situated in Thames alluvium to the north-west of one of the sand and gravel islands (eyots) on which the early settlement of Southwark took place, in an area of channels and marshy, alluvial clays and silts. The surrounding area has been constantly subject to inundation from the Thames and reclamation from the Roman occupation of Southwark (AD c.43–410) onwards. The alluvial nature of the soils, while good for the preservation of organic remains (timber, leather etc) can make difficult conditions for the retrieval of archaeological information.

Archaeological background to the site of the Globe

Previous archaeological investigations within the vicinity of the site have uncovered evidence of occupation from the Neolithic period (c.4000–2000 BC) onwards. An excavation at Skinmarket Place, to the north-west of the site, revealed a previously unknown eyot plus Neolithic pottery and flint artefacts, whilst Neolithic activity to the south-east of the site is illustrated by the recovery of a leaf-shaped arrow-head from the Old Courage Brewery site close to the junction of Park Street and Redcross Way.

Much of the Roman settlement in Southwark was around the Borough High Street where there was a dense concentration of first and second century Roman buildings. The settlement extended westwards on the higher, dry, sandy land and it seems likely that the Anchor Terrace car park site is too far north into the lower, wetter surrounding clayey soils to have been attractive for substantial Roman activity.

Archaeological excavations, close to the junction of Park Street and Redcross Way, have however uncovered Roman domestic and industrial activity, evidence of the road system within the Roman settlement and a large, well-preserved Roman timber, waterfront building (Brigham et al 1995).[2] To the south-west of Anchor Terrace at 38–42 Southwark Bridge Road a Roman timber post-and-plank revetment – part of the reclamation programme associated with the main Roman settlement to the east – was recorded. Dating evidence retrieved from behind the revetment suggested it was not constructed before the late third century.

The area surrounding the site was the subject of land reclamation schemes in the medieval period and by the fourteenth century river defences had been constructed although 'it seems clear … that large areas, probably on both sides of Borough High Street, remained water-logged until the 16th or 17th century' (Graham 1978, 516).

Evidence of post-medieval activity has also been recorded on sites in the vicinity of the Globe, the most notable of these being the Rose theatre some 100 metres to the north-west of the Globe. Excavation took place during the Winter and Spring of 1988–89 (Bowsher & Blatherwick 1991) and revealed the foundations of two phases of the Rose, the first theatre to be built on Bankside. Constructed in 1587, the remains of phase one appear to indicate that the building was a twelve or fourteen sided polygon some 72 ft in diameter (*see* fig. 10, p. 40 *above*). The main foundations of the polygon consist of chalk and brick walls and chalk foundation pads. The line of the external foundation was paralleled by an internal foundation some 11 ft 6 in. away – the foundations providing the base for the superstructure of the timber-framed gallery and so giving some indication as to the width of the lower gallery. The stage at the Rose, within the northern half of the building, appears to have been an elongated hexagon tapering towards its front edge. Although no evidence of the timber galleries was recovered during the excavation, the floor of the first phase yard (on which the groundlings stood) was uncovered, and indicated that the surface was raked in such a fashion that it sloped downwards to the brick and timber foundations of the stage – possibly as a means of maintaining sight-lines for those who stood at the back of the yard.

During 1592 the Rose underwent structural alterations and the physical remains for this second phase of the building appear to indicate that the northern half was extended, altering both the outline of the building and resulting in an alteration of the stage to a more rectangular, thrust shape. Pillar bases found inside the corners of the foundations of the second-phase stage suggest that it was covered. Wooden roofing shingles were amongst the artefacts recovered in this area of the site. Cartographic evidence from John Norden's *Civitas Londini* (1600) shows the Rose with a hut above the stage. The reason for these alterations is not fully understood although it may have been related to a change in the requirements of the plays being performed. The Rose went out of use in the early seventeenth century, probably as a result of the direct competition it received from the newly constructed Globe theatre.

The excavation at the site of the Rose revealed an almost complete ground plan of an Elizabethan theatre and produced significantly more information than was recorded at the site of the Globe. As a result of the work at the Rose, there has been a marked effect on the thinking related to the structure and format of such buildings, with assumptions relating to theatre size and stage location and size being challenged. Scholars of the early-modern theatre have had to accept that there may not be such a thing as a 'blueprint' for the design of theatre buildings. Contemporary illustrations and building accounts of the Swan, Globe, Fortune, Hope and Rose combined with new archaeological evidence suggest that each theatre may be as different as the people who built it and the locations in which they built.

Documentary background to the site

The importance of the borough of Southwark in the history and development of London cannot be stressed too greatly as Southwark developed as a suburb long before the City had reached saturation point with its population. Its riverside location, which provided it with a direct route to markets at home and abroad, enabled it to enjoy the prosperity brought by the development of trade, while its freedom from the jurisdiction of the City proved attractive to those who wished to live within a less restrictive environment. At the same time 'Those who resided on the north bank were not unaware of the advantages which accrued to them when odorous or dangerous places like tanneries, slaughter-houses, or gunpowder stores were relegated to the far side of the river.' (Johnson 1969, 1)

The use of the name Southwark first appears in the Burghal Hildage in the early tenth century when it is recorded as *Suthringa geweorche*, 'the defensive work of the men of Surrey' (Johnson 1969, 7). The Domesday Book records fifty households which were maintained by eleven Surrey lords within the borough. Whether these were occupied by military personnel or merchants is open to debate.

Initial ownership of land is difficult to ascertain. Southwark appears in the Domesday Book under the name of the Bishop of Bayeux. Undoubtedly the Crown had an interest in Southwark as Edward the Confessor is recorded as being lord of a manor there with sixteen houses. From the confusion of ownership records the King emerges as lord of the Guildable Manor (at the Bridge-head) although the name 'Gildable' does not appear until 1377 in *Rotuli Parliamentorum*. The Liberty of the Clink (the manor of the Bishop of Winchester in which Anchor Terrace is situated) whilst of marginal importance to the borough, remained beyond the reach of the City authorities and developed a reputation for bawdry and lawlessness.

Documentary evidence, from the sixteenth century onwards, provides detailed information concerning the usage of the land on which Anchor Terrace and the Globe are located, most of which is dealt with by W.W.Braines (Braines 1924). Braines disproved the theory that the Globe lay to the north side of Maiden Lane (now Park Street) and established the correct boundaries of the land leased for the building of the Globe to the south of Maiden Lane, which he called The Globe Estate (fig. 22). Herbert Berry (Berry 1981), working mostly from documents in the Public Record Office, has also explored the ownership and leasing of the site in the seventeenth century. Braines effectively proved his case and his attention to detail means that his conclusions are not open to challenge. It is nevertheless useful to summarise the land transactions for the site in the sixteenth, seventeenth and eighteenth centuries, adding more recently discovered facts where appropriate as the evidence illustrates the changing land use around the site.

During the greater part of the sixteenth to eighteenth centuries, the site formed part of an estate lying between the ditch of the Bishop of Winchester's Park to the south and Maiden Lane to the north, stretching from Deadman's Place in the east to a line immediately to the west of Southwark Bridge Road in the west. The land had formerly been part of the Bishop's estate in Southwark, and in the sixteenth century still owed him a payment of sixteen shillings per annum. During the 1590s, the Surrey and Kent Sewer Commission several times ordered the landlord and tenants of the estate to clean out the ditch that

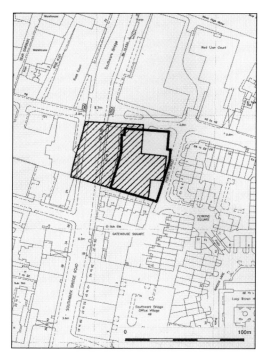

FIG. 22 The Globe estate. Approximate location of the Globe Estate, located by W.W. Braines, shown in relation to the site outline and the 1991 Ordnance Survey map.

formed the boundary between their lands and the Bishop's Park to the south. The Bishop's property still bordered the estate to the west and the south in the nineteenth century (Braines 1924, 36. LCC 1950, pl. 59).

From 1554 until the mid-eighteenth century the land was in the freehold of the Brend family. Thomas Brend purchased land, in October 1554, from John Yong (a member of the Skinners Company) who had inherited the land from his grandfather, Thomas Rede. Brend bought the land under the description of houses and gardens in Maiden Lane in the parish of St Saviour (Braines 1924, 17).

Brend held the estate until his death in September 1598. At this time there were about fifteen tenants living there in tenements with gardens. It was alleged, in 1601, that these were small and ruinous houses which no-one wanted to buy (PRO WARD 9/94, f.632). Brend and one of his tenants, George Archer, were accused by the Sewer Commission of filling in the east end of a drainage ditch which ran along the south side of Maiden Lane and building houses on it.

It was Thomas Brend's son and successor Nicholas who, in February 1599, leased two plots of land to the company of players consisting of Richard and Cuthbert Burbage, William Shakespeare, John Hemings, Augustine Phillips, Thomas Pope and William Kemp. Effective from the previous Christmas, the lease was for thirty-one years. The northern plot of the lease lay alongside Maiden Lane at the west end of the Brend estate and had recently been divided into three gardens, whilst the southern plot was separated from it by a lane and was divided into four gardens abutting the boundary ditch of the Park to the south. The yearly rent for each plot was seven pounds and fifteen shillings and the lease granted right of access along the lane which divided the two plots. Although the original lease does not survive, it was quoted extensively in a case in the court of King's Bench in 1616 between Hemings and his daughter, Thomasine Osteler. Braines showed that this court copy had reversed all the points of the original, thus misleading some historians into believing that the Globe lay to the north of Maiden Lane (Braines 1924, 43).

The lease was also mentioned in the Court of Requests in the 1630s, in a case between the company of players and Sir Matthew Brend. Evidence given mentioned that the lease allowed the players to pull down any buildings on the plots, provided they replaced them with better structures within a year. Although drained by the ditches running along their north and south boundaries, the plots were said to be subject to flooding at the Spring tides, because there was no embankment or fence to keep the water out. This description of the nature of the leased land conforms to Ben Jonson's image of the Globe, in his 'An Execration upon Vulcan', as 'Flanck'd with a Ditch and forc'd out of a Marish'.

The players' witnesses said that there were no houses on the plots at the time of the lease, but according to George Archer there were two, each consisting of two rooms (Berry 1987, 173). This statement of Archer's appears to be borne out by the evidence presented by John Norden's *Speculum Britanniae*, published in 1593. In this map Norden illustrates properties fronting on to Maid Lane which may well lie within the boundary of the Globe Estate and therefore have existed on the Anchor Terrace site.

It was on this land that the Globe Theatre was built from the dismantled timber framework of the Theatre in Shoreditch. Thomas Brend's post mortem 'inquisition', taken on 17th July 1599, refers to a newly-built house with a garden occupied by William Shakespeare and others. This may have been the theatre, but is more likely to have been the house which is known to have adjoined it. That the theatre may have been constructed on a piled wharf is suggested by the fact that, in February 1606, the Sewer Commission ordered the owners of the Globe Playhouse to pile, board and fill up eight poles (a pole equals 16.5 ft) of the wharf beside the playhouse and to remove the posts they had driven into the ditch under their bridge on the north side of Maiden Lane. The wharf, it therefore seems, was 132 ft (40.23 m) long.

The Globe is depicted on Norden's panorama of London, *Civitas Londini*, drawn in 1600. In the map inset published with this panorama (fig. 19, p. 58), Norden illustrates houses adjacent to the Globe, plus properties fronting on to Maid Lane. Norden's record of the development of architectural detail in buildings appears to be corroborated by his depiction, in 1593 (in *Speculum Britanniae*) and 1600, of different phases of the Rose Theatre. These phases appear to have been borne out by excavation at the site of the Rose.

Access to the Globe was through Globe Alley from Deadman's Place to the east and through Horseshoe Alley from Bankside to the north. Globe Alley is first mentioned in the St Saviours Sacrament Token Book in 1612 and was described as leading to the playhouse in 1626 and 1723 (Braines 1924: Appendix B). It originally ran to the west side of the leased land but is depicted on later maps as turning north, to the east of the Globe leases. Horseshoe Alley was described as leading to the Globe in 1669 and 1681 (Braines 1924, 82) although the theatre no longer survived at those dates.

In October 1601 Nicholas Brend, on his death-bed, mortgaged his estate in Southwark to his step-brother Sir John Bodley and others. The description of the property included a playhouse with Richard Burbage and William Shakespeare, gentleman, listed among the

FIG. 23 Wenceslaus Hollar's Long View of London from Southwark (1647). The labels 'The Globe'
and 'Beere bayting h' are mistakenly transcribed: the Globe is marked 'Beere baytin h'.

tenants. Bodley had effective control of the land for the next twenty years (Berry 1981, 39.
Braines 1924, 21,27). Two years after Brend's death, Bodley repaired the tenements on the
site, in order to attract new tenants.

During this period the Globe flourished but was destroyed by fire on 29th June 1613,
along with the dwelling house which adjoined it (Winwood 469). Within a year, the company of players rebuilt the theatre with brickwork, timber and plastering, a tiled roof
replacing the original thatch where the fire had started (Berry 1987, 167). The adjoining
house was also rebuilt and another house added. That the rebuilding took place on the
original ground-plot and re-used the original foundations is specified in a Buildings Return
of 1634 which mentions:

> The Globe playhouse, nere Maid Lane, built by the company of players with the dwelling house
> thereto adjoyninge, built wt timber, aboute 20 years past upon an old foundation, worth 14 li to
> 29 li per ann. and one house there adjoining, built about the same time with timber, in the
> possession of Wm. Millet, gent., worth per ann, 4 li (Braines 1924, 26).

Hollar's *Long View* of London from Southwark (fig. 23) published in 1647 (but sketched
between 1636 and 1644) only shows one of the two adjoining houses.

In February 1622, following a case in the court of Wards, Sir John Bodley surrendered
the Southwark estate to Matthew Brend, the son and heir of Nicholas (Berry 1981, 44). In
March 1624, Matthew (now Sir Matthew) settled the west part of the Southwark estate,
including the playhouse, on his wife Frances as a jointure property for her lifetime, after the
reversion of the rights of his mother, Lady Margaret Zinzan. This arrangement was extended, in June 1633, to a holding by Frances in perpetuity. Braines has demonstrated that
the jointure property consisted of the two plots originally leased for the building of the

Globe, and Lombard's Garden to the east of the southern plot (Braines 1924, 40,42). Other parts of the Southwark estate to the east of the Globe leases were sold by Sir Matthew Brend in the 1620s and 1630s to Hilary Mempris and Henry Smyter (Braines 1924, #68,73,76).

Throughout the period, the Globe continued to be profitable to the company of players. The original lease of the plots was due to expire at Christmas 1629 but the players negotiated a six-year extension at the same rent with Bodley in 1613, when they were planning the rebuilding of the burned theatre. Between 1633 and 1637 the players fought a protracted case against Sir Matthew Brend in the court of Requests, to force him to honour a promise of a further nine-year extension which he had made whilst still a minor. Brend wanted to recover the land in order to build tenements on it. The players were eventually successful, but their rent was increased from fourteen pounds and ten shillings to forty pounds per annum (Berry 1981, 54. Berry 1987, 155). They held the lease until Christmas 1644. They did not, however, require the entire area of the leased land for the operation of the playhouse and the extra house, built after the fire of 1613, was rented out. In 1634 it was in the occupancy of William Millet, gentleman, and by 1638 in that of Richard Hodges (Braines 1924, 25). Since the beginning of the lease, the company had received rents of six pounds per annum, probably for gardens on the southern plot (Berry 1987: 168).

There are several references to a house built adjoining both the first and second Globes, and another adjoining house built at the same time as the second. The original house was a tap-house built and occupied by the actor John Hemings, perhaps as a private venture (Berry 1987, 173). One of these buildings was probably on the Maid Lane frontage (Concanen & Morgan, 224). Hollar's *Long View* shows a gabled house immediately to the south of the Globe (mistakenly labelled as 'Beere Baiting h') which is aligned from north-west to south-east, with a chimney at the east end and with a southward extension (fig. 23).

Parliament ordered the cessation of play performances in 1642. When Brend recovered the land, he pulled down the Globe, though probably not as early as April 1644, as the evidence for this is widely thought to be a forgery (Berry 1981, 31). Berry argues nevertheless that 'evidently the Globe really was pulled down in the 1640s or soon after' (Berry 1987, 79). In its place Brend built twelve tenements, most of which covered the site of the playhouse. Braines demonstrated that they lay along the south side of Maiden Lane, on either side of Fountain Alley, with the eastern-most property being occupied by Edward Symons. Symons' house was located at the north-eastern corner of the Globe Estate. These tenements certainly existed when the jointure property was settled on Sir Matthew's daughter-in-law Judith as, in the settlement dated 17th October 1655, Sir Matthew Brend set aside ' all those messuages ... most of which last before mencioned messuages or tenements are erected and built where the late playhouse called the Globe stood and upon the ground thereunto belonging'. The settlement lists twelve individuals who occupy those tenements and then continues to list thirty-one 'messuages and tenements in or neare Maiden Lane'. This settlement was later quoted in several Chancery lawsuits (Berry 1981, 31. Braines 1924, 27, 28, 35, 36).

The second set of tenements is located by a settlement dated October 26th 1655, which describes them as being situated 'upon Mayden Lane on the north, and on an alley called Globe Alley on the south, on the tenement of one Smiter, baker, on the east, and on the house and ground of one Edward Symons on the west' (Braines 1924, 29). Braines has established that Symons' house was at the north-eastern corner of the Globe Estate, thus indicating that these properties extended eastwards from the north-eastern corner of the Globe Estate, along the Maid Lane/Park Street frontage.

The February before the settlement of his property, Matthew Brend sold 'unto John Goodspeed ... All that piece or parcel of Garden ground ... abutting on the Common Sewer called the Park Ditch on the south side and for the most part a certain Garden ground belonging to the parish church of Saint Saviour on the north and turning with a little Nook into Maid Lane at the north west corner thereof' (Southwark Local Studies Library (S.L.S.L.) S C 942. 16431 WAR). When Goodspeed sold the land in 1657, four houses are mentioned in the title deed. Upon the death of Frances Brend (1673), the jointure passed to Judith Brend, wife of Sir Matthew's son, Thomas and mother of Elizabeth. In 1708, after the death of Francis Brend (brother of Thomas) and as the result of litigation, Elizabeth Cason (nee Brend) received the jointure.

Along with tenements, it is noted that a Presbyterian Meeting House was erected in Globe Alley, 'most probably ... in 1672' (Wilson 1814, 149). This was established at the west end of Globe Alley, on the south-east part of the Globe leases, when John Chester was licensed to preach there. By 1687 Chester had moved to the Zoar Street Meeting House and the Globe Alley Meeting House was out of use by the time it was leased to Sarah Peck in 1715. She built a messuage and a shop on the site whilst the ground to the east and south of these was let as a leather-dresser's yard. This land was later used as the parish workhouse (L.C.C. 1950 n.6:79).

Elizabeth Cason and her husband, Timothy mortgaged part of their land in 1721 (the mortgage deed lists twenty four occupants of the tenements on the mortgaged parcel of land) and in 1726/7 sold a portion of their property, at the west end of the south side of Globe Alley, 'to John Lade, James Kinder and others for the purposes of a parish work-house' (Braines , 24:37). Built around a yard measuring 34 by 25 ft, with a ditch running through, its kitchen, 'cookry' and laundry were all in basements, which still suffered from flooding from springs and tides (S.L.S.L. St Saviour Parish Workhouse Trustee Minutes 423 f.3). The position of the workhouse is located on Rocque's map in 1746 (fig. 24).

In the minutes of the Saint Saviour Workhouse Trustees, dated 26th July 1774, the work-house is described as 'surrounded by other Buildings some of which are lately built very near and very lofty' and one side of Fountains Alley is described as 'containing nine small tenements' (S.L.S.L. 423 f.3v). It was too cramped for its needs and so it was moved to a new site in 1774.

Most of the land to the east of Fountain Alley was acquired piecemeal from the Casons and others by the Barclay-Perkins brewery. The company's acquisitions during the eighteenth century included the nine tenements on the east side of Fountain Alley in 1778 and the Workhouse site in 1777 (Braines 1924, 38). On a map of the Brewery estate in 1774 by George Gwilt the area south of Globe Alley (and therefore on the southern of the Globe plots) was occupied by a square yard with stable stalls on all sides and a circular dung-pit in the middle. To its east was an open yard. To the north, adjacent to Fountain Alley, a small building which was used as an infirmary for horses is illustrated. This stable block covered the site of the nine tenements and the Workhouse, and some of the Lombard Garden. On a later map, also by Gwilt, the stables have been turned into a two-storey cooperage and

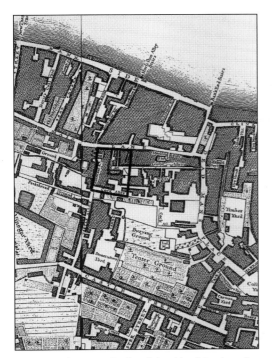

FIG. 24 John Rocque's *Plan of the Cities of London and Westminster and Borough of Southwark* (1746) showing the approximate location of the site and its development in the eighteenth century.

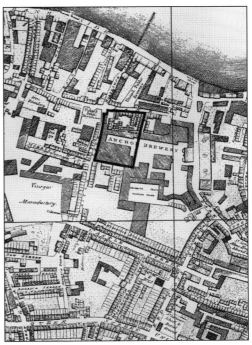

FIG. 25 William Faden's 1813 revision of Richard Horwood's *Plan of the Cities of London and Westminster the Borough of Southwark* showing the approximate location of the site and the development of the Anchor Brewery.

storehouse. The northern edge of these buildings was about 80 ft south of the New Park Street (formerly Maiden Lane) frontage. The Brewery therefore owned very little of the northern plot of the Globe leases. Faden's 1813 edition of Richard Horwood's 'Plan of the Cities of London and Westminster, the Borough of Southwark and parts adjoining shewing every house' (fig. 25) indicates tenement properties still standing on the northern plot of the Globe leases. In 1831 Edward Cooper was rated for a skittle ground between the northern arm of Globe Alley and Fountain Alley. A large part of the Brewery burned down in 1832, but it was rebuilt shortly afterwards (L.C.C. 1950:80).

The parts of the jointure property (and therefore of the Globe leases) which lay to the west of Fountain Alley were purchased by the Southwark Bridge Company for the new road in 1816. Part of this had been used as another leather-dresser's yard. The narrow area between the new road and Fountain Alley was subsequently bought by the Brewery, and the houses of Anchor Terrace built on it.

Archaeology 1989

The 1989 evaluation on the site of the Globe, to the east of Anchor Terrace, was a large, open area evaluation aimed at both examining any significant archaeological remains on the site and attempting to establish whether any remains of the Globe Theatre survived. That any remains of the Globe did survive appears to be largely fortuitous in light of the 20th century constructional activity that has taken place on the site. However, in the north-west

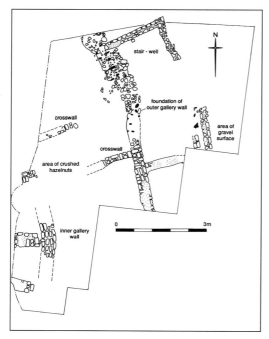

FIG. 26 Archaeological remains of the Globe
recorded during the 1989 evaluation
of the site.

corner of the evaluated area, against the western limit of excavation, remains thought to be associated with the Globe were uncovered. The alignment of the remains indicated that further remains could be expected to survive beneath the foundations of Anchor Terrace to the west.

The recorded remains (fig. 26; *see also* figs 11 and 13, pp. 40–1), part of the north-eastern circumference of the polygonal building – consisted of a series of chalk and brick foundations. The main, central foundation survived to approximately 6.30m long and varied in width from 0.40m at the southern end to a maximum width of 0.80m. This foundation consisted, at its northern end, of chalk rubble apparently set around timber stakes. Lying to the south of and partially over this chalk and timber foundation, along the same alignment, was a foundation of red brick set within a chalk-flecked mortar.

Immediately east of this main foundation is a brick structure which appears to butt up to the main foundation. The northern part of this structure extends 2.0m east of the main foundation and then turns to run parallel to the main foundation for a length of 1.55m. At a distance of 1.80m south of this and on the same alignment (parallel to the main foundation) is a similar brick foundation. This survives for 1.50m before it is destroyed by a modern intrusion but then emerges from the intrusion to run west and rejoin the main foundation. It is this foundation which could be interpreted as forming the base of a stair-well and which could correspond with that shown by Hollar in his *Long View*.

Approximately 3.0m west of the main foundation is a fragment of a brick and mortar foundation, surviving for a length of 1.40m and to a width of 0.50m and robbed out both to the north and south (i.e. the building material removed at a later date to be re-used elsewhere). In both the alignment of the brickwork and the alignment of the robbing cut there is an indication that this was an angled piece of foundation, running parallel to the main foundation to the east. This is interpreted as being the surviving remnants of the foundation of an inner gallery wall, suggesting a gallery width of between 3.0m (9 ft 11 in.), measuring between the inner faces of the foundations and 3.80m (12 ft 6 in.) measuring between the outer faces. Between the two parallel inner and outer gallery walls are the remnants of two cross-walls, similar to those recorded between the inner and outer gallery walls at the Rose. It has not yet been possible to account adequately for three fragments of brick foundation recorded to the west of the inner gallery wall.

Against the south-east angle of the 'stair-well' a gravel layer, possibly indicative of a surface, was recorded and deposits of crushed hazelnuts within a matrix of dark brown silt are recorded in close proximity to the 'cross-walls'. This has parallels with the hazelnut deposit found adjacent to the *ingressus* (or entry) at the Rose. The phasing of these deposits at the Globe, however, is not properly understood.

Archaeology 1991

Listed Building Consent and Scheduled Monument Consent were granted in 1991 for the excavation of trial pits within the standing Anchor Terrace building, both to provide information about the foundations of the building and to assess the likelihood of the survival of archaeological remains beneath. At the time the condition of the foundations of Anchor Terrace was not known, although it subsequently came to light that the building was sitting on a huge concrete raft foundation, some 1.40m to 1.67m thick (Blatherwick 1991) presumably laid to prevent the building from sinking into the wet, alluvial soils.

Three trial pits were opened and one, located against the eastern foundation of the building, was of particular interest. Immediately beneath the concrete raft foundation of Anchor Terrace was a dark-grey clay containing occasional charcoal, mortar and brick flecks and lying within this clay was a ragstone, brick and mortar 'structure' measuring at least 0.55m by 0.44m, although its full dimensions were not revealed. Due to the depth and restrictions on the evaluation it was not possible to assess the importance of this feature fully, but it has provisionally been interpreted as a pier base, inferring from the knowledge of similar features on the site of the Rose. It is assumed that this newly uncovered feature is related to the Globe, the assumption being based on the recovery of a Nuremburg trading token (1580–1630) which was removed from the clay surrounding the feature.

Conclusion

Archaeological work that has taken place at the Anchor Terrace car park site indicates that (as is often the case with post-medieval archaeological deposits) activity subsequent to the demolition of the Globe has caused large scale disturbance and destruction of the site's archaeological deposits. The nature of the work that has taken place on the site means that definitive conclusions are hard to come by and that speculation about the size and shape of either of the two Globe theatres remains no more than inference. It may be that future generations of archaeologists and historians will gain access to the land beneath the standing Anchor Terrace building and so develop a better understanding of the archaeology of the Globe Estate and its buildings. Until that time nobody can fully understand the significance and meaning of the remains so far uncovered. Until more information comes to light we have to rely on the amalgamation of documentary and archaeological evidence combined with comparisons with evidence from similar structures. In the context of this book, I leave that to others.[3]

Notes to Chapter Four

1 Planning guidance to local authorities emphasising the role of archaeology in the planning process but also stressing the increased desire to practise the policy of preserving remains for future generations.

2 The chapter uses the form of notation common in social science research. The reference will be located by consulting the appropriate entry in the Bibliography below.

3 The Museum of London Archaeology Service has been helped by a great number of people and organisations in undertaking the work described in the previous pages. We would like to acknowledge their contributions to this work and also acknowledge the contributions of colleagues too numerous to mention individually.

Bibliography

BERRY, H., 1981 'The Globe: Documents and Ownership', in C.W. Hodges, S.Schoenbaum and L.Leone (ed.), *The Third Globe: Symposium for the Reconstruction of the Globe Playhouse*, Wayne State University.

BERRY, H., 1987 *Shakespeare's Playhouses*.

BOWSHER, J.M.C. and BLATHERWICK S, 1991 'The Structure of the Rose' in F.J.Hildy (ed.) *New Issues in the Reconstruction of Shakespeare's Theatre: proceedings of the conference held at the University of Georgia, February 16–18, 1990, 55–78*.

BLATHERWICK, S., 1991 *Report on the Archaeological Evaluation at 1/15 Anchor Terrace, Southwark Bridge Road, London SE1*.

BRAINES, W.W., 1924 *The Site of the Globe Playhouse*.

BRIGHAM, T., GOODBURN, G., TYERS, I. with DILLON, J., 1995 'A Roman Timber Building on the Southwark Waterfront, London' in *The Archaeological Journal*, 152, 1–72.

CONCANEN, M. and MORGAN, A. 1795 *History and Antiquities of the parish of St Saviour's, Southwark*.

FOAKES, R.A., 1985 *Illustrations of the English Stage, 1580–1642*.

GRAHAM, A.H., 1978 'The Geology of North Southwark and its Topographical Development in the Post-Pleistocene Period', *Southwark Excavations 1972–74*, 2, 501–17. London & Middlesex Archaeological Society and Surrey Archaeological Society joint publication.

JOHNSON, D.J., 1969 *Southwark and the City*.

LONDON COUNTY COUNCIL, 1950 *Survey of London*, vol. XXII, *Bankside* (*The Parishes of St Saviour and Christchurch Southwark*).

WILSON, W., 1814 *The History and Antiquities of Dissenting Churches and Meeting Houses in London, Westminster and Southwark*, vol. IV.

WINWOOD, R., *Memorials of Affairs of State*, vol. III.

PLATE 1 (*above*) The galleries and thatch during the construction process.

PLATE 2 (*left*) Benches within a gallery.

PLATE 3 Model showing the frame structure.

PLATE 4 Frame nearing completion.

5

DESIGN AS RECONSTRUCTION: RECONSTRUCTION AS DESIGN

Jon Greenfield

RCHITECTS DESCRIBE the starting point of their designs rather prosaically as 'the idea', and see design as a cyclical process of development and refinement. The original 'idea' is drawn out, examined, criticised, modified. It is then drawn out again at a larger scale, examined and criticised again. This process is repeated many times, in gradual increments from the initial 1:500 blocking-out to the final full-size drawings of details. The design process is *iterative*, as it is by the repeated application of the same procedure that the design advances. In the Globe project, by contrast, the design didn't start with the architect's idea. That had already been established over four centuries of scholarship and energised by Sam Wanamaker's enthusiasm. Ownership of 'the idea', the vision that set the design process in motion, lies with the scholars and with Sam Wanamaker, but all of the subsequent effort has been very similar to architectural design for any other building, except that it was carried out over a much longer period and incorporated the opinions of many more people than usual. For over three decades the project has been redrawn when new evidence has come to light, circulated to everyone with an interest, their comments evaluated and the drawings modified.

The reconstruction of a building that disappeared four hundred years ago clearly cannot use modern techniques. The original was a *craft building*, each part fashioned by the skill, control and dexterity of a human hand. Difficult work was carried out by the most experienced and accomplished craftsmen, the simpler parts by apprentices. Clearly our reconstruction also had to be hand crafted, but more than this, it needed to be informed by the specialist knowledge of a building craft that no longer exists; a building craft which had died out in this country by about 1830. So the end of the architectural design process was again unusual. It was not, as is normal, a series of tightly-drafted specifications and fully-developed details, accompanied by an instruction to the contractor not to deviate from the contract documents. The end point of our design of the Globe was hours of discussion with McCurdy and Co, drawing on Peter McCurdy's vast knowledge and practical experience of historic timber framing and the very active influence of the craftsmen over the final details.

The design, as this account makes clear, was started by scholars and finished by craftsmen. With so many other disciplines involved with the design, what was left for the architect to do?

In the late 1960s, even before his eventual architect-partner, Theo Crosby was drawn into the project, Sam Wanamaker was working in collaboration with an architect. The task of architectural design has therefore taken place over a period of some three decades. There is a vast effort that links the initial vision of the playhouse and the final working of a mortise and tenon joint. There is the need to ensure that academic fancy doesn't take the reconstruction away from a building technology that was possible in 1600. There is the need to ensure that practical considerations don't make the reconstruction too leaden and ordinary. The architect's role has therefore been one of enabler, of ensuring that the vision is able to be achieved, and that all of the appropriate specialisms are able to be represented in the finished building.

To demonstrate these points it is useful to consider two aspects of the architectural design. The first describes the processes we have undertaken to get the necessary permissions from the authorities. This not only covers normal permission to build but also permission to use the oak framed building for public performances. The second is about drawing. As each new idea has been proposed, or new piece of evidence unearthed, it has been drawn out, for circulation to all concerned, for criticism, development and modification.

I. THE DESIGN PROCESS
The Fire Regulations

Getting Permission

When the idea of building the Globe as an authentic reconstruction finally took over from the various other ideas that had been canvassed before 1980, ranging from a large hangar-like structure with a flexible, multipurpose interior to a modern theatre with a neo-Elizabethan facade, Theo Crosby and his architectural collaborator Edward Armitage visited the GLC to see what the health and safety parameters might be for such a venture. They went with a clear conception of what they wanted to build: an oaken structural frame with timber seats 'divisions and conveniences', as the internal work is described in the Fortune contract, and a thatched roof. They met the GLC theatre controllers on Tuesday 7 October 1980, where they discussed means of escape from fire, and the Southwark District Surveyor two days later. In a letter to Wanamaker commenting on his meeting, Crosby reported that the District Surveyor wanted to be helpful, but had no powers of discretion, so would be forced to apply the regulations without favour. At that time the London Building Acts were still in force and were the principal building codes that would be applied to the proposed reconstruction, rather than the Building Regulations which applied throughout the rest of the country. Theo left the meeting under no illusion about what was required. The structure would have to be non-combustible, and this meant that it could not be made of timber. Crosby offered Wanamaker a number of alternatives, ranging from building the theatre in timber as a full size exhibit that no one could enter on one extreme to making the structure entirely from pre-cast concrete on the other.

This was the conundrum. While the Building Regulations demanded a structure conforming to modern safety requirements, the design brief was for a reconstruction made in every detail as close to the original as possible, modified only as much as was necessary to make the auditorium safe so that a paying audience could be admitted. The central requirement was for this building to become a perfect *instrument* for acting. Actors would be searching for insights into the play texts of Shakespeare and his contemporaries. Discoveries about the nature of playing classical texts would be found by the process of staging plays in the reborn Globe. But these experiments could only be valid if the acting took place in a space which was the closest thing we could make it to the original of 1599. It has been vital to resist any temptation to extemporise, building only that which can be justified by records of the building that have come down to us or by defensible inference from contemporary records. We have had to work with the same priorities as an instrument maker recreating early musical instruments for Baroque music. Everything in the construction of the instrument matters: the choice of the wood, the shape of the sound box, the construction of the bridge, the choice of gut for strings and even the choice of varnish. All are essential components in the final response and tone of the instrument. The same is true of the Globe. It is an instrument for acting. It will respond to the sound and tone of an actor's voice, to the sound and tone of the audience's reaction, and will define the play's visual spectacle. Clearly the shape of the auditorium is of immense importance, and so is the position of the stage. But so too are the materials that we have used: structural green oak, haired lime plaster, oak boarding and thatch are all vital and characteristic components of the building, its aura and its acoustic response. The choice offered by the GLC District Surveyors in October 1980 for either authentic materials in a building that no audience could enjoy, or a usable auditorium made from concrete simply wasn't going to meet the project's needs.

In 1980, then, there was a seemingly insurmountable problem as the controlling authorities would not allow a working theatre that was made from the original 1599 materials. When faced with a seemingly insurmountable problem the best technique is to break the problem down into a series of smaller problems, and to attempt to solve each one at a time. This we did with the Globe, dealing separately with the fire resistance of the structure, the fire resistance of the walls, the spread of fire across the surfaces and the construction of the roof. As each of the separate problems has been tackled and solved over the past 15 years the proposed reconstruction has been able to get incrementally closer to what we believe the original was like, and convince the authorities to allow the reconstruction to be used as a working theatre.

The Oak Structure

Theo Crosby had persuaded Sam Wanamaker to appoint the firm of Buro Happold as structural engineers for the project in 1980. It was Buro Happold, and most particularly Ian Liddell, who were first able to suggest a way of showing how a timber structure could be suitably resistant to fire. Ian Liddell and his former colleague Terry Ealey had completed the refurbishment of warehouse G at St Katharine's dock when they both worked for Ove Arup and Partners in 1975, a timber frame structure within a brick enclosure dating from the eighteenth century.[1] They did not want to spoil the original structure by cladding or replacing it and had used British Standards and a Structural Engineering Code of Practice, CP 112 (which was then still in draft form) to convince the GLC Special Projects Division that hardwood, and particularly oak, is indeed a good material for resisting fire. It burns, but only slowly, and if the rate at which the wood chars and the size of the timber balks is carefully balanced, it is possible to contrive a situation where a structural timber remains large enough to carry its load even after a fire has eroded its surfaces for one hour. Any longer and the argument becomes invalid. Liddell and Ealey provided Theo Crosby with

FIG. 27 (ABOVE) The charring rate of structural timbers: The British Standards indicate that structural hardwoods will char at the rate of 1¼ in. (30 mm) per hour, or ¼ in. (6 mm) in 12 minutes. Our own tests, carried out in conjunction with the Fire Research Station, indicated a rate slower than this.

FIG. 28 (RIGHT) The three photographs show the major test stages when a sample joint was subjected to fire for 1 hour. The first photograph shows the sample as it looked when made by McCurdy & Co. The second photograph shows the sample as it looked when it was taken from the kiln. The third photograph shows the sample after the char has been removed, revealing blackened but sound timber beneath.

experimental evidence and encouraged him to try this approach with the District Surveyor in relation to the Globe (fig. 27).

Theo Crosby confirmed the new specification for the proposed reconstruction in a letter dated 27 August 1982:

> We agreed a timber structure for the Globe with a one hour fire rating. I also agreed we would omit the thatch roof and substitute plain (clay) tiles. All soffits would be plastered, as would both sides of the external wall. Balustrades and railings all of solid oak. In general it would be a heavy Tudor Oak Structure and would be constructed in the old way: joints, pegs and so on, as authentically as we can.

A project with such a long design development period is bound to be buffeted by political changes, and the Globe has certainly had its fair share of these, some of which have been formative. For example, in 1986 the GLC was abolished and the combined experience of officers who were responsible for the West End theatres was dissipated to the boroughs. Secondly, the London Building Acts were replaced by the Building Regulations, bringing London into line with other parts of the country. Finally, and most significantly, the Building Regulations were themselves completely revised in philosophy as well as content in 1985. This last change may seem unspectacular, but it was a change of the greatest significance for the project. The old regulations were full of what were generally referred to as 'deemed to satisfy' clauses. This means that forms of construction were specified which had to be used. Put simply, clay tiles could be used, thatch couldn't. The intention behind the old regulations was to give a building designer a limited range of options that the authorities themselves had proved met the necessary criteria. But like all menu options it was necessarily restrictive and excluded any unusual proposals, like those needed for the Globe. After 1985 the Building Regulations contained very simple performance clauses. Under the new regulations you can use whatever material you like, provided you prove, with scientific test data, that the proposed material meets the stated performance standards. The door was opening for us to use not only green oak for the structure, but haired lime plaster for the walls and thatch on the roof.

The proposal that hardwood is a suitable material to use in fire rated structures has now been fully legitimised and the subject has its own British Standard, BS 5268. However this code still doesn't cover the Globe construction adequately, and in June 1994 we made arrangements for the charring rate of green oak to be tested at the Fire Research Station, then in Borehamwood. The Fire Research personnel had agreed to help the project by undertaking indicative tests. They had a small kiln measuring one metre by one metre by one metre, and we devised six different oak joint samples for them to test at a temperature of 1000° centigrade for one hour. Three of the samples were simple straight balks which varied in their moisture content, grain pattern and surface figure. The remaining three samples were all full-size joint assemblies, taken from different parts of the structure, so that we could see how the joints themselves would perform. Fire tends to exploit any natural weakness in a material, and we were concerned to see if the flames would erode deeply around the peg holes, timber junctions and drying checks (surface cracks).

When they were winched out of the kiln the burnt samples looked terrible, blackened with fissures and cracks in the characteristic charcoal grid pattern. However, once the char had been removed, by simply scraping off the loose material and getting down to the raw unburned timber, the test samples took on a wonderfully smooth appearance, like huge pieces of driftwood. All the edges and arises were rounded, but the peg positions and joints had not been singled out for specially intense action by the flames. Samples of joints had been affected by the fire as if they had been monolithic, unjointed shapes cut from one imaginary huge piece of timber, and the material loss on all exposed faces had been steady and even. Measurements were taken from all faces and compared with the measurements taken before the test. The British standard had led us to expect a steady erosion rate of 30mm. Our measurements showed a rate 33% slower than this (fig. 28).

In historic structures the sizes of the timbers are generally much larger than the minimum needed to hold up the loads. The sizes were determined not by calculation but by experience, and it was common for the carpenters to size the timbers very generously. Almost every timber in these structures is therefore at least 30mm larger than it needs to be on all faces, so the timbers already have a casing of enough sacrificial material to have a fire resistance of one hour.

Walls

One of the main problems we had to face as architects was devising an acceptable Means of Escape Strategy. This is summarised in the illustration (fig. 29) and has three principal components. Firstly, the two external stairs, so clearly drawn by Hollar, have been enlarged. Enlarging the two external staircases has brought them to a size that concurs exactly with the stairs in the Queen Elizabeth Hunting Lodge at Chingford, dated mid-sixteenth century, so there is historical precedent for our decision. Secondly, two additional stairs have been added for which there is no known documentary evidence. These fit very nicely in the interface between the backstage (or Tiring House) and the auditorium, and take up space that otherwise has little use, as the sight lines for the audience at this position would be very poor. Thirdly, we have four six-foot doors serving the yard, rather than the 'two narrow doors' mentioned in John Chamberlain's account of the 1613 fire. These three measures were necessary because the audience capacity permitted in the theatre is directly related to the capacity of the exits, and the number of people who can be conveyed from the building in two and a half minutes. These stairs and escape ways allow a capacity of nearly 1400 people in the reconstruction, which is also all that can be accommodated in the three galleries and open-air yard without squeezing up the audience unacceptably. The exit widths we have employed are therefore at their optimum size. An increase in width would not give an increase in the audience size because the building is at capacity, but a reduction in width would necessitate a reduction in the permitted audience numbers. The reconstruction will hold just under half of the three thousand people it is believed could be accommodated in the original building.

This means of escape strategy will only work if we can use a wall construction that has a fire resisting capability of one hour. Historically, there are two possible types of infill panel that could have been used at the Globe: 'wattle and daub' or 'lath and plaster', each of which fits into panels formed by the beams and posts of the oak structure. There is some evidence, although not conclusive, that the Rose Theatre had wattle and daub infill panels, with the more refined lath and plaster construction used around the stage only, and possibly in the Heavens. Wattle and daub is generally associated with rural areas (and Southwark was

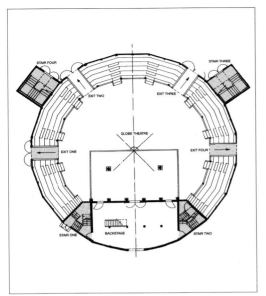

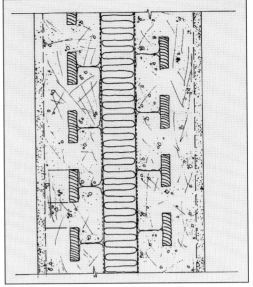

FIG. 29 Means of escape: stair towers and doors. The plan of the Globe had to be modified in three ways to achieve the required means of escape. Firstly, the two stair towers were enlarged to accommodate wide stairs. Secondly, two additional stairs were added either side of the Tiring House and thirdly, the access to the Yard was enlarged from two small doors to four six foot wide ones.

FIG. 30 Wall section prepared for the fire test. This section shows the construction used in the fire test. Traditional materials (oak staves and laths and lime plaster) are supplemented with a fire board placed centrally in the construction. Also, the plastering technique had to be modified, and the lath spacing, so that as much plaster as possible could be placed behind the laths.

at least semi-rural in 1600), and is the more yeomanly method of the two. The wattle is made from coppice offcuts, generally hazel or willow 'withies', woven around cleft oak staves sprung into the structural oak. Daub can be a mixture of anything that is suitable and varies greatly from region to region. Loam, brick earth, sand, tallow, lime, straw and animal hair and dung are all constituents that can be found in a convincing recipe. Lath and plaster, in a more sophisticated way, involves the formation of chestnut or oak laths, split or 'riven' from straight-grained timbers. The laths are nailed at close centres onto staves (relatively substantial secondary timbers that are retro fitted into the panels of the oak frame at close centres). The whole is then covered with a plaster mix, made from lime putty, sand and animal hair (fig. 30).

It is important to note that both of the variants described here result in plaster panels within the oak frame, giving the characteristic 'half timbered' look. It was historically very common to plaster over the oak frame completely, particularly on domestic first floors, giving a very plain appearance that was then enriched with painting or low relief plaster decoration (pargetting).

Lath and plaster infill panels suited the Globe reconstruction. Their pedigree and appropriateness are unquestionable – lath, lime and hair definitely *were* used at the Fortune, which was based on the Globe – except perhaps in being a little smarter than material found in the robbed-out remains of the Rose Theatre. The panels also could be adapted to give a satisfactory fire performance, and could be batched and applied on site in a controlled way, giving a quality that matched a test sample. Unhydrated lime, or putty, once the mainstay of the British building industry, has almost completely been superseded by gypsum and cement for plasters, mortars and renders, and there was almost no modern laboratory data on how lime plasters would perform in a fire.

When we first proposed using lime plaster panels we met with considerable resistance. Most Fire Officers had encountered a lime plaster ceiling at some time in a fire, generally in a historic building, and had found that it collapsed after only a few minutes. Some test data existed from the 1940s but it was not comparable with modern standards and disappointingly gave a fire resistance of only 19 minutes. Our solution had to be practical and pragmatic. We had worked with a company called Rockwool to modify one of their standard products, a fire board, which we proposed to use buried in the wall construction behind the lime plaster. The product was 'Conlit', a material generally used to encase steel columns and beams. It came with a jute scrim on one side (a scrim being a light gauze that helps with the bond between plaster and the fibreboard). We had boards specially made with a scrim on both sides. Our wall profile is summarised in the illustration and has the fibreboard hidden in the centre of the construction, carefully cut between the staves (fig. 30). Plastering is then carried out in the historic way, being a sand, lime putty and animal hair mix, except that a method had to be devised to get plaster behind the laths so that the walls could form a solid barrier.

A fire test was carried out on 29 March 1994 at the Loss Prevention Council, again in Borehamwood. A sample panel, ten feet square, was built, first as a green oak frame and then infilled with the fire board and plaster. Much care had been taken in preparing the sample with advice and help from personnel of the Fire Research Station and Bruce Induni of Bournemouth University's Building Conservation Department. The test started at about eleven in the morning, with the kiln reaching its full temperature of 1000 degrees centigrade after about ten minutes. It was possible to observe the condition of the test panel on its hot side through two small windows in the kiln, but the heat and bright orange glow concealed much of the fine detail. After about twenty minutes a layer of plaster delaminated and, although the sample was still intact, this event was ominously close to the time that the 1940s samples had failed. Detailed examination was only possible after the test had been completed and the test panel had cooled down. We discovered that the delamination was just a surface effect as the plaster had failed at its interface with the laths, a naturally weak line. Half an hour into the test went by without further incident, which meant that we had passed the first recognised point of certification (forms of construction are classified for their fire resistance as 'half hour', 'one hour', 'two hour' etc.). Then the one hour point also passed without further incident and we had achieved our objective, a certified classification for the lime plaster construction of 'one hour'. We made the spot decision to continue with the test until the sample failed, which eventually took place just seven minutes short of three hours.

Thatch

It was not until 1989 that we were able to find a way of challenging the last major constructional compromise: the District Surveyor's insistence on clay or concrete tiles rather than thatch. The first Globe, built in 1599, was known to have been a very expediently produced

building, re-erected in about six months from the dismantled structural timbers of the Theatre, first built in
Shoreditch in 1576. It was certainly thatched, as the
accounts of the ruinous fire of 1613 prove. This is the
theatre that Sam Wanamaker wanted to reconstruct,
because it is the one associated with the first productions of many of Shakespeare's plays. The Second
Globe, rebuilt after the fire on the foundations of the
first Globe, was a quite different structure and had a
tiled roof. The proposed reconstruction, featuring tiles
on the first Globe, would inevitably be seen as a confusion between the two versions. But until 1989 it was
either that or no Globe at all.

It came to our attention that chemicals had been
developed by a commercial organisation called the
Thatching Advisory Service that enhanced the
performance of thatch to the point where it might now
be possible to use it. But rural, isolated, squat cottages,
which are the usual locations for thatch in the twentieth
century, are a very different proposition from tall urban

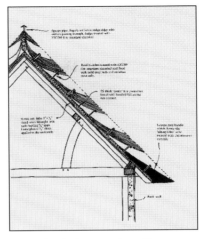

FIG. 31 Thatch: fire precautions: Three
measures have been taken to improve the fire
performance of thatch. Firstly, the thatch
has been laid on fire boards. Secondly, the
thatch has been treated with a chemical fire
retardant and thirdly, a drencher system has
been incorporated in the roof.

structures like the Globe. Thatch had been seen as a dangerous material in cities from the
earliest times. London's first Building Regulation, the ordinance of 1212, had banned the
use of thatch, although the regulation was by no means strictly enforced.

The Thatching Advisory Service, like ourselves, had worked with Rockwool, who were
well known in the building industry for their fire protection mineral fibre boards and quilts.
They had tried to address the concerns of the insurance industry in relation to owners of
thatched dwellings by discussing the matter with various fire officers in rural areas. Rockwool
felt that the greatest problem was with fire spreading up through a building and engulfing
the roof, and had commissioned the Loss Prevention Council to carry out a comparative test
using an insulation board lying between the rafters. Despite the good sense of this approach, it did not meet the requirement of the Building Regulations which are more concerned with the spread of fire from above, from a firework or a burning ember landing on
the roof and igniting the building's thatch. The intention of the regulation is to prevent the
'Great Fire of London' effect, when a mischievous wind was able to cause rapid spread of
fire from one building to its neighbour. There was clearly much more work to be done.

We made preparations to stage a fire test of our own. We checked out the requirements
of the standards, and we asked for, and received, help from the Thatching Advisory Service
and Rockwool. Fire tests are expensive, however, and these talks were taking place at a time
when the project was particularly short of money. We decided to take a different route. On
paper we had all of the essential components of a successful construction. We had a chemical treatment for the thatch called FRT 80 (developed and marketed by the Thatching
Advisory Service). Together with the specialist sprinkler consultants GEM we had devised a
sparge pipe drencher system to run along the ridge of the thatch, just under the surface (fig.
31 and plate 11). And we had a high performance fire board and plaster to protect the

underside. The drencher was needed because the FRT 80 chemical is a water-based treatment, which gets washed out of the exposed last inch of reed. This end 'washing out' is not particularly significant, but we felt it was better to cover all possible eventualities, and the drencher could be shown to be a good way of dousing any smouldering thatch before it started to flame. On our behalf, Rockwool presented our data to the Loss Prevention Council along with other data that they had collected, and they were able to give us an official Assessment Certificate three classes higher than we required (AA rather than BC).

It had taken fourteen years, but we had now managed to devise protection methods for all of the major elements so that original materials, not concrete and clay, could be used to build the Globe.

II. THE DESIGN PROCESS
Drawing

The design process, as it applies to the Globe project, is best illustrated by concentrating on the development of the stage (including its cover) and tiring house. All good architectural design starts with good briefing. A designer needs to know in the fullest sense what the client wants, and finding this out can be a lengthy process. It is not uncommon for an architect to find a difficulty in obtaining a clear briefing and there is a great deal of work to be undertaken even before the back of the envelope receives its first scribble. Often the funders or managers responsible for the administration of the construction work are not the end users and therefore may not themselves know precisely what the end user's needs may be. A similar dilemma prevailed at the Globe. The decision to aim for the most accurate reconstruction possible placed the task of briefing the architect with the academic community. The form of the Globe must follow the latest scholarship, even taking into account conflicting opinions and interpretations.

Theo Crosby decided to host a one day seminar on the Globe at Pentagram on 29 March 1983. This device was repeated in 1986 and 1992, with a number of other smaller gatherings between. By bringing the scholars to the architect's office it was possible to follow all of the debates, opinions and counter opinions in full, and to present schemes and options to be adopted or discarded. Tracing the development of ideas through these conferences shows how the design has progressed, but the story is equally told in images, in the basic plan, section and elevation drawings that were associated with each phase (fig. 32 a to d).

The starting point (fig.32a) for work on the stage, stage cover and tiring house is shown by drawings provided by Richard Hosley, adopted by Pentagram and modified in minor respects. They show a tall superstructure over the stage, its shape bearing a close resemblance to Visscher's famous gabled huts. The 'wooden O' of the auditorium is complete and the stagehouse with its turrets is set within the yard. This design has two major elements, the circular auditorium and the hutted stage structure.

This version of a hutted structure had become a familiar one for the Globe, not least because Richard Hosley and Richard Southern had produced a compelling description in the *Revels History of Drama in English* (*vol. 3*) *1576 to 1613*. Hoseley's work was particularly convincing to the mind of an architect because it had confronted some of the important constructional issues of timber jointing. However at the seminar held on 12 April 1986 a

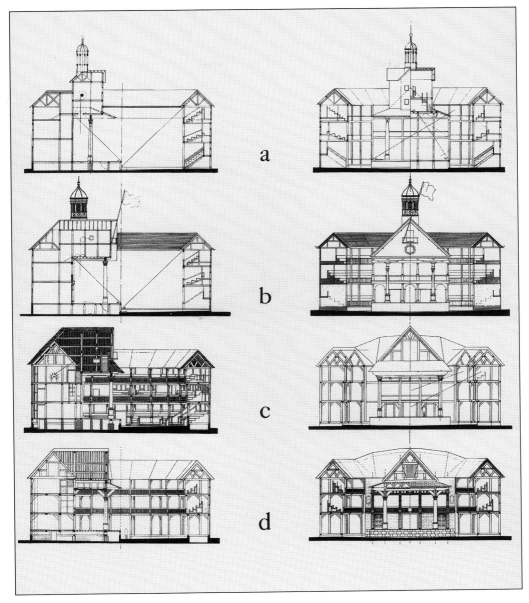

FIG. 32 The development of the design in the longitudinal and cross sections

a **1983.** A design based largely on Richard Hosley's proposal showing a hutted stage structure. This proposal has a tiled roof and Gallery heights of 13 ft 6 in., 10 ft 6 in. and 9 ft.

b **1986.** After adopting the Norden view of the first Globe, which clearly shows a pedimented stage structure rather than a hutted structure. The lantern was included as an acknowledgement that the tiled roof came from Hollar's view of the second Globe.

c **1990.** The introduction of thatch as the roofing material increased the pitch of the roof from 45° to 50°. Gallery heights were also modified at this time to conform with the Fortune Contract: 12 ft, 11 ft and 9 ft.

d **1996.** Following the debate in Summer 1995 after the Workshop Season the stage columns were moved together and the height of the stage roof reduced. A boarded pentice roof was also added.

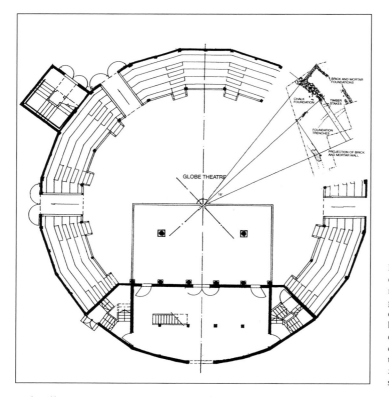

FIG. 33 Archaeological excavations: the derivation of measurements. The information generated by the archaeological excavation was small, being barely two bays, but it was enough to confirm the overall diameter, the Gallery width and to bring about a revision from a 24-sided structure to a 20-sided structure.

radically new interpretation was discussed and adopted. Professor John Orrell had been arguing since 1983 that Norden's view showing a single gabled attic with a ridge running at a right angle to the tiring house front, in the manner of Hollar's view of the second Globe, was a more reliable source than Visscher's (*see* figs 19 and 20, p. 58). Much of the discussion considered the value and ranking of the source material, but a most significant contribution came from Theo Crosby's drawings of three versions of the new proposal. The previous stagehouse had been constructionally convincing, but the new Nordenesque superstructure came to be seen as even more so and was adopted from that point onwards.

The next point at which the issues were brought into sharp focus was in 1992, when the seminar group was reassembled to debate the now fully-digested findings of archaeologists from the Museum of London on the Globe and Rose sites. The archaeological evidence, one could expect, would be conclusive. In fact it was not and the small area of the Globe excavation raised more questions than it answered. The main point at issue was the diameter and number of sides of the playhouse. The upshot, from very careful analysis of the two bays that had been unearthed, was a confirmation of the 99 foot diameter previously adopted, but a challenge to the division of the circular plan into 24 structural bays (fig. 33). The twenty-four divisions had worked out very nicely, giving an *ad quadratum* rationale not only to the inner and outer gallery diameters, but to the placing of stair turrets and stage as well. The stage, as predicated by this configuration, was almost exactly 43 feet by 28 feet, and the *frons scenae* was situated in relation to a chord generated from five of the twenty four perimeter bays. Convenient divisions were also provided for the tiring house. As a five-bay struc-

FIG. 34 The Tiring House designs

A Early designs for the Tiring House had shown it as a structure set within the 'wooden O' (*See* fig. 32 a and b.) Although this was a defensible interpretation of the description of the Fortune Theatre in Peter Streete and Philip Henslowe's contract of 1600, it was hard to justify in terms of timber framing. The junction between the inserted Tiring House and five bays of the circle was awkward.

B Later designs for the Tiring House show it as a separate structure, with the horse-shoe shaped auditorium abutting at each gable. (*See* fig. 32 c and d.)

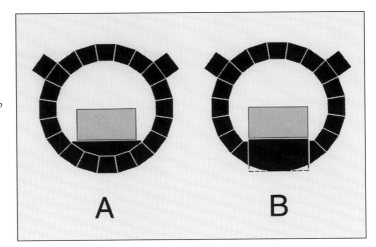

A   B

ture the *frons scenae* worked well. It had a wide central opening (the 'discovery space') and two flanking openings separated by blank panels. A twenty-sided polygon, the result of interpreting the archaeologists' findings, did not work nearly as neatly, but the evidence could not be ignored and the revisions had to be made.

The designs that were presented in 1992 again showed the tiring house taking up five bays of the 'wooden O'. Now, however, the chord for the *frons scenae* had become proportionately and actually larger. Not only was it generated by five twentieths of the circle rather than five twenty-fourths, but it was also generated at wall plate level (the eaves) as the galleries had by this time been designed with an eleven-and-a-half inch jetty at each inner level. This gave a fifty foot long chord, providing rather too wide a stage for most of the scholars, so the chord length was taken as divided into seven structural bays, the central five bays of which formed a forty four foot wide stage. These stage dimensions are comparable to, but not exactly the same as, the ones shown on the previous solution.

We started detailing work on this version straight away, and immediately ran into problems. Constructionally it made little sense to continue the 'wooden O' around all three hundred and sixty degrees and then to superimpose a fully integrated tiring house structure onto it (fig. 34a). The problem was exacerbated by the adoption of a jettied structure for the auditorium. Joining a secondary frame onto such a complete face as a frame with a jettied front was very hard to justify in any surviving structures. Furthermore, the term 'house', as in 'tiring house', common in contracts of around 1600, referred to a wide range of building types well beyond the domestic, but did always mean a discrete self-contained structure. It made no structural sense to divide the tiring house between stage and 'wooden O' so that it was made up from two quite separate structural systems. Could it be that the Globe comprised three major elements: a three-quarters circular auditorium , a tiring house, and a stage with its roof bearing up against the house? (Fig. 34b.) This is certainly what the Hollar drawing seemed to show, and was a plausible solution to the inconclusive remains of the second phase of the Rose theatre. Constructionally it worked very well, except that the span between the stage columns was slightly too large for comfort and the roof ridge of the stage house was higher than the roof ridge of the tiring house. Yet despite these anxieties, this plan was adopted in 1993. The new dimensional system, with 33 feet between the main columns, gave rise to a comprehensive geometry based on fractions of rod measures (one rod being sixteen feet six inches). The *frons scenae*, for example, was now a three bay structure, with each bay two thirds of a rod wide (eleven feet). Three rods allowed for a wide central opening and two secondary narrower openings.

It had not proved possible to build the stage and tiring house by the summer of 1995, but there was a strong desire to hold experimental performances so that the actors could get a first sense of a stage which was bound to challenge the basic precepts of their experience of modern stages. A mock-up stage was therefore devised and built. These were the months immediately prior to the lottery grant, and money was tight, so the mock up went ahead on a miniscule budget. The stage, stage roof and *frons scenae* were built from modern steel scaffolding, clad in plywood without decoration or modelling. All of the major elements were represented, but the overall effect was crude and charmless. Many different groups took part in the workshop season from all around the world. The reactions were varied and mixed, but British classical actors spoke with convincing consistency. They were not happy.

The actors' comments were of great interest in themselves, as they were the first true reaction to the recreated Globe's stage. The issues raised by the actors were:

a   concerns over the size of the stage
b   concerns over the shape of the stage (some believed that it would be better if tapered)
c   A feeling that the stage cover was too large (did it need to cover the whole stage?)
d   A strong feeling that the stage columns were too far forward and too close to the edge of the stage, giving too little space to circulate around them.
e   A certainty that the two side entrances in the *frons scenae* were too close together.

Having recognised previously that the true client for this project was the scholars, another voice now had to be recognised, that of the actors. The matter was more delicate than one might at first think. Sam Wanamaker, when giving one of his persuasive talks to a potential funder, would dwell on the hierarchy of voices that should inform the design. To put the scholar's voice above all others, he would argue, paradoxically made this an actor's theatre. All modern traditions of staging had to be stripped away. Providing an unvarying back wall for the stage, the *frons scenae*, in which the actors' entrances and exits would remain constant for every performance, would make it easier for them to become familiar with the stage and reduce the need for direction. There would be no new sets or designs that had to be learnt so all effort could be focused on the actors' interpretation. But now it looked as though these arguments carried no conviction with the actors. We couldn't ignore the comments coming from the first groups to try out the stage. Their message was too strong and consistent. Lord Birkett, chairman of the Artistic Directorate, said that actors in a group never agree about anything, and to hear them speaking with almost one voice was alarming. What's more, the last thing we wanted was a dark house, one which had been an interesting experiment for a season or two but which no decent actor wanted to play.

The questions being asked by the actors also revived doubts, based on quite different grounds, about the huge dimensions of the gabled cover for the stage roof, supported on just two columns, and the unusual spectacle of the secondary structure (the stage roof) being higher than the primary structure (the tiring house). All of these points are directly related to the size and position of the stage columns. The actors' objections were based on the effect the siting of the stage columns had on their use of the stage. They provided obstacles on the stage and divided the stage into unusable areas at the edges and corners. The repercussions of their comments, however, affected almost every part of the tiring house and stage cover structures. Furthermore, it was proving very difficult to find good vernacular models as precedents for this design, even though we had widened our consultation to include timber frame experts from all parts of the country to see if there was one good model that we had missed. We were also troubled by other features of the structures. Doubts that lay in the mind of the construction team were:

a   that the stage roof span between columns was too great to justify with historic examples
b   that the stage roof span from the *frons scenae* to the columns was too great
c   that the cantilever from the stage columns to the edge of the roof could not be justified by surviving examples of Elizabethan structures.

All of the decisions made so far for the reconstruction were based on the best evidence available, but no piece of evidence on its own was conclusive, so a process of confirmation and verification was used to give a high degree of probability or plausibility about this enigmatic structure. Yet it remained enigmatic, and it was not possible to give a conclusive and unarguable summary of evidence to quieten the experts' concerns. It was going to be necessary to review every decision made over the last fifteen years to see if the same conclusions would be reached.

The issue quickly boiled down to one major point. Given that the stage was to be fully covered by its roof (as we concluded on historic evidence it must be), what was the size of cantilever that could be justified for the heavens? The size and shape of the stage was reaffirmed from the same evidence that had previously informed our decisions. Sir Peter Hall summarised his concerns arising from his experience of working on the temporary stage. He suggested that the stage columns should be 12 ft 6 in. or so back from the front of the stage and 12 ft 6 in. or so in from the sides of the stage. On the experimental stage they were only 5 ft 6 in. from the front of the stage and 5 ft 6 in. from the sides. This would have implications for the structure of the 'heavens' as a whole.

The Globe's carpenter, Peter Streete, was part of a vernacular tradition, one without architects and one in which the problem-solving mentality was against looking for radically new solutions to problems, preferring rather to seek a solution that came from an adaptation to an existing technique. Great care had been taken throughout the design process to find existing examples for every structural feature, every frame junction and detail in the reconstruction. Yet the playhouses were clearly not ordinary structures, but extraordinary ones. Nothing remains among historic buildings that looks anything like the de Witt Swan stagehouse. Nothing remains that looks anything remotely like the Hollar second Globe stagehouse. Perhaps, even, the very extraordinary and experimental nature of these structures is why they lasted so badly? It was in the midst of reflections such as these that we had to take our final decisions about the design of the stage house.

Ten options for the stage house roof were drawn out as discussions reiterated the points made over all of the fifteen preceding years. The solution adopted was to increase the cantilever from 5 ft 6 in. to 8 ft 3 in., which moved the columns closer together (from a separation of 33 feet down to 27 ft 6 in.) as well as further from the stage edges, and therefore reduced the size and overburden of the stage roof and ridge height to exactly the

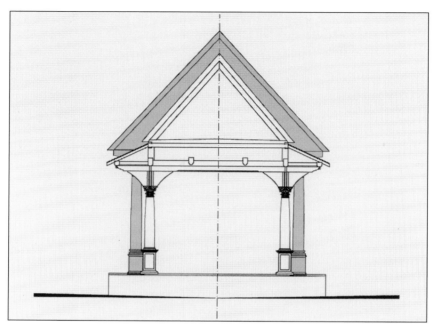

FIG. 35 Stage elevations showing the 1996 modifications: The shaded elevation shows the structure that was mocked up for the Workshop Season in 1995. The columns are spaced at 33 ft between centres and there is a 5 ft 6 in. cantilever on either side to cover the full 44 ft of the stage. The superimposed elevation shows the effect of the modifications: the column spacing was reduced to 27 ft 6 in., which increased the cantilever to 8 ft 3 in. on either side. A light pentice roof (or lean-to) was used at the lower level to both decrease the burden on the cantilever and to lower, and therefore lighten, the main stage roof. This configuration was mocked up for the Prologue Season in 1996.

same as the tiring house (fig. 35). To maintain an acceptable geometry for sight lines the cantilevered section of roof was now treated as a low pitch skirt, clad with riven oak shingles, which has the added advantage of reducing its weight to a minimum. Formally, the *frons scenae* changed again from a three bay structure back to a seven bay structure, with five central bays adjacent to the stage and two flanking bays. The principal difference here is that the bays are all of different widths, starting with an eleven foot wide central bay, flanked by two 8 ft 3 in. wide bays which are in turn flanked by two 6 ft 2¼ in., a diminishing proportion of three quarters.

This is the stage and stagehouse structure that was simultaneously fabricated in its final form in the carpenter's yard and fabricated in temporary form for the prologue season in August/September 1996. The mistake of the workshop season of summer 1995 was not repeated and the temporary stage was used as an opportunity to experiment with the mouldings and painted decoration of the *frons scenae* (plates 26, 27). The success or otherwise of this solution, and the persuasiveness of the design as a whole, will be tested by actors, audiences and scholars as the years go by.

Notes to Chapter Five

1 *See* the account in *The Structural Engineer*, October 1975.

PLATE 5 The first two bays, with the balusters in place.

PLATE 6 Wooden beams, showing split in timber.

PLATE 7 A wooden joint assembly.

PLATE 8 Frame laid out flat.

PLATE 9 Playhouse frame showing complex jointing.

PLATE 10 Thatch being applied to the reconstructed Globe, across the river from St Paul's.

PLATE 11 The finished thatch showing an ornamental pattern on the ridge, with the nozzles of the sprinkler system protruding.

6

TIMBER FRAMING, THE TWO BAYS
AND AFTER

Jon Greenfield

*This chapter was written by Jon Greenfield, drawing on his own expertise as an architect and on the vast experi-
ence of Peter McCurdy as master carpenter and researcher of timber-framing techniques. Peter has worked for
twenty years on the construction of timber-framed buildings. His firm, McCurdy and Company, is one of the
country's leading specialist firms in the construction and conservation of timber buildings. He has undertaken
wide practical research on workshop fabrication techniques, and studied forty to fifty historic buildings in preparation for his work on Shakespeare's Globe. His research has provided the essential underpinning for the discussion
that follows.*

IN 1992 Peter McCurdy and I, master carpenter and architect together, set out to make
two whole bays of the Globe Theatre, in precise detail, at a time when the archaeological discoveries had thrown the generally adopted design back into a state of flux.[1] In his
presentation to the Atlanta conference in February 1990, following the discovery of the
Globe's foundations, John Orrell presented what he described as 'a few tentative conclusions
from these scant remains'.[2] We could not improve on his conclusions, however tentative, and
used them as the basic setting out of the two bays. The conclusions became less tentative
and were adopted for the design of the reconstruction shortly after. Conclusions made at
that time about the form of the auditorium have remained current, and subsequent opportunities to re-examine the design of the timber frame have tended to reinforce the conclusions
made for the two bays. The construction of the remaining thirteen auditorium bays from
1993 to 1995 has followed a repeating pattern that was set by the first two bays.

I. SETTING OUT

The setting out of the theatre in plan had become a polygon of 20 equal bays set inside a
circle of 100 ft in diameter. Confusion can arise if it is not clearly understood that these
diameters are measured across opposite corners of the polygon, not across opposite faces,
which is a slightly shorter dimension. To derive the gallery widths it is necessary to consider
the dimension across 'flats', from one facet to the one opposite. Across flats the twenty-sided
figure measures 98 ft 9 in. from the outer face of the outer ring. Both the remains of the
Globe theatre's footings and the Fortune contract give a gallery width of 12 ft 6 in. and this
simple arithmetic reveals a yard 73 ft 9 in. wide (98 ft 9 in. − 12 ft 6 in. − 12 ft 6 in. = 73 ft
9 in.), a most significant finding when we consider, as we do below, the use of *ad quadratum*
geometry to establish the yard's dimensions.

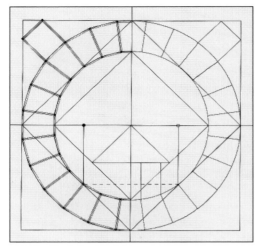

FIG. 36 *Ad Quadratum* setting-out of the inner and outer galleries and 24 structural bays

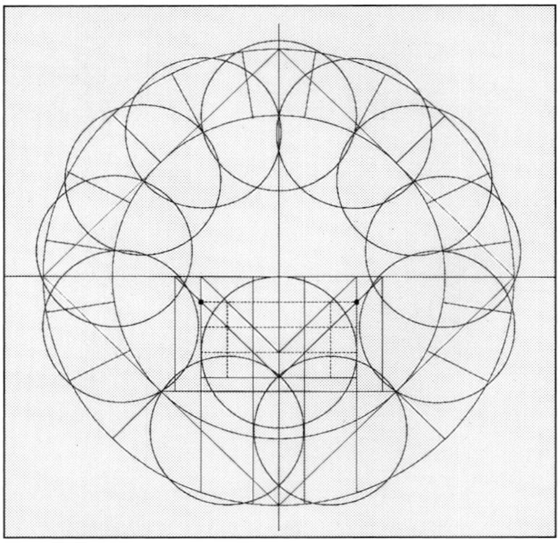

FIG. 37 *Ad Quadratum* setting-out of the inner and outer galleries and 20 structural bays

Orrell, in his initial analysis of the remains, was the first to see that the diameter of the Globe as deduced from the remains, and the gallery width as deduced from the same source, did not seem to concur with the *ad quadratum* setting out that had been the basis of the reconstruction up to this time:

> If true, it demonstrates that the Globe was not designed *ad quadratum*, as I had often suggested was the case, for an *ad quadratum* setting out in a theatre 100 ft in diameter would result in a gallery depth some three feet greater than this (12 ft 6 in.).[3]

Ad quadratum had been a vital ordering principle for the theatre before the archaeological discoveries, as demonstrated in the setting out diagram. It is a method of linking the diameters of two concentric circles with a square, in which the square is set within the larger circle so that the points of the square touch the circumference of that larger circle, and the smaller circle is set within the square so that its circumference touches the sides of the square. In the playhouses this *ad quadratum* principle was thought to describe the relationship between the inner and outer ring of the galleries. Despite Orrell's initial misgivings subsequent consideration of the frame in three dimensions showed that *ad quadratum* could still be an essential part of the theatre's setting out (figs 36 and 37). Exhaustive geometrical studies were carried out on plots of the fragmentary remains, fragments which were disappointing in their geometrical precision as they were of footings that had been dug with the equivalent of pick and shovel. These studies tended to concentrate analysis exclusively on the lowest members of the timber frame, the sill beams. Peter Streete, the Globe's master carpenter, would have been thinking beyond this at the outset. His first task, after felling the trees and converting them to usable balks, would have been to set out sill beam and wall plate together, the sill being the lowest component of the structural frame and the wall plate being the highest (beneath the roof trusses). By this he would have established his upper and lower datum from which all of the vertical frame elements that lie between sill and wall plate could be positioned (fig 38). So Peter Streete had in his mind not just one set of dimensions (those for setting out the sill) but a second set for the wall plate too, both of equal importance.

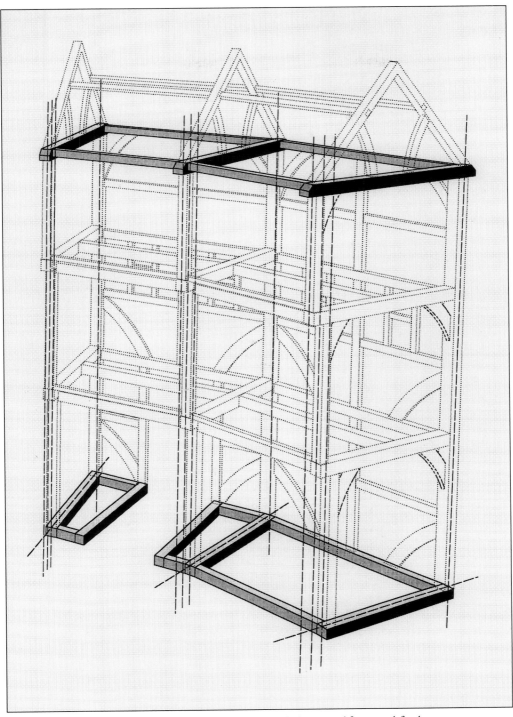

FIG. 38 The setting-out dimensions of the whole structural frame are defined
by the sill and wall plate frames.

The possible presence of jetties at the storey heights on the inner ring means the setting out of the wall plate and the setting out of the sill could be quite different. If we apply an *ad quadratum* setting out to the *wall plate*, rather than to the sill, we can see that this was the case. Using *ad quadratum* we produce a diameter across corners of 70 ft 8½ in. and 69 ft 10 in. across flats. The inner wall plate is therefore set 23½ inches further in than the inner sill beam, which can be accounted for by two jetties, each measuring 11¾ inches. The Fortune theatre was contracted to have two jetties of ten inches each. We are convinced that this is how Peter Streete would have worked, using *ad quadratum* geometry applied to the wall plate and then working his dimensions back to the sill.

Perhaps these figures are hard to follow, which only emphasises the mental dexterity with which Streete would have been able to work the numbers. After calculating the figures for fabricating sill beams and wall plates in his yard to a very high degree of accuracy, perhaps even after cutting the timber, he would have taken on a gang of labourers to dig and lay the foundations within the setting out he had devised and marked out for them. It is unfortunate that we are only left with this, the least accurate of the operations on which to base our theories of setting out.

It is important here to pause and consider the accuracy with which carpenters making structural frames have to work. So many of the examples of oak frames left to us are three, four and five hundred years old and have suffered natural decay, fire, beetle, subsidence or thoughtless modification. All major structural elements of historic English timber framing use 'boxed heart' timbers. This means that the natural circular section of the tree was hewn to a square section with the heart of the annular rings at the centre. Elizabethan craftsmen were not wasteful, and would use as much of the trees as possible, including the outer, much less durable sap wood and perhaps, on some of the secondary timbers, they might even have included a bit of bark too. The frames that have survived the ages often show where the less durable sap wood has decayed, leaving timbers with gnarled and rounded arises (corners) which has enhanced the erroneous popular image of rough and inaccurately jointed work. The timbers were not originally cut like this, but were made in sharply defined sections with very tightly fitting joints, particularly on timbers of primary importance like the sill beams and wall plates.

With modern saw mills we are too used to squared up and easily available timber sections, which leads to the other common misunderstanding about the accuracy of traditional timber frame work. 'Boxed heart' timbers were hewn to shape with a side axe and their faces were smoothed off with an adze. Secondary timbers were also framed from 'boxed heart' timbers which were sawn in a pit down their length, or 'halved'. Tertiary timbers were sawn down their length a second time, or 'quartered'. All of this was done by hand and as with all hand-crafted objects, the timbers had small undulations and deviations along their length, and the squared-off faces would not necessarily be quite perpendicular to one another. But this does not produce inaccurate work or poorly-fitting joints, as the carpenter's method of forming the joints worked directly from the timber itself and therefore took account of the deviations. This method is called 'scribing' and was used on the two bays and throughout the reconstruction thereafter.

It will already have been noted that the gallery setting out dimensions referred to the outer face of the outer wall and the inner face of the inner wall, not to the centre lines of the respective walls. This is precisely how the timbers would have been set and measured when the frame was made in 1599, with measurements taken from the external face of one timber to the external face of another timber. It is bothersome for a craftsman constantly to establish a centre line when taking measurements, and it was not common practice when working with sill beams, wall plates and bressumers. In almost all building projects Peter Streete would have worked his frames from one common face, using that one side as a datum, then working all the joints and dimensions from that 'fair' face. All timbers in the frame would be lined up flush on the fair face, and deviations and differences in section would be taken up on the other faces. This method was used for all of the reconstructed Globe's frames, except the radial cross frames, as it would have looked very curious to have the timbers in each radial cross frame 'weighted' to one side. For these radial frames it was decided to depart from the more common 'fair face' method and use the less common centre line method: all cross frames have been set out from their centre lines. A notable example of the centre line method can be found in the hammerbeam roof of the Middle Temple Hall which was set out from centre lines . Carpenters' centre line marks scribed onto the timbers with a draw knife in 1562 can still be found today.

II. METHODS OF CONJECTURE

Undisputed, clear evidence of the Globe's superstructure is very sparse, so we had to accept at the outset that many of the decisions that were made about the frame were inferences from the limited evidence available, and that many of the decisions made about the reconstruction were therefore conjectural. However, if the exercise was to be of any value at all we had to avoid the temptation to invent. It was necessary to devise a method and formula for decision-making, so that our conjectures could be reasoned and justified and not be mistaken for whimsy or fancy. Two methods of conjecture were used. The first came from the examination of prototype buildings and the second from an understanding of the carpenters' methods.

Prototypes

The four important criteria for a useful prototype are: (a) it should be as close in function as possible to a playhouse; (b) it should be as close in geographical location as possible to Bankside; (c) it should be as close as possible in date to the Theatre of 1576 and the first Globe of 1599; (d) it should be as close in form as possible to the polygonal structures shown in the panoramas and proved by the archaeological remains of the Globe and Rose Theatres.

Some idea of the usefulness of our prototypes can be gained by setting a rank order which depends on how many of the four criteria are met. For example, a prototype that meets all four criteria is the most useful to us and could be freely copied, a building that meets only three of the criteria is clearly a less 'safe' source of evidence and so on. No standing buildings survive that meet all four criteria, as no Elizabethan playhouses have survived in Britain, let alone on Bankside. Very few of the buildings that survive for us to use as prototypes even meet three of the criteria, a number meet two and most buildings only meet one. Appendix A (p. 115 *below*) contains a list of all the buildings used as prototypes, with an indication of date and type.

Prototype Dates

Although the first Globe was erected in 1599, it used the timbers of the Theatre erected in Shoreditch in 1576, which were transported across the Thames with dubious legality during the Christmas festival of 1598. How much of the building was re-erected without modification? Which date should we follow when searching for prototypes? Herbert Berry, in his consideration of the legal documents arising from the dispute over this 'theft', draws attention to the owner Giles Allen's account in which he claims that sixteen people dismantled the building. The sixteen people would have included Cuthbert and Richard Burbage, Peter Streete, William Smyth (an old friend of the Burbages) and twelve workmen (presumably Streete's men). Ellen Burbage, mother of Richard and Cuthbert, looked on. In his account Allen claims that Burbage's people started on Boxing Day 1598 and took four days, finishing before he could arrange for them to be stopped by power of attorney; Allen himself was out of London and too ill to travel back.[4] Four days is very fast work, even for sixteen men, and it seems that they could only achieve such speed by stripping out and discarding all the secondary elements: thatch, plaster, partitions and seating tiers. In such a short time only the primary structural frame could have been dismantled with the necessary care and method needed for reuse. On the other hand, the Globe was erected from the reclaimed timber by 16 May 1599, if E.K. Chambers, following C.W. Wallace, is right in identifying the 'house' (*domus*) in an inquisition of that date with the Globe. In any case, the work must have been finished soon after, so that there was simply no time to do anything much more than re-erect the Shoreditch building. The secondary elements were all remade as new, but the primary structure was unchanged. The involvement of Peter Streete is of some significance to this point, as Irwin Smith has suggested:

> Any crew of unskilled wreckers could have dismembered the Theatre if the mere salvage of the lumber were all that was required. Streete was one of the most skilful and sought after contractors of his day; and the fact that he was employed for the precedent dismembering as well as for the subsequent re-assembling suggests that something more than a mere wrecking job was required of him.[5]

It is with some confidence, therefore, that we have concentrated our search for prototypes of the structural frame on 1576 rather than 1599, although the stylistic treatment of the fitting out of the first Globe is certainly of the later date.

The legal records of the Theatre show that the building was opened in 1576 before it was finished and that it needed 'further building' in January and February 1592, at much the same time as Henslowe made substantial alterations to the Rose. Henslowe added stage columns and a stage roof at this time; could the Burbages have done the same at the Theatre? The arrangements in Shoreditch involved the Burbages in the management of a reasonably large range of buildings as well as the theatre, including an impressively large barn and a number of dilapidated out-buildings that were repeatedly raided to provide a cheap source of building materials for repairing other buildings, including the Theatre. However, expenditure on the Theatre in 1592 of up to £40 over six or seven weeks does not seem a large enough sum to have paid for a substantial alteration of the primary structure in comparison with the £700 total it cost to build the playhouse originally. Henslowe's expenditure on enlarging the Rose in January 1592 was over £105.

We are well advised, therefore, to bear in mind building details of the last quarter of the sixteenth century, and have taken note of buildings erected up to 50 years before our key date of 1576, as the development of timber frame technology was slow and occurred over generations. Skills were passed from Master Carpenter to apprentice, with the occasional introduction of a new method by a journeyman who had learnt a useful new skill on his travels. Book learning of Italian methods was soon to become an important part of a build-er's learning and the architectural profession was soon to grow, but not until some years into the next century and after the completion of the Globe.

Prototype Locations

London has suffered many calamities over the last four hundred years, the Great Fire and Blitz being particular catastrophes for the stock of timber frame buildings that have been left for us to study. Even discounting 1666, the timber city constantly suffered from wasting fires, as exemplified by the George Inn in Borough High Street, Southwark. Being south of the river it survived the Great Fire, only for part of the Inn and all of the Stables and Barn to be consumed by a 'sad and violent fire' in 1670. The publican borrowed heavily to rebuild the damaged parts, only for the whole building to be destroyed again, this time in a fire which razed Borough High Street in 1676. It is, therefore, great good fortune that has allowed one wing of the again rebuilt Inn to survive to this day, but it is of much too late a date to inform our research into the Globe's primary structure. Southwark, at the heart of our search, is disappointing in that it has not revealed any good prototypes for us to use.

We have had to look for prototypes throughout modern Greater London but have gener-ally concentrated on buildings in the central boroughs. We have a number of good, if somewhat disfigured, examples from Fleet Street, St Bartholomew's and the Tower of Lon-don, buildings which stood right on the eventual edge of the Pudding Lane fire. We have included examples as far away as Chingford and Eltham, where the royal or aristocratic owners used metropolitan craftsmen and so compensated for their then rural location.

Prototypes chosen by Form

Of course the most singular feature of the Globe was its shape: the 'wooden O'. Forgetting the variations of site and topography for a moment, most of the buildings left to us that are of the right date and right general location are rectangular, not polygonal. To research polygonal jointing details we had to travel some distance from our preferred time and place to find useful examples.

Timber frame jointing methods are remarkably tolerant of changes in angle, allowing almost any shape to be constructed. A cursory glance at the plans of the Elizabethan sur-veyor Ralph Treswell, which show various tightly packed London blocks, reveals that even supposedly rectangular building plans have corners whose angles are mostly anything but right angles. Walls are rarely parallel and elevations change direction, demonstrating how familiar Elizabethan carpenters were with buildings of highly irregular shapes. However, the 18° angle of a twenty-sided polygon is enough of a deviation from a right angle to change the generic nature of the timber joint employed. We feel certain that Peter Streete would have encountered the problem of making a polygonal joint infrequently enough to have thought it out carefully, and even to have done some research himself. This would be by examining similar structures, which he would have used to inform his own life-long accumulation of knowledge. We have examined two categories of building: the market cross, both examples of which are octagonal, and religious buildings (chapter houses and apsidal ends of chancels or chapels). Although the Market Crosses are far from London and the Church and Cathedral architecture is of a higher order of design and construction than the lowly playhouses, important conclusions can be drawn from both, particularly about the wall plate to main post junction. For example, Wymondham market cross has avoided the complexities of joining the wall plate on a polygonal angle by employing a butt joint for the wall plates and relying on the jowl and principal rafters to hold the joint together. This is an adaptation of the standard dovetail lap joint. Later wrought iron and steel strapping shows the failure of this solution. The Chapter House of Lincoln cathedral was made by an engineer in the nineteenth century, and uses a scarf joint on the angle to make a complete ring beam that restrains the spreading forces. The solution works well, but at the expense of a very complicated joint which must have been time-consuming and expensive to make. Does this fit with the known history of expediency in both Shoreditch and Bankside? Our conclusion was quite different from both of these, and was to tenon the wall plate into the truss tie beam, effectively treating the wall plate like a butt purlin. This solution is discussed as part of the cross frame further on.

Peter Streete's Methods

The first and most informative aspect of Streete's work is that it falls into the vernacular tradition. The Burbages did not employ an architect or engineer, but went straight to the Master Carpenter for what we call today a 'Design and Build' service. The size and layout was agreed between the Burbages and Streete, but the carpenter was largely left to make the enclosure as he saw fit. Furthermore, it must be remembered that this was not just one way of building from many, like today, but the only way of building. Summerson states:

> Nothing remotely like an 'architectural profession' existed. The word [architect] was rarely used in the sixteenth century and its connotation was in every sense ornamental … The title seems to have been adopted by or applied to craftsmen who knew how to handle the new architectural grammar [of the Elizabethan renaissance] in any material. The truth is, of course, that the craft of building was still conducted as it had been for hundreds of years: that is to say, by master craftsmen who were apprenticed and trained in the quarry or the workshop.[6]

In France and Germany there are still established apprentice-based timber framing guilds, if small and highly secretive. Not so in Britain, and it is largely through the research of Peter McCurdy and the Weald & Downland Museum that it has been possible to rediscover, to a large extent, traditional English methods. It would be inappropriate to describe these in exact detail here. The use of reference planes and points, 'face up' alignment from sawn faces, scribing of joints, the selection of trees, their conversion and the procedures used in the framer's yard before reaching the site are all complex matters. However, there are three aspects of framing that do need further clarification to help make the relevant points.

The first is that the method of erecting the frame on site was 'piece-on-piece' construction. Each post, beam, joist or rafter was set into the frame one piece after the other, following a strict sequence. Among other sources, film recordings showing the Amish raising a barn in the United States have given the impression that wall frames were assembled on the ground and hauled up into position. 'Raising' in this way was common in the New World, but was not used in England for this type of building. A gin pole, sheer legs or rope and pulley would have been used to lift in one structural timber after another.

The second point is nicely summarised by Irwin Smith:

> Tudor carpenters knew well that jointed timbers were not interchangeable, and because they knew it they went to considerable pains to mark each timber with a distinguishing device which would enable them to return it to one relative position which it, and it alone, was fitted to fill.[7]

The playhouses were prefabricated buildings, but they were not made like meccano. Modern machine-produced prefabricated buildings tend to be a 'kit-of-parts' with each part mass produced to precisely the same dimensions. In this case it would be possible to substitute one part with another that is exactly the same from another similar position in the building (if the structural bays are repetitive) or from the same position in another similar building. Prefabrication methods for historic framing work quite differently. It has already been noted that all of the timbers are hand hewn or pit sawn, giving deviations from one timber to the next. In section the timbers may not be square and can vary in dimension significantly along their length. When a frame is made up, therefore, it is not cut with standard joints for standard timbers, but each joint is precisely scribed to receive a particular timber, taking account of all of its special deviations and characteristics. So, for a timber to be interchanged in an historic frame it had to be uniquely re-cut for its new position. A number of joints may be similar in principle, particularly thinking of a repeating structure like the Globe's auditorium with fifteen similar bays, but the exact dimensions of each timber and therefore each joint are unique.

Thirdly, the sequence and division of work were clearly defined. Orrell had already divined the stages of building in the Fortune contract,[8] realising that the terms 'made erected and sett upp', and 'made erect, setup and fully finished' were not, as they first seemed, just overly ponderous legal language but were, in fact, precisely sequenced terms. They fit exactly with the newly rediscovered traditional framing methods of 'piece-on-piece' construction. Using Orrell's terms, *making* describes the selection of growing timber, felling and converting it and the fashioning of the frame in the carpenter's yard, perhaps a considerable distance from the building site. *Erecting* describes the raising of the primary structure on site. Orrell includes the binding joists, braces and roof trusses in the following stage, but as they are essential parts of the primary frame it seems more likely that they would be included in the 'Erecting' phase. *To Set Up* refers to the secondary timbers: partitions, carcassing, seating, tiers, 'conveyances and divisions withoute and within', indeed all of the parts of the Theatre that would have been ruthlessly smashed out to allow careful dismantling of the primary structure in the short time available over Christmas 1598. *Finishing* clearly refers to the lath and plasterwork, and painting.

III. NOTES ON THE FORM OF THE GALLERIES

Having established the two-dimensional setting out of the bays, and armed with a framework for decision making, we set about devising the form of the galleried bays. Our first effort was to set out the cross section, and in doing so a jetty system was adopted.

Jetties

A jettied form of construction makes a fundamental difference to the frame configuration, particularly the inner wall. By 1576 there were buildings with and without jetties in almost equal number in the London area. Within a few years jetties were to become illegal within the City. Without a jetty, the principal posts, front and back, will rise full height, a length of some thirty-two feet without a break. One bressumer beam only will be required at each floor level, to receive the wall studs from below and to support the floor joists and wall studs above. In a jetty system there are two edge beams at each floor level: the lowest beam, the bressumer, rests on top of the lower posts and studs and supports the joists above, which in turn oversail the bressumer beam and cantilever by the length of the jetty. The second beam, or jetty sill, lies on the projecting ends of the joists. It provides support for the posts and wall studs of the next floor. So in a jetty system we have, on the inner face, posts no more than one storey high, a feature which cuts costs, increases stability and makes erection easier.

We followed the Fortune contract in this respect '... All of which Stories shall conteine Twelue foote and a halfe of lawfull assize in breadth throughoute, besides a juttey forwardes in either of the saide twoe vpper stories of Tenne ynches of lawfull assize ...'.[9] We interpreted the 'juttey forwardes' as a jetty into the yard, having found ourselves commonly referring to the outer wall as the back wall which implied that a jetty forwards was a jetty on the inner wall. It was also this evidence which made us reject the configuration of a jetty on both the inner wall and a jetty on the outer wall, a plausible design but one which did not concur with the Fortune contract. We interpreted 'in either of the saide twoe vpper Stories' as one jetty on each storey, although we accept that there is another reading which would give one jetty that carries forwards past both of the other storeys. The Elizabethan lawyer's 'either' could be translated into modern language as 'each' or 'both', and could therefore describe either of the two different forms equally well. I have already indicated how the jetties fit into the setting out, which has led us to 11¾ in. jetties rather than the 10 in. ones. With a jetty forwards we are clearly left with full-height thirty-two foot posts on the outer frame, but as the inner wall is open the jetty sill is only carrying balusters rather than wall studs, and therefore need not be a large timber. Again we have clear savings with this method of construction.

The jetty gives one clear constructional advantage: the lower floor can be finished off, posts and beams laid in position as well as the floor joists and perhaps even the floor boarding for the next lift up, all quite independently of the timbers for the upper storeys. Several bays-worth of back posts, three storeys in height, with the rest of the structure built to first floor level, can be left as a stable structure during erection. Work can begin again the next day, or later, without excessive temporary propping, and the second level can be built using the first floor as a working platform.

A constructional advantage such as this should not be underestimated. Using the English piece-on-piece method of erection, described above, is like playing a large-scale three dimensional chess game. Each section of the frame must be added in exactly the right sequence, otherwise the frame will close up leaving no room for an out-of-sequence timber. A major timber, like the long back post, has many secondary timbers jointed into it. Twenty-six timbers are jointed into three of the post's four faces in all. As each new post is brought into the frame it receives the tenons of ten timbers, all of which have to be guided into one of the faces of the main post simultaneously. This is a tricky job which can only be achieved using blocks placed under the shoulders of the main vertical timbers, to prevent these joints fully engaging and therefore closing up while all ten of the tenons are being offered into their appropriate mortices. If we didn't have a jetty on the inner ring we would have to have full-length posts there too, and when these were offered into the frame they would have to receive timber from *two* directions: sixteen tenons in all. This is not impossible, but very difficult indeed.

The use of jetties on only the inner side of the galleries has had another noticeable effect on the structure. Due to its cellular nature, timber shrinks as it seasons considerably more across its width and breadth than along its length. The outer wall of the Globe is made from one full-length post, so shrinkage here has been minimal. The inner wall, by contrast, is broken by two jetties, each of which have jetty beams and rails under the short jetty posts. Shrinkage in the jetty posts is minimal, but shrinkage in the intermediate beams and rails is significant. The result is that the inner wall is shrinking more than the outer wall, with the result that the structure is tending to lean in towards the yard.

Associated with the jetty solution is the use of a flat floor, fully boarded-out at first and second floor level, onto which the tiers of seating are set in a later construction phase. This fits neatly into Orrell's separation of constructional phases, with the structure, including flat floors, falling into the 'Making' and 'Erecting' phases, and the seating tiers falling into the 'Setting up' phase.

Our conviction that this is the correct interpretation is deepened by a consideration of the alternative, which is to 'frame in' the raking members that support the seating degrees. This would involve including the raking members as part of the primary frame to be constructed in the 'Making' and 'Erecting' phases, considerably enlarging the size and complexity of the framing task. At first we had thought that 'framing in' rakers for the seating would give useful bracing to the structure in an out-of-the-way place, below the seats, but this consideration was outweighed by the constructional advantages outlined above. We will see the positive aspects of this later on when considering braces generally, and it should be noted that the adopted method had other cost and practical advantages as well. The seats were designed as separate discrete frames in themselves, completely independent of the main frame. We were therefore able to follow the implications in the Fortune and Hope contracts that carcassing and secondary elements like the seats were made from the cheaper and easier-to-work imported softwoods generally referred to as Baltic Fir. The Hope contract also stipulates that the main posts should be made from fir although the rest of the primary structure was to be from oak. Baltic softwood was commonly available in London and was sold in a number of standard board sizes, ready sawn. The seats in the reconstruction were also made from Baltic Fir, framed up from members that could have been cut down from 9 in. x 3 in. boards, one of the standard sizes available at the time (*see* plate 2). This separation of the building into its primary oak structure and its secondary softwood carcassing is an appropriately disciplined division. The greatest difficulty it posed was finding softwood (*pinus silvestris*) of the appropriate grade. The Elizabethans would have used first-growth trees from Sweden and Finland, trees grown slowly in a cold climate and therefore having a very durable internal composition of densely packed annular rings. The fast grown 'farmed' trees available today have significantly different characteristics.

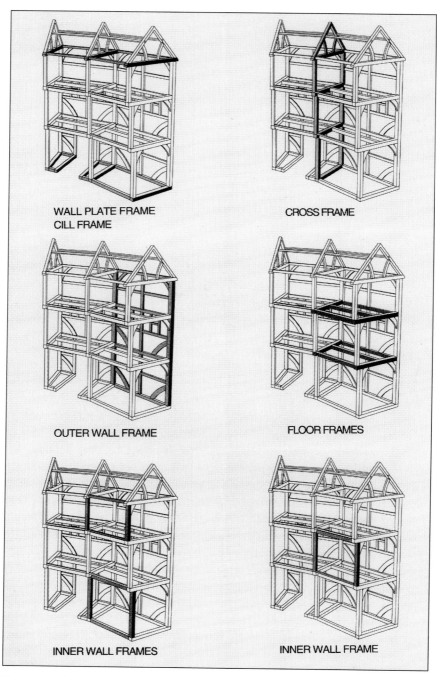

WALL PLATE FRAME
CILL FRAME

CROSS FRAME

OUTER WALL FRAME

FLOOR FRAMES

INNER WALL FRAMES

INNER WALL FRAME

FIG. 39 The structural frame of two bays is illustrated here, with its constituent two-dimensional frames highlighted. McCurdy & Co. constructed each two dimensional frame in turn, laid out horizontally in their yard. As each frame was completed it was dismantled, carefully stored and the next frame started. The new frame had some timbers from the previous frames, which were taken from the stack, rotated to reveal the appropriate face and cut into the new frame. In this way the whole structure was fabricated in McCurdy's yard in two dimensions and each joint offered together before any site work. Only on site was the frame finally assembled in three dimensions.

As touched on above, a three-dimensional frame is made up from a series of two-dimensional frames, in much the same way as it can be said that a cube is made up from six two-dimensional squares, one for each face. Extending the analogy further into framing terms, each of the squares making up a cube would be made in the framing yard, laid out flat and then dismantled, so that the next square could be fabricated. However, it can be seen that the edge of one square also makes the edge of another square, so one of the timbers from the first square would have to be used in the fabrication of the second square, and so on. It could be said that the whole of the cube could be put together in the framing yard as a series of flat faces, but it would only be fully constructed as a three-dimensional cube once, at the very end, on site. So it is with timber framing. The back wall, for example, would be laid out in the yard, each joint scribed, cut, offered up and marked with a reference like the ones described by Irwin Smith. The back wall frame would then be dismantled and a side wall frame constructed using the shared corner post from the back wall appropriately rotated so that the carpenter could work on another face. As before, each joint would be scribed, cut, assembled and referenced, after which the side wall frame would be dismantled and another frame laid out. The process would continue until each two-dimensional frame had been assembled in this way. And herein lies the problem with 'framing in' the seating tiers: even when only considering the seating tier rakers they are not in orthogonal planes, and therefore do not form a frameable two-dimensional configuration (fig. 39).

A further indication that the Globe was constructed with flat floors in the first instance can be found in the legal documents of the Theatre. Herbert Berry tells us:

> At one point, towards its end, Allen and Cuthbert Burbage spoke about using the Theatre as a playhouse for only five more years, and then converting 'the same to tenem, or upon reparacions of the other houses there'[10]

If the floors were flat, converting the playhouse structure to tenements would be a relatively simple matter, by blocking in the open front wall. If, however, the floor was banked up in seating tiers that could only be removed by cutting out a piece of primary structure, and an important bracing member at that, then Allen and Burbage would not even have bothered to discuss the conversion. It seems much more likely that it was a flat-floored frame, with the seating tiers built as secondary elements on the floor.

Storey Heights and Braces

The cross section through the auditorium does not look unlike the Richard Hosley/Richard Southern reconstruction of the Swan Theatre,[11] which is unsurprising as we have worked from similar evidence, namely the heights given in the Fortune contract. This is the very best evidence for the height of the galleries, and we could see no substantial reason to make a new departure. Certainly there was a development of the playhouse type over the years from 1576, and it cannot be that the Theatre as the first building of this type was the optimum in every respect. One would expect the Curtain to improve on the Theatre, the Rose to improve on the Curtain, the Globe to improve on the Rose (inasmuch as it could within the bounds of the re-erected structure) and the Fortune to improve on the Globe: a steady development over twenty-four years. There is evidence that the stage and stage roof developed from one playhouse to the next, as did stair locations, but there is no

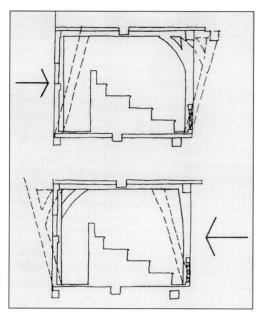

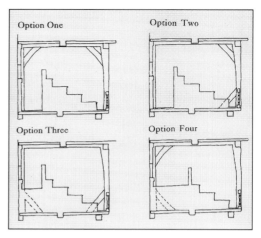

FIG. 41 Middle gallery timber braces. The pair of braces are equally effective in any combination, except diagonally with the braces opposite one another, when they would both be resisting the same force. The choice of brace positions is therefore dictated by the patterns of use in each gallery. In the middle gallery (illustrated) Option 1 positions the braces where they do not restrict the use.

FIG. 40 Timber braces are used to resist wind load, and they are much more effective in compression than in tension. As the wind can act on either the inner or the outer walls a minimum of two braces is required.

evidence that the storey heights changed.

Without doubt, the Fortune dimensions of 12 ft, 11 ft and 9 ft for the height of the galleries are floor to floor dimensions, not floor to ceiling heights. The floor is the accepted reference plane when framing, and of course the timbers are set flat up to the floor, with the difference in their depth set down from the floor plane. A floor-to-ceiling measurement is affected by the depth of the ceiling timbers, each of which varies slightly giving uncertainty about where the measure should be taken (to the underside of joist, bridging beam or summer beam?). Our study of the prototypes has not been particularly conclusive for the floor heights, as examples are mostly of domestic architecture and not always three storey height. However they reveal dimensions that are not far off the standard storey heights for urban buildings. 17 Fleet Street is typical and has been measured as 11 ft 3 in., 10 ft 7 in. and 9 ft 9 in., and the wall plate at Staples Inn almost exactly matches the 32 ft elevation of the Fortune.

What's missing from the Hosley/Southern section is the positioning of wind braces in the cross frame. Speaking in structural terms, the essential feature of the playhouse frame is that it has an open front. Any extra timber in the front wall would restrict sight lines. Handrails and balustrades contribute to the stiffness of the open front wall to some extent, but not very much, so it is essential that stiffness is transferred to the front wall from the back wall, which is very stiff, via the cross frames and floor frames. When boarded out, the floors provide a very stiff 'diaphragm', so it is only necessary to brace the cross wall sufficiently and the structure becomes stiff enough to resist the movement caused by the vast 'live load' of the audience, or a gust of wind from the Thames. There is no concern over the strength of the timbers, as they are all well over the minimum size needed structurally. The concern is to make a suitably stiff frame.

Braces prevent the rectangular frame from distorting into a parallelogram under load (fig. 40). They are very effective at resisting loads in compression, but much less effective with tension loads when all of the forces are directed into the pegs holding the tenon. Depending on the direction in which the load is applied it is possible for the rectangle to distort in either sense. It is therefore inadequate to position the braces in corners diagonally opposite one another, as they would then provide resistance to the applied load in one direction only. If the load is applied in the opposite direction, the braces would offer no resistance to collapse other than the intrinsic stiffness of each joint. The diagram shows the correct positioning of the braces (fig. 41). Streete would have been well aware of this structural system, although he would have been so as a result of his craftsmen's learning, passed down from previous generations, who had discovered the most effective position for the braces by trial and error, rather than through any formal study of structural behaviour. Option 1, with the braces positioned in the two upper corners, is the least problematic when considered in relation to the seating tiers and the access way, but it does restrict the layout to some extent. Clearly, the circulation space at the rear of the gallery must remain at a low enough level if there is to be sufficient headroom, which strongly suggests that the access way was simply set at floor level, and not set at the top of the highest seat as has sometimes been shown. There is a certain expediency in using the floor level, but it does suggest a particular layout of access and seating, with the tiers punctured at intervals to allow a connection between the access and seating.

The braces have been made with a slight concave curve, although consideration was given to straight braces, which were coming into fashion in the early seventeenth century. Our prototypes have a wide range of brace shapes, from ogee to straight, but we followed the examples of Queen Elizabeth's Hunting Lodge and St Bartholomew's gatehouse. Arch braces, pushed tight into the elbow of the joint, were also considered, but rejected because of their inferior structural performance and because sufficient headroom was achieved without using such special methods.

It is worth re-examining Hollar's drawing of the Globe here (not the engraving of course), looking particularly at the windows (fig. 8, p. 37). Hollar shows a single line of windows, perhaps slightly over half way up the outer wall. Windows need additional timbers to form them, trimming them within the pattern of the frame. They involve additional effort and additional expense and would therefore not have been included unless they were absolutely necessary. Why are windows needed onto galleries that are only 12 ft 6 in. wide and which are completely open on the inner face? On our cross section through the auditorium the access way at first storey level would be dark and gloomy as it is set behind seating degrees; windows would be absolutely necessary for lighting the way. The natural height of windows to coincide with our floor-level access way comes out about halfway up the rear wall, just as in the Hollar drawing. If the access way were set at the top of the seating tiers firstly there would be no reason to have windows, as there would be ample light at the back of the gallery from the open front, and secondly the windows would be set much higher up the frame than Hollar shows. Of course, this argument uses the Second Globe for information about the First, and the 'View of London from the North towards the South' made before

1599 shows a somewhat different configuration of windows on the Theatre (fig. 2, p. 17). Nevertheless we remained faithful to Hollar's version, particularly as his drawing style and survey method as described by Orrell gives a greater assurance over such a detailed matter as the windows.

Roof Form

The two bays and subsequent auditorium were built with a standard Queen Strut trussed roof, with curved and slightly raked queen struts. The span across the diagonal corner of a gallery bay is only 14 ft 8 in., easily within the capabilities of this common truss form. However, it is important to note that we examined an alternative in some detail. Inspired by the section of Staples Inn published by Cecil Hewett,[12] which shows an Upper Cruck (or 'Knee Principles') roof form, and knowing from contemporary illustrations that the half storey was a very common domestic feature, we felt it was worth further consideration. Staples Inn, as a prototype, must be considered as one of our better examples, being both geographically close to Bankside, and close in date at 1586. We were unable to find good survey information on the original work, however, and mistrust much of what we see due to some creative renovations in 1866 and 1937. We were further inspired to examine the Upper Cruck formation after finding a reference to a roof made with 'crooked postes' fixed with 'iron boltes' in the Beargarden gatehouse contract of 1606, a contract also made with Peter Streete only seven years after he had completed the Globe and not one hundred and fifty yards from it. Applying an Upper Cruck to a playhouse is very interesting, but not convincing in the final analysis. The third gallery is the least commodious part of the building in terms of sight lines, and therefore of little commercial value to a theatre manager. The Upper Cruck gives greater capacity here, or even gives room for a small *fourth* gallery: poor seats very high up. However, adding a further five feet or more to the height also changes the proportion of the building somewhat, and it is worth remembering that most of the prospects show tall buildings, although only Hollar's second Globe can be relied on to any great extent.

IV. NOTES ON JOINTING

We have already touched on the frame configuration of the polygonal form but closer examination reveals a problem with the junction between timbers running around the concentric rings (bressumers, jetty sills and particularly wall plates) and the timbers in the cross frame that connect the inner and outer concentric rings. The back post being continuous in height from sill to wall plate is not interrupted by the bressumers at each intermediate storey. The bressumers are simply tenoned into the post. The jetty configuration on the inner ring gives a different solution, whereby the bressumers meet over the post, and tenons on the post engage in mortices at the ends of the bressumers. The joint is strengthened by a gradual jowl on the post, which is tenoned into the summer beam, and this beam then laps over the jointed bressumers and locks the assembly together.

Straightforward traditional mortise and tenon joints therefore work well until we consider the wall plate/ tie beam/ main post junction mentioned earlier. The traditional lap dovetail joint is the most common way of joining tie beam, post and wall plate, but could

PLATE 12 (*above*) Sixteenth-century architectural cabinet, *c.*1550, German, supposed to have been designed by Holbein and to come from the palace of Whitehall.

PLATE 13 (*left*) Street fountain in Mainz, Germany, *c.*1526.

PLATE 14 (*above*) Overmantel from the library chamber at Langley Marish church, nr. Slough, *c.*1620s.

PLATE 15 (*left*) Woodgraining at St Mary's, Bramber.

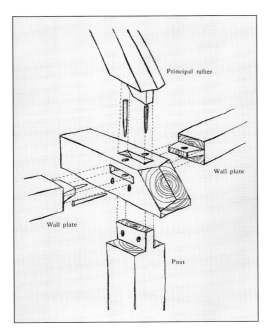

FIG. 42 The wall plate/tie beam junction. If the structure had not been polygonal the common dovetail lap joint would have been appropriate in this position. Instead the wall plates are jointed with the tie beam.

It is important to note that much of the timber at the heart of the joint in the tie beam has been cut away to form the four mortices required. This final timber to be positioned on site, the principal timber rafter, cannot be pegged.

only work on the polygonal angle of 18° if we could find a suitable way of joining the wall plates within the tie-beam/post junction. We could find no suitable prototypes for this, and feared both the complexity of the junction and its strength; it would inevitably involve cutting away a large part of the timber at a point where strength is most needed. There is a way of avoiding the problem altogether, for which there are good prototypes. This is to run the tie beam over the top of the post and simply tenon the wall plates in from either side, a straightforward and economical solution (fig. 42).

The same rationale was applied to the purlins. Clasped purlins would have necessitated another complicated junction, as they too would have to be jointed at the truss junction where they change direction by 18°. This negates the principal advantage of a clasped purlin, namely that it has greater strength because it is not broken at truss junctions. Furthermore, the junction would have to be angled in another direction as well, because the purlins are not set horizontally but lie at the angle of the roof. It is much simpler, and therefore more appropriate, to adopt a butt purlin system, with the purlins tenoned into the side of the principal rafters.

It can be said, therefore, that we have devised a cross frame building where, in simple terms, the cross frame has been expressed from the outer face of the outer wall to the inner face of the inner wall, and the concentric timbers have been jointed into the cross frame, not vice versa.

CONCLUSION

The slow advance of the project has been a frustration to many people, but for the design and construction process it has been a great help. Time has been one of the project's greatest resources and has enabled a wide consultation process. After the two bays were built in June of 1992 each of the decisions recorded here were re-examined and evaluated. The result, however, was that very few changes were made to the design of a typical auditorium bay. The two bays were moved to their correct location in 1993 and construction of the remaining auditorium bays, together with the stair towers, secondary seating carcassing, plastering and thatching proceeded as and when money became available until November 1995, after which the funding arrangements changed.

For the stage and tiring house, the carpentry methods remained the same but the nature of the work changed considerably. The tiring house is the largest single element in the theatre, but is in many ways the most straightforward. Its model is a domestic three storey structure, as the word 'house' implies, without jetties, and with a roof span of about twenty four feet: a form that was very common throughout London in 1576. Its curved back wall is its most striking feature. By contrast the stage roof is almost without precedent, and the use of just two columns to carry such a substantial structure provided a constructional challenge and quite a different research methodology (as described in my chapter 'Design as Reconstruction/Reconstruction as Design' elsewhere in this volume) from the one recorded here for the auditorium.

Notes to Chapter Six

1   This chapter is reprinted, with alterations and additions, from *The Design of the Globe*, edited by Andrew Gurr, Ronnie Mulryne and Margaret Shewring (International Globe Centre, 1993) pp. 53–88.

2   John Orrell, 'Beyond the Rose: Design Problems for the Globe Reconstruction' in Franklin J. Hildy ed., *New Issues in the Reconstruction of Shakespeare's Theatre* (New York, 1990), p. 79.

3   Ibid. p. 100.

4   Herbert Berry, ed., *The First Public Playhouse: The Theatre in Shoreditch* (Montreal, 1979), p. 33.

5   Irwin Smith, 'Theatre into Globe', *Shakespeare Quarterly* 3 (1952), 116. Chambers refers to the inquisition in *The Elizabethan Stage*, II, 415. W.W. Braines, *The Site of the Globe Playhouse, Southwark* (2nd edition, London, 1924), p. 13, is not convinced by the reference.

6   John Summerson, *Architecture in Britain 1530 – 1830* (Harmondsworth, 1953), p. 56.

7   Irwin Smith, op cit., p. 116.

8   John Orrell, 'Building the Fortune' *Shakespeare Quarterly*, 44 (1993), 127–44.

9   From the Fortune Contract (*see* pp. 180–2 *below*).

10 Irwin Smith, op cit., p. 116. John Orrell comments (privately) that 'there are numerous accounts of the construction of galleries and degrees, in the Works accounts and elsewhere, which show that the normal form was for raking joists to be constructed on a level floor, with the seating boards and risers attached to them (nailed, usually) by means of brackets. This form is shown in the 1605 Christ Church section, and the Inigo Jones 'Cockpit' drawings.

11 Richard Hosley, 'The Playhouses' in J. Leeds Barroll et al. eds., *The Revels History of Drama in English, 1576 –1613* vol. 3 (London, 1975), p. 152.

12 Cecil A Hewett, *English Historical Carpentry* (London , 1980), p. 232.

13 Richard Hosley, op. cit. in note 11.

Appendix A

Prototype Buildings

A	**SURVIVING LONDON BUILDINGS**	**DATE**	**TYPE**
1	41 & 42 Cloth fair, London EC1	mid 17C	Domestic
2	34–38 Court Yard, Eltham	mid 16C	Domestic
3	32 Court Yard, Eltham	mid 16C	Domestic
4	Spotted Dog Pub, 22 Upton Lane Forest Gate	16C	Domestic
5	Charterhouse, London EC4	1576–1610 (modifications)	Aristocratic
6	17 Fleet Street, London EC4	1610	Domestic
7	Queen's House, Tower Green London EC3	1540	Royal
8	Bayward Tower, Tower of London London EC3	mid 16C	Royal
9	St Thomas' Tower, Tower of London London EC3	1532	Royal
10	Queen Elizabeth's Hunting Lodge	mid 16C	Royal
11	St Bartholomew the Great Gatehouse	early 17C	Domestic
12	Middle Temple Hall, London EC4	1562–70	Institution
13	Staples Inn, London EC1	1586	Domestic
14	Canonbury Tower, London N1	1523	Aristocratic
15	No. 229 The Strand, London WC2	1625	Domestic
16	Hoop & Grapes, Aldgate, London EC3	mid 17C	Domestic
17	16 Old Buildings 12 & 13 New Square Lincoln's Inn London WC1	1534	Chambers
18	18, 19 and 20 Old Buildings, Lincoln's Inn, London WC1	1524	Chambers
19	Lauderdale House, Waterlow Park	1580	Domestic
20	Chapel Cloister, Charterhouse Square London EC1	1613	Religious
21	Calverts Buildings, Southwark	1542	Inn
22	Carbis Cottage, The Green Walk Chingford	17C	Domestic
23	13 & 14 Portsmouth Street London WC1	17C	Domestic
24	Wymondham Market Cross, Norfolk	1615	Commercial

B BUILDINGS THAT HAVE BEEN WORKED ON BY McCURDY & CO AND WHICH INFORMED DECISIONS ABOUT THE GLOBE

1	137, 139 & 141 High Street, Watford	early 17C	Domestic
2	Reigate Town House now at Singleton	17C	Domestic
3	15 to 17 High Street, Uxbridge	16C	Domestic
4	Harmondsworth Great Barn	mid 15C	Agricultural

C LOST BUILDINGS, WELL RECORDED

1	Sir Paul Pindar's House, London EC2	1624	Domestic
2	Brooke House, Hackney, London E9	1530 (Modifications)	Aristocratic
3	Tennis Court, James Street London SW1	1635	Sports

D RELIGIOUS BUILDINGS (TIMBER ROOFS)

1	St Andrews Undershaft, London EC3	1520
2	St Giles Cripplegate, London EC1	1545–50
3	St Catherine Cree London	1628–31
4	St Mary Aldermary, London EC4	1511–1629
5	Savoy Chapel, London	1510–16
6	St Margaret's Westminster London SW1	1504–23
7	Westminster Abbey; Henry VII Chapel and apsidal end of chancel	
8	Chapter House, Lincoln Cathedral	c.1820

Appendix B

A STRUCTURAL SIZES GIVEN IN THE HOPE CONTRACT (*after Hosley*)[13]

All dimensions in inches
Bracketed figures represent conjectural dimensions

	PRINCIPAL POSTS (inner only)	BINDING JOISTS (or Summer Beams)	BRESSUMERS OR GROUND SILLS d x w	PRICKPOSTS
4th level		(tie beam) (7 x 8)	(wall plate) (8 x 6)	
3rd storey	7 x 7			6 x 6
3rd level		7 x 8	8 x 6	
2nd storey	8 x 8			7 x 7
2nd level		8 x 9	9 x 7	
1st storey	10 x 10			8 x 8
1st level		(10 x 11)	(11 x 9)	

B STRUCTURAL SIZES USED IN THE TWO BAYS (*see* figs 43–9 *below*)

All dimensions in inches

	PRINCIPAL POSTS (inner only)	BINDING JOISTS (or Summer Beams)	BRESSUMERS OR GROUND SILLS d x w	PRICKPOSTS
4th level		(tie beam) 10 x 10	(wall plate) 7 x 8.5	
3rd storey	8 x 9			6 x 6
3rd level		11 x 11	10 x 9	
2nd storey	9 x 9			7 x 7
2nd level		11 x 11	10 x 9	
1st storey	10 x 10			8 x 8
1st level		11 x 9	9 x 9	

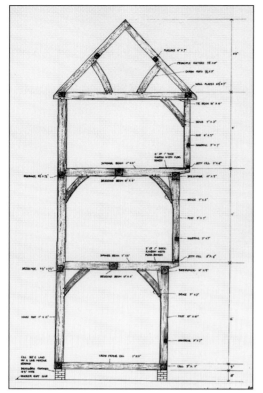

FIG. 43 A typical cross frame

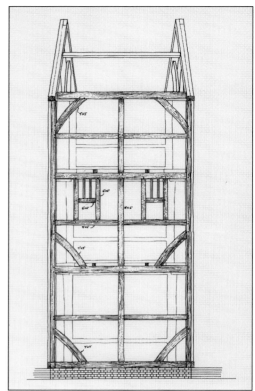

FIG. 44 A typical outer wall frame

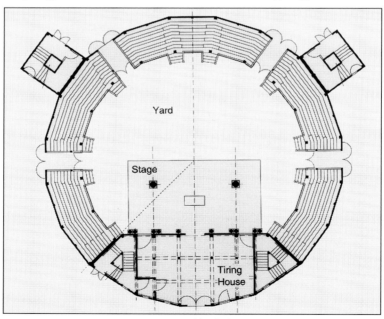

FIG. 45 Yard level plan

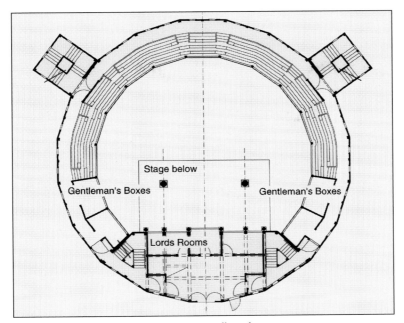

FIG. 46 First gallery plan

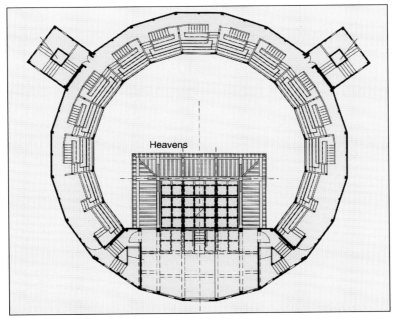

FIG. 47 Second gallery plan

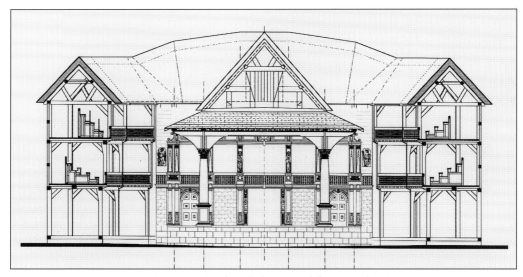

FIG. 48 Cross section through the stage and *frons scenae* elevation

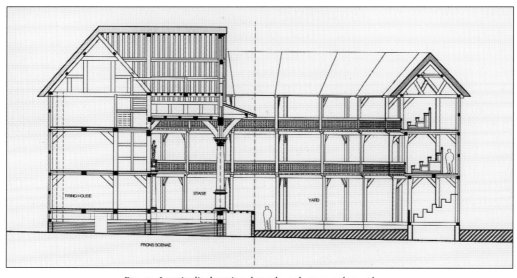

FIG. 49 Longitudinal section through yard, stage and stage house

∽ 7 ∽

TOTUS MUNDUS AGIT HISTRIONEM
[The Whole World moves the Actor]
The Interior Decorative Scheme of the Bankside Globe

John Ronayne[1]

WE HAVE very little direct evidence to bring to the development of a plausible scheme of interior painting for the 1990s Globe. To date, no trace of timber, let alone any decoration of the 1599 Globe, has been found. Half a baluster was recovered from the site of the Rose theatre, but if it had ever had a surface coating, this was lost.[2] Fleeting glimpses of theatre decoration are offered in contemporary travellers' descriptions and contracts, but always of other playhouses. When considering whether and how the Globe might have been decorated, it has therefore been necessary to find analogous contemporary examples, and build up an idiom which arises reasonably from such evidence as there is. We have had to develop a visual vocabulary, which has then had to be applied in practice. This chapter is an attempt to collate some of this evidence, and to explain the nature of the temporary decorative programme adopted for the new Globe's 'prologue' season of 1996, together with those modifications incorporated in the permanent scheme of the theatre.[3]

The Exterior

So far as our research takes us, the Globe would in all probability have offered a different appearance externally from that of its inner space, by analogy with the inside and outside contrast of 'architectural' cabinets produced in the 16th and 17th centuries (plate 12). The exterior of such cabinets is noble, but relatively plain. But when the cabinet doors are opened, the sparkling and bejewelled interior takes away the onlooker's breath. In similar fashion, as playgoers approached an Elizabethan theatre they would have seen its high white walls (plaster over half-timbering) suggesting perhaps some grave and substantial Roman temple or arena. But once through the doors, they would have entered a world of imagination and possibility far removed from the lath and plaster familiar from everyday life.

Roman amphitheatre prototypes of the round wooden playhouse were beginning to be known in England at this period, through Vitruvius and Serlio. Sebastian Serlio's *Five books of Architecture* was first available in English in 1611,[4] but available earlier on the Continent. These were taken as inspiration rather than model. The exterior views of playhouses shown on bird's-eye maps such as Norden's *Civitas Londini* (1600), Visscher's *View of London* (1616) and Hollar's *Long View of London* (1647) convey a desire for these timber rings to look like solid stone. The thatch and protruding huts give the game away, but we do know that the Fortune was to be 'enclosed withoute with lathe lyme & haire', which was doubtless to give the playgoers the impression that they were entering a solid stone building.

Examples survive of sixteenth-century buildings rendered over their timber framing, for example the Market Keeper's Lodge at Lavenham (Suffolk), and the Wyckhurst House at Singleton. Evidence of lath nail-holes and nails can also often be detected in surviving buildings on external timbers which have been exposed by later restorers, a feature which betrays the process of 'enclosing'. The outer renderings of such buildings were doubtless often left smooth and plain but there is much evidence that they were sometimes decorated as fictive stonework. For example, at Woking in 1593–4, Ellis Johnson and John Allen of the Works were paid at the expensive rate of a shilling a yard for 'newe lathing layeing plastering and drawing with stonewoorke Joyntes all the syde of the house towardes the garden'.[5] Similarly, at Nonsuch in 1599–1600 Richard Dungan, the Master Plasterer who was responsible for the ceilings at Knole, was paid 6d. a yard (workmanship only) 'for lathing, laying and rendering with Lyme and haire all the outsides of the stables: being drawne ashlar woorke'.[6] These buildings at Nonsuch were all timber framed, and had just been erected by Paul Warde and William Brice. At Greenwich in 1610–11 a plasterer was paid 4d. a yard for 'striking out ashlar wise' 50 yards of work in the Conduit Court.[7] Eric Mercer cites numerous examples of other detailing used for the same purpose, including 'pencilling' of brickwork.[8]

Our re-creation of the 1599 Globe is a timber-framed building, and we have elected to leave the 'green' oak exposed to weather and fade to grey over the years. The majority of buildings in pre-fire London had their timbers exposed (Claes de Jongh's painting of London Bridge, of about 1612, now at Kenwood, shows this vividly). As our reconstruction is the first major timber-framed building in the capital since the Fire, our decision, on balance, was to expose the structure of what is a rare sight in London, rather than cover it up as the Elizabethans may have done, taking for granted the frameworked appearance. For them, outer rendering was grander. For us, half timbering is more generally evocative. The point is no more than a quibble as long as the essential balance between a decorated interior and plain exterior is maintained.

Monochrome visual chastity in the Roman mode was literally foreign to the Elizabethans. Not until Inigo Jones's return around 1605 from his Italian sojourn was there anyone to convey Palladio's message about classicism to the English, and then it fell on deaf ears. When Jones created the first convincing classical building in Britain, the plain Queen's House at Greenwich, it was greeted in 1619 as 'some curious devise',[9] though the curiosity perhaps relates to its road-straddling plan rather than to its whiteness. Late sixteenth century understanding of classical design was not that it was plain.[10] A street fountain in Mainz dated 1526, (re)painted in garish, almost fairground colours may serve to illustrate the point (plate 13).

While in terms of exterior plainness true classical purity was becoming established during the seventeenth century (for instance in the Whitehall Banqueting House of 1619–22), Stuart England continued to have a taste for symbolism, texture, colour and grotesquery. The result was a stylistic mélange which persisted until the Restoration. It took the Puritans of the 1640s and the Great Fire of 1666 to scorch the strapwork off the half-timbered face of London.

The Interior

The Globe would certainly have been decorated within. Except where there was some overriding practical reason, Elizabethan architectural surfaces tended to be polychrome where possible. To quote from standard works on this point: 'Throughout the greater part of the period the only reason for leaving anything unpainted seems to have been the physical impossibility of reaching it with a brush',[11] and, 'Every surface that was free of tapestries or wall hangings and that could be reached with a brush was painted ... '.[12] Mercer contends that 'Under Elizabeth the most noticeable feature of painted decoration [was] the love of bright colours and bizarre effects'.[13] An example of this colourful decoration is preserved in the c.1620s Kederminster library in Langley Marish Church (plate 14). The colourful and busy backgrounds to be found in Elizabethan and Jacobean interiors are also evidenced indirectly in a number of Early Modern portraits, for example, those by Robert Peake, or 'The Brown Brothers' by Isaac Oliver (1598).[14]

Modern scholars have often shied away from the notion that the Globe's internal appearance shared this vibrantly painted character. It has been felt that such a backdrop would have detracted from the elaborate, colourful costumes worn by the players. Yet this is to read the Elizabethan spectacle with modern eyes. Contemporaries appear to have revelled in displays of colour and pattern. We can gain some sense of the Elizabethan taste for bright, intricate display by considering the c.1585 painting of 'Queen Elizabeth receiving the Dutch Ambassadors'. The finely-wrought, coloured patterns of Elizabeth's dress are juxtaposed with the bright colours and designs upon the walls and the intricate patterned work of the ceiling.[15] The room depicted is relatively bare of furniture and the splendour of the scene is created through the accumulation of colour and detailed designs. In similar fashion, the spectacle of the richly costumed players set against a vibrantly painted auditorium could have created a visually striking scene which functioned as a whole to generate splendour.

In a culture which accustomed people to the study and interpretation of visual display (whether in the form of symbolic royal and civic pageants or the cross-culturally employed emblem) it is no surprise to find that it was equally conventional for Early Modern buildings to follow systematic iconographic schemes. The degree to which this is the case is easily underestimated. Like Elizabeth's elaborate costumes, portraits and pageants, Early Modern buildings often made symbolic statements and were expected to be 'read'. A particularly interesting example of this fashion for symbolic painted schemes is indirectly revealed by the Early Modern poet Henry Vaughan in his preface to 'A Rhapsodie'. There he describes a tavern chamber 'painted overhead with a cloudy skie, and some few dispersed starres, and on the sides with Land-scapes, Hills, Shepherds, and sheep'. The pub was called the 'Globe taverne'.[16]

As a product of this artistic, architectural and intellectual milieu, decorated by craftsmen trained in such design work, we can expect the 1599 Globe to have been adorned in similar symbolic fashion. Unfortunately, greater precision in our reconstruction of the Globe's interior is difficult, for a simple reason. While, thanks to Richard Dutton's 1988 *Shakespeare Survey* article, we can confidently assume that the Globe's sign featured Hercules carrying the Globe and the motto *totus mundus agit histrionem*, there is virtually no other direct evidence of the Globe's internal appearance.[17] However, there are numerous indirect sources of information upon which we can draw, including analogous material afforded by other Elizabethan playhouses and the wider world of Renaissance design and Early Modern decoration. In addition, information can be inferred from plays believed to have been first performed at the 1599 Globe and contemporaries' general accounts of sixteenth century auditoria, where the playhouses are admired or criticised for their ornate decoration and 'sumptuous' splendour.[18]

Decoration and the tiring-house façade

The tiring house wall, known as the *scenae frons* or scenic frontispiece, is inescapably the theatre's visual focus, the central part of the architectural cabinet's sparkling interior. In our re-creation, the wall's structure has been established by Jon Greenfield, in consultation with scholars including Andrew Gurr and John Orrell. There have been practical considerations to bear in mind, such as the distance Romeo has to climb, or how a bed can be revealed. Beyond that, there were aesthetic considerations, such as how to take account of the relationships between the architectural orders, and how the overall 'wooden O' could accommodate the lines of the façade.

As far as content is concerned, Peter Davidson has proposed an iconographical arrangement for the *scenae frons*, integrated with the modelling, which is set out in the next chapter. Like every deliberately visual product of the age, such a presented structure would have been intended to be read like a book. We have therefore integrated the visual planes of the *scenae frons* as symbolic divisions of the levels from the heavens down to the earth, in which every figure has a name and a role.

Looking at Elizabethan stone-built façades, tombs, gateway crestings, wooden hall screens, bed heads and title pages, one can get a reasonable impression of the style, manner and treatment that would be at least consistent with surviving examples. Architecturally, the style was meant to be classical, but with that curious and Flemish twist of mannerism familiar from the pages of John Shute, one of the earliest English artists to visit Italy.[19] A similar blend of classical and mannerist styles may be seen in the flattened cut-out classical style of John Thynne's recladding of Longleat, completed in 1580.

The argument for visual splendour in the scenic wall is indirectly strengthened by studying contemporary decorative and applied arts, costume and jewellery, coloured title pages, paintings and interior decoration. One can also consult the Works accounts which give a year-by-year tracing of the developments of fashion in matters of Westminster/London based Court décor, and for exterior work, surviving street furniture, coats of arms, ships' figureheads and, of course, written descriptions. We can reach the same conclusion more directly from such evidence as the Fortune contract ('carved proporcions Called Satiers')[20] and from de Witt's description of the interior of the Swan ('pillars marbled so as to deceive the most prying').[21] None of that suggests a bland monochrome. Drawing on all the evidence, our belief is that the Globe interior and especially the tiring-houses façade would have been richly carved and painted, and we have attempted to make this a reality in our reconstruction.

Another key source for decorative materials and techniques is the surviving trade painters' manuals. The increasing literacy of skilled tradesmen combined with the decreasing cost of printing meant that by the late sixteenth century the ancient process of instruction through apprenticeship was regularly supplemented, for many crafts, by actual textbooks, which give us an unprecedented access to information on materials and techniques. The most important sixteenth-century example is Richard Tothill's *A very proper treatise wherein is briefly sett forthe the Arte of Limming* (London 1573), which can be supplemented by the some-

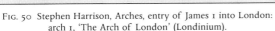

FIG. 50 Stephen Harrison, Arches, entry of James I into London: arch 1, 'The Arch of London' (Londinium).

FIG. 51 Stephen Harrison, Arches, entry of James I into London: arch 3, 'The Flemish Arch'.

what later John Guillim's *A Displaye of Heralderie* (London, 1610), John Smith's *The Art of Painting, Wherein is included the whole Art of Vulgar Painting according to the best rules for preparing and laying on of Oyl Colours* (London, 1674), and an anonymous handbook preserved in the British Library, *A Short Introduction to the art of painting and varnishing* (London 1685), which may also be by Smith. Though the latter two treatises are a century later than the Globe, they describe centuries-old materials and techniques with great clarity, and are thus useful sources. These national treasures are indeed glossaries of the trade painter's art, displaying a lexicon of terms and a hierarchy of finishes from masonry to jewels. The tradesmen's handbooks explain how to get the whole range of effects, and we have tried as far as possible to emulate them in our decoration of the Globe.

Visual exemplars

One way of inferring the decorative style of the Globe interior is to search out visual parallels or analogues. The key reference here is the Painted Staircase at Knole, 1605, not only on account of its theatrical manner but also because many of the tradesmen in the 1603–5 renovations at Knole were from the Office of Works and thus represented Westminster traditions (plates 19 and 20). Other major references are the Kederminster Pew (fig. 56, p. 130) and the painted Library chamber at the church of Langley Marish near Slough (plate 14). Painted around the 1620s, this last is relatively remote from the 1599 Globe in time and distance but can help to give us some sense of how overall colour coverage was employed, since the artisans who created it are clearly working some distance behind metropolitan changes of fashion.

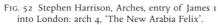

FIG. 52 Stephen Harrison, Arches, entry of James I into London: arch 4, 'The New Arabia Felix'.

FIG. 53 Stephen Harrison, Arches, entry of James I into London: arch 5, 'The Garden of Plenty'.

Another vital source for our work was the set of designs for triumphal arches published by Stephen Harrison (figs 50–55). These relate to the arches proposed in 1603 for the entry of James I into London, and used when, after a year's delay due to plague, the entry actually took place.[22] The arches were painted illusionistically to resemble stone and other features, and the designs were put into effect by craftsmen of the City, in all probability acquaintances of Peter Streete. They are therefore likely to provide convincing analogues for the decoration of the Globe, since many of those associated with them were also playwrights in the public theatre, notably Jonson and Dekker.[23] The Harrison arches were comparable to the Globe's scenic wall in their scale (as large and sometimes larger) as well as arguably in their decoration. We are fortunate that their designer left ground plans and scale-staff on his drawings so that they can be minutely inspected and scaled. The first arch ('Londinium') measured approximately 50 ft wide (fig. 50), while the seventh arch, 'The Temple of Janus', towered 60 ft high (fig. 55). These dimensions compare with a height for the Globe's exterior walls (to the eaves) of approximately 32 ft, and a width (for the *scenae frons*) of 43 or 44 ft. The openings in the arches made for live actors and musicians to stand inside scale off at comfortably life size, with the central 'discovery space' in the third arch ('Flemish') measuring 15 ft square (fig. 51). The arches offer us therefore implicit guidance in our attempts to build a plausible scenic wall at the Globe.

In terms of decoration, the arches encapsulate the tension between near-correct classical and grotesque 'antick' styles. Since the arches are festive structures for outdoor use, and are not dissimilar in scale from the scenic wall at the Globe, they offer a guide to the visual idiom we should employ. They show a cheerful muddle of styles. Arch six, for example,

FIG. 54 Stephen Harrison, Arches, entry of James I into London: arch 6, 'The Arch of the New World'.

FIG. 55 Stephen Harrison, Arches, entry of James I into London: arch 7, 'The Temple of Janus'.

employs Corinthian upon Corinthian (fig. 54), while the *Londinium* arch shows Tuscan pilasters obscured by heavy strapwork and obelisks (fig.50). Arch seven offers twin Corinthian pillars supporting a lugged cornice of mannerist bulbousness (fig. 55). These are examples of the 'dissonance' commonly found in decorative schemes at the time.[24]

Harrison's drawings are painstakingly three-dimensional. When his engraver, the renowned Willem Kip, draws surfaces which look as though they are flat painted (on arch six, for example, the 'types' and round turrets down each side), one is convinced that this methodical draughtsman is attempting to represent a combination of flat-painted, relief-carved and fully-carved decoration that surely was the 1604 reality. We can return time and again to these drawings for features, motifs and details. There are satyrs (on arch five) probably carved in relief if not 'pilaster wise', as well as herms and terms, the figure of Fame (on arch four) and heraldry (on arches one, six and seven). Pictures are presented on arches three (over doors), one (bottom centre) and five (top centre), even if we do not take the central discovery space (arches four and six) as representing paintings, but rather *tableaux vivants*.

The only ingredient missing from the drawings of the arches that would make them a complete model for our reconstruction is colour. Here we can turn to other sources such as the hand coloured 'architectural' title pages of contemporary books and a highly comparable drawing of a Dutch Rederyker stage erected in Antwerp in 1582 which has survived in full colour. This has all the ingredients of ashlar stonework, precious stone inserts and marbled columns, as well as heraldry, obelisks, flags, grotesques, cartouches and strapwork which we believe we are right to incorporate.

A hierarchy of stone

A perusal of examples such as the Knole stair, the Langley Marish pew and the backgrounds of paintings, soon leads to a feeling that the representation of stones and the variety of geological specimens was of interest to contemporaries, including in all probability those working on the decoration of the Globe. A parallel interest in mixtures of stone materials is picked up by commentaries on triumphal arches, some of them built for real. Similar decorative schemes are found in the Cavendish 'prodigy houses' at Hardwick and Bolsover. Stone implies cost, substance and permanence, the very qualities that festive structures lacked. It was for the painter to put these qualities back into the wood, plaster and canvas forms. There was, as Mercer observes, a 'fondness for painting one material to look like another. The material chosen for imitation is not always more colourful but is invariably more expensive'.[25]

There seems to have been a code or hierarchy in the way that stones could be organised in these decorative schemes. A typical scheme assumes a basic utilitarian stone, the one that was generally covered by the phrase 'stone colour'. This was used for flat walling, but also for 'mouldings and cornishes and pendaunts', column bases and the like. Smith tells us (chapter IX) that 'Pales and Posts are sometimes laid over with White which they call Stone Colour'. So the basic stone can be run over almost any shape. It serves also as the main bordering outside the more precious minerals. If we imagine this omnicompetent material to be a pliant freestone of some generalised kind which could be worked with a saw, we can soon accept that it could also serve as the material for more complex forms and shaped members such as rafter beams and braces. The evidence for this in real stone may be found in the crestings over gateways and parapets such as those at Hardwick Hall and Bolsover, with lettering and strapwork. An example in imitation stone is the Knole staircase, where a stone colour was the basic component, a strong yellow ochre applied in three shades, light, mid and dark. This achieves the modelling required. Stone is also the material for the slender stair balusters at Knole as well as for flat surfaces such as walls.

The shadows of stone blocks and lines of mortar in painted stonework could be quite convincing. In 1501, when Catherine of Aragon was received into London, one of the pageant arches was 'empeynted like frestone and whight lyme, so that the semys of the stone were preceyved like as mortur or sement had been between.' One of the most spectacular rustications was known as diamond point, of which a remarkable surviving example is the 1567–8 courtyard murals at Ambrasin (Austria) by Heinrich Taufelin.[26] It was also used on one of the triumphal arches that welcomed Louis XIII into Paris in 1629. In England, it can be found both carved and painted on hall screens (e.g. at Cuckfield, Sussex, in the 1580s) and on furniture (e.g. the claviorganum, 1579, discussed below).

The interior of the Globe, as we have developed it, is painted to look like expensive stone. If we ask where an Elizabethan painter in London might have gone for his visual reference and samples, the most plausible answer would be to the workshops of the Southwark school of sculptors, right on the Globe's doorstep. Their work provides much of the detail we need: coloured marbles, dot/dash gadroons, ribbon work, and so on. Figures like Cornelius Cuer, Maximilian Colt and the Jansens or Johnsons all lived and worked near the Globe and did nearly all the best decorative stonework in the country. Probably the outstanding example of this expert work is Garret Johnson's tomb for the 4th Earl of Rutland at Bottesford Church, Leicestershire, sculpted in 1591 in Southwark, and then transported to

PLATE 16 (*top*) Detail of painted cloth at Hardwick Hall.

PLATE 17 (*left*) Detail of bedhead from Bed of Ware,
*c.*1590.

PLATE 18 (*above*) Claviorganum decorated by a Fleming in
London in 1579.

PLATES 19 and 20 The Great Staircase at Knole, c.1605.

Bottesford.[27] The Southwark-made tombs of Elizabeth I and Mary Queen of Scots in Westminster Abbey remained nearer to hand.

The stone used by these Southwark sculptors could be cut and shaped, but also carved and incised with fielded panels, or manipulated into bands of amazing narrowness to border higher-status, more expensive stones. At Langley Marish, painted marbles are separated by a vivid line of glossy black (fig. 56). The workaday material (freestone, alabaster, or their painted equivalents) was normally the outer, basic or first stone material in the sequence. Rarer and costlier stones would then be added, preferably framed by the humbler freestone. Marbles and hardstones such as granites, porphyry and serpentine would be next, which would, in turn, sometimes have semi-precious minerals like chalcedony, agate, and cornelian set within them. The sequence might climax with a jewel.

Similar techniques were employed in festive architecture. Illustrated books were published to record the magnificence of triumphal arches with their marbled pillars and panels. An account of an entry into Pesaro in 1621 mentions 'the wonderful imitation of valuable marbles and precious stone ... paragone ... lapis lazuli ... and oriental granite'. Vasari's introduction on technique to his famous study of *The Lives of the Artists* (1550) shows how widespread the practice was in more permanent architecture, listing the imitation of porphyry, serpentine, and red and grey granites on the walls of houses and palaces.

The whole decorative programme, in tombs as well as ephemeral and permanent architecture, was capable of variation, with elements omitted and added, but the view that it can be read like a code or sequence does seem to accord with the developed sense of propriety in visual and iconographical matters which appealed to the designers and workmen of such structures as the Globe stage wall. One would never, for example, expect to see a marbled capital on a column shaft made of plain stone. A typical and well-provenanced arrangement is a stone base of a column with a field incised into each side. Into this is laid a marble, which in turn contains a bullet or lozenge. Borderings could be provided in the plain stone if desired, in very low relief like straps. These might also need gilding if they are on a noble level of the structure.

Once this hierarchy of stone, akin to the orders of architecture, is perceived, it can be called upon to provide answers to some of the problem shapes and combinations on our scenic wall. For example, at the top of the main stage columns (gilded of course, for nothing less would do for the highest order in the scheme, Corinthian, on top of a marbled column), there is a set of braces which branch outward from a stem. This arrangement is necessary in terms of carpentry, but how should the painter treat its forms? The stem can be rendered as granite (column shafts at Knole are granite), but for the curved braces stone makes the best sense, due to their sawn shape. If they were to be elaborated, then marble might well be placed within a field set inside the stone, with perhaps a hardstone bullet or lozenge inside that. An example in the right spirit is the claviorganum decorated by a Fleming in London in 1579. This organ-case, now in the V&A, is painted with shaded strapwork on blotchy red marble (rance?) with red and black hardstone diamond points at each centre, highlighted to look as sharp and spiky as possible (plate 18).[28]

In completing a decorative scheme such as ours, extra shine is sometimes added by a touch of gold at the sharpest point. This is not naturalistic, but agrees with the trick of manuscript painters of the period, and earlier, as being the way to get light to 'jump about'

FIG. 56 Detail of marbling on the Kederminster
family pew, Langley Marish.

FIG. 57 Detail of sixteenth century painted door
in the V&A collection.

regardless of its yellowish colour. Examples of various techniques for embellishment and heightening are found in the Notebooks of John Guillim, the author of *A Displaye of Heralderie* (1610):[29]

> To towche any Jewell: The right towche of any Jewell ys fyrst to laye over in Browne ocker, then trace yt out with Redd Leade and Masticotte and lastly heighten yt with masticot alone.[30]

Figure carving

The Fortune contract, while specifying that this theatre differs from the Globe, tells us that its *frons* had satyrs 'wroughte palasterwise'. This implies they were like pilasters rather than pillars, that is, engaged to the wall surface, not free-standing in the round. Stylistically, some carved satyr figures (e.g. the bed head at Adlington Hall) are blockish to an almost Polynesian degree. Such figures would fall between fully carved and flat painted illusion of reality. The distinction between high relief and in the round was, it seems, worth making in the contract, indicating there was a choice and therefore a need for guidance. The choice of 'palasterwise' seems right for the herm figures carved on our screen, since these accord with the kind of carved figure work that one sees on bedheads and hall screens. Square-sectioned herms (known as terms) are a probable interpretation. In the Harrison arches, the engaged form appears in the right-hand entry of the *Londinium* arch (as it does in the second gallery in the great Hall at Hatfield), while the square-sectioned type can be seen in the *Hortus Euporiae* arch at Cheapside in the Harrison engravings (fig. 53). A spectacular surviving example of this kind of decoration is offered by the carved house-front of the house owned by Sir Paul Pindar, which is London craftsmanship dating from 1600 (fig. 58).

The work might be rendered in local colour, as it seems to have been in the final scene of *The Winter's Tale* ('The ruddiness upon her lip is wet; / You'll mar it if you kiss it, stain your own / With oily painting' V.iii.81–3). The same was the case with the Bed of Ware (plate 17), on ships' sterns, and representational images on several title pages. Alternatively, the herms might be given an overall material finish, such as the marble of a carved bracket at Ockenden church, or stone. We have chosen to follow the former route.

FIG. 58 Carved satyr and panelled work on façade of Sir Paul Pindar's House, Bishopsgate, 1600, now in V & A.

Painted illusions of reality

In court theatres, the steps leading from the stage to the floor of the hall were sometimes not actual, but merely painted on the flat parapet. In Elizabethan England it was conventional to paint duplicate banisters on the blind wall of a staircase. Examples of this illusion survive at Knole (*see* plates 19 and 20), Aston Hall, Mapledurham House, Harvington Hall and the 17th century Merchants' House in Marlborough. An engraving in Turberville's *Noble Art of Venerie* (1576) shows flat palings shadow-painted as spindly, round balusters. The same effect can be seen on many vernacular buildings.

Many of the figures, niches and decoration shown in illustrations of triumphal arches were painted, one may suppose, rather than modelled. This is suggested by several details on the Harrison engravings of 1604. A good example is the 'Arch of the New World' (*see* fig. 54, p. 127). The two belvedere towers at the sides are drawn exactly as though they were closed in with canvas. The central panel between them might as well have been painted, since by Harrison's scale it was 40 feet above the ground. The niches that contain the Four Kingdoms and Four Virtues measure only 4 feet in height. Even if they were intended to accommodate children, the drawing of those niches positioned on the round towers suggests that they were two-dimensional; they curve with the walls instead of showing any depth, while the two niches at the extreme sides are drawn in an impossible perspective.

The figures at the Globe have been treated in *grisaille* (shades of grey) with the images propagated by Continental engravings, for example those by Virgil Solis of Nuremburg (discussed below). The V&A has a series of English plaster grisaille panels painted in about

FIG. 59 Detail of Grisaille murals from Stodmarsh Court, near Canterbury, Kent.

1600 (fig. 59) that are based firmly upon Solis (fig. 60) and show classical gods including Mercury in heavenly surroundings. This *trompe l'oeil* technique is used appropriately in our reconstruction for the figures represented on the solid panels at the extreme sides of the *frons* walls: Apollo on the left and Mercury on the right. Much illusionistic painting was done in *grisaille* rather than full colour. Mantegna had championed this technique in Renaissance Italy, giving his patron a convincing coloured marble monument in two dimensions. *Grisaille* panels based on Martin de Vos are prominent features of the Knole stair (*see* plates 19 and 20).

A SPECIFICATION FOR THE BANKSIDE GLOBE

The entire theatre, not just the stage-house, requires to be decorated. This discussion outlines the choices made and the reasons for making them, and starts from the ground and works heavenwards, covering all the areas of the building in turn which require decorative treatment. Reference and illustration relate to the mock-up devised for the 1996 Prologue season (plates 26 and 27), and to the modified *frons scenae* which has replaced it.

Sub-stage

At the sub stage level of the playhouse yard, we are actually below ground, perhaps in the grotesque world from where (through the stage trap) the *Hamlet* ghost would emerge, where Yorick lies buried, and whence filters up the sound of hautboys in *Antony and Cleopatra* as the god Hercules departs. The sides of the stage have been boarded in and painted with a heavy rusticated stone reminiscent of grottos and caves. This is in parallel with the canvas-covered walls of the Westminster Banqueting House, which were painted 'most artificiallie with a worke called rustike much like to stone' in 1581.[31]

The stage boards were evidently meant to be painted (as was the stage at the Rose),

FIG. 60 Print of Mercury in his chariot by Virgil Solis in V & A.

although the records for the Fortune might superficially suggest that they were not, since Peter Streete was 'not chardged wth anie manner of pay(ntin)ge in or aboute the saide fframe howse or Stadge or anie parte thereof'.[32] This is actually because that work was for another contract. It looks in fact as if the stage front and sides were afforded much the same degree of finish as the rest of the auditorium. Apart from references in Sabbatini,[33] and a few incidental scraps, the nearest source of visual information here is Inigo Jones, who drew several stage fronts for Court theatres intended for plays rather than masques. He favoured painting them as heavily rusticated masonry, as at Somerset House for *Artenice* in 1625, for example, where the five-foot-high stage is represented as five courses of massive stone.

Ordinarily, Jones is not a satisfactory source for us, but his most Jacobean design, for *Oberon* in 1610, is more relevant than most, since it is for the Jacobean Banqueting House with which Peter Streete was connected and draws quite obviously from Harrison's *Londinium* arch (for the battlements and ashlar, among other elements). It is therefore within the Globe's stylistic milieu. The *Oberon* design, like that of *Artenice*, has a a five-foot-high stage painted as five courses of massive rusticated masonry, acting as a basis for a more refined ashlar storey above, with a Doric storey above that.[34] Similarly, in 1601–2 at Richmond, Leonard Fryer painted six 'footspaces' (platforms, like stages) with 'stoneworke like unto the pavements'.[35] This repeated design points to a tradition of raising the stage as rusticated masonry, with each course one foot deep, and we therefore imitated this as the basis of the design for the Globe. Presumably the oak boards would be nailed on horizontally so that they could be painted as coursed masonry. Such 'palings,' though undecorated, were commonly shown in illustrations of Whitehall tilts.[36]

At the Globe, because the block shape of the stage must be defined by this stone, it is not continuous, but painted as though cut into gigantic blocks piled onto one another. The colour is 'sad' (dark) and dull earth pigment, say 'spanish brown', burnt umber and lamp black. This is carried round to the face of the scene wall to provide a five foot plinth for the whole of the microcosmic world presented to the audience.

The Stage Surface

The stage boards have been painted earth green (*terre verte*), to represent ground level, the playing-green space of medieval tradition. Certainly it was common enough to paint vertical boarding green. There was a dark green colour scheme of this kind in the 1540s Orton Tower at Lambeth Palace. A painting by Holbein of the Hanse merchant George Gisze in his office at the Steelyard (1532) shows dark green painted on the boarded wall. It may be that rushes were scattered over the stage (though the risk of slipping perhaps makes this unlikely).[37] A rush mat could have been spread over all, or part, of the stage to define a smaller area or show a contrast between the indoor world and the world of nature. A painted finish for the stage would be practical, since it may well have needed to be refinished after performances, if, for example, stage blood had been spilt, or to ensure that it did not look unevenly stained at its front edge from the dripping of roof water. The green paint could have been water based, for cheapness and speed, and sealed by varnish. Gerbier in 1663 lists 'painting of the fairest green, that can be in distemper, and varnisht is one shilling a yard'.[38] Nearer in time to the Globe itself is the evidence of 'leonard ffryer ... pryming and leying on rownce water cullour coated with mastricke xvij seates for the garden and orchard ...' [39] While the stage surface would be practically invisible to the groundlings, its appearance would be more important than the scene wall to those sitting in the highest seats to the sides, since they would only have a plan view of the stage.

The SCENAE FRONS: *The First Level*

This is the practical level, 2.7m high (8 ft 9 in.) with doors and a central space, and the level against which the actors are seen by the majority of the audience. It is time to set out the palette to be used for articulating the scene-wall structure.

Stone: wall surfaces

The hierarchic sequence of decorative stone has already been described: stone, marble and hardstones and ultimately semi-precious stones, gilding and jewels, which must all be properly lined and framed. As already indicated, triumphal arches, and perhaps also theatres, were often decorated with masonry simulated in paint. Thus, at the Globe, we have chosen to paint the main ashlar wall surfaces stone colour, shadowed in dark and light shades. An appropriate model here is the 1575 painting by Hans Eworth, *Elizabeth and the Three Goddesses,* showing Queen Elizabeth I stepping through an arch painted with obviously fictive stonework.[40] The central panel face of each stone is picked out in the darker tone, a pattern which Sabbatini illustrates in 1638 in his *Pratica di fabricar scene e machine ne' teatri.* Diamond point would also be appropriate. The lower three courses of ashlar at the Globe could justifiably have been painted as *vermiculated* ('worm eaten') to represent a ruder nearness to the earth, since a vermiculated finish appears on one of the Antwerp arches illustrated in Scribonius' album of 1550. Our decision however was to represent these ashlar courses in simpler terms.

Marble: columns

Each exit door in the Globe scenic front is flanked by a pair of columns. These are marbled as *rosso antico* with gilded capitals and bases, and can be taken as referring to the pillars of Hercules. Such columns on triumphal arches were often flat cut-outs, shadowed at each side, pretending to be expensive turned columns. The tools for marbling are simple – a rag for dabbing and flogging, a brush handle for scoring in the vents and a feather for fine blending. As Guillim describes it, 'Take blacke & a portion of whyte & medle them by equall portions and deepe yt with blacke & marble yt with blacke & white'.[41] In fact, painting convincing marble requires years of practice. As Smith rightly says, the skill 'must be attained by ocular inspection, it being impossible to deliver the manner of the Operation by Precept without Example.'

The material of the pilaster behind the columns, and the architrave beam which they support, is painted as white veined marble. It is not stark white, but is clouded pale grey and dulled by veining (such a two-marbled scheme appears at Langley Marish: *see* plate 14). Our spandrels are of red marble with a centre-piece of dark green serpentine. The door frame is in granite and the keystone is a gilded lion mask. The cornice beam above the Ionic capitals is white marbled.

Hardstone: the door frames

At Knole the granite (as in the Globe door frame) is rendered by splotching various lighter tones over darker grey. The rendering of lustrous hardstones and semi-precious stones could be done by more sophisticated means. Among the 'items for colours' in the Greenwich accounts of 1527 is mentioned '½ lb of ground glass', which was perhaps used in the French way, to add a sparkle to varnish. In the anonymous pamphlet of 1685, directions are given how 'to lay on your Mettle Speckles: First wet your work with varnish, with a soft brush, then while 'tis wet dust your speckles upon it thro' a piece of Tiffany, and then varnish it twice, to keep 'em from rubbing off, 'tis enough.'[42]

Woodwork: the doors

The doors at the reconstructed Globe are plain timber ('deal' or 'wainscott') boarded, as shown by de Witt, a structure which could be extremely tight-joined. Their surface is enriched by fictive panelling and grained to mimic walnut. The lively manner of this work is exemplified by a surviving seventeenth-century wood-grained room at St Mary's Bramber, Sussex (plate 15). Smith (chapter x) lists recipes for 'new oak', 'Olive-Wood' and 'Walnut Tree' graining. The last, he says, was made up from burnt umber plus white, and could be 'veined with Burnt umber alone, and in the deepest places with black'. Leonard Fryer used 'wallnuttree cullore for the lower Creste and the soyles [sills?] of wyndowes' at Oatlands in 1597–8.[43] Wainscotting too could be rendered as walnut. Gerbier prices 'Wainscott put into Wale nut red colour, in distemper at six pence a yard'.[44]

Each of the fielded door panels at the Globe has a bold diamond point (or 'nail head') at its centre, proportioned and shaped by its surrounding moulding. Real ones can be found on fully carved hall screens. A good example is that at Knole.

The Tiring Room

The rear wall of the loggia or 'green room' space is painted as panelling, and can be hung with painted cloths. It is, in effect, a series of rooms and follows the existing grammar of contemporary interiors. The ceiling is plaster limewashed white, with some relief-modelled stamping. The wainscot is painted. At Oatlands in 1597–8, Leonard Fryer was paid 'for pryming and stopping with white leade all the wenscott about the gallery and after leying the pannelles and battens of the same with sondry Cullours curyously graynerd with a grayne called flotherwoode'. In the following year 118 yards of the work were fixed with 'Sweete varnishe'. In 1598–9, payment was made to 'Leonarde ffryer … for layinge lij yerdes of olde wenscott in that roome [a room between the privy and presence chambers at White-hall] in Draperie woorke'.

Painted cloths

The central opening of the *frons scenae* is in our reconstruction covered by a painted cloth to be drawn aside to reveal pre-set tableaux or grand entries (plate 26). Painted cloths would have been familiar to playgoers as the *default* decoration of citizen and prosperous yeomen's houses. Shakespeare's grandfather, Robert Arden, left eleven painted cloths in his will. Henslowe's inventory of properties used at the Rose theatre refers to at least two painted cloths, 'a cloth of the Sunne and moone' and 'Tasso's Picture'.

Woven cloth, and tapestries, despite mentions in theatre texts of 'cloth of arras', seem in practice less likely to have been used on the Globe stage. They would be vastly more expensive and would be at some risk in use on an outdoor stage. They are bulkier, harder to tie back, and their pictures could not be adapted. The point of painted cloths was their iconography and stories, not their intrinsic material quality or other properties. They were in a sense the economy version of tapestries. Only a handful of examples survive. Tapestries survive in much greater numbers because they were precious and therefore carefully preserved. On the other hand, painted canvas which is stretched rigid on frames – the practice in the Netherlands – survives in a comparatively large number of seventeenth century examples. This is not to say that if the company owned a woven arras this would not have been deployed where appropriate. The 'arras' which Polonius hides behind could have been literally that, or generically any cloth.

Shakespeare's play texts make quite frequent reference to painted cloths. These references suggest something of the pictorial quality an audience would have in mind when the cloths are mentioned. For example:

> You will be scraped out of the painted cloth for this (*Love's Labour's Lost*, V.ii.576)
>
> I answer you right painted cloth, from whence you have studied your questions (*As You Like It*, III.ii..273)
>
> As ragged as Lazarus in the painted cloth (*I Henry IV*, IV.ii.25)
>
> Good traders in the flesh, set this in your painted cloths (*Troilus and Cressida*, V.x.45)
>
> There's his chamber, his House, his Castle, his standing-bed and truckle-bed: 'tis painted about with the story of the prodigall, fresh and new (*The Merry Wives of Windsor*, IV.v.5–7)

The most relevant and best preserved, though restored, painted cloths to survive are the complete set by 'John Painter', Bess of Hardwick's Clerk of Works and domestic painter, at

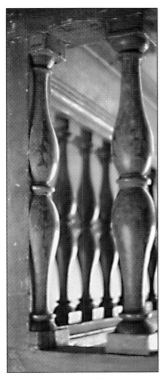

FIG. 61 Detail of balustrade,
Queen's House, Greenwich, c.1630s

Hardwick New Hall (plate 16). They depict scenes from the story of St Paul, based on contemporary engravings, broadly and competently painted, stylistically like much middle-rank contemporary wall-painting. Figures are labelled with their names. Where the series is really invaluable as an example for imitation is in its surviving foliage and 'antick' borders. These relate to the central biblical scenes they depict exactly as border does to central image in contemporary tapestries. The colouring is not unsubtle, tending generally towards blues and greens. A further example is the painted cloth depicted behind the gentlemen of the Somerset House Conference of 1604.[45] This shows a soldier bringing news to a king. It has a red/brown colouration, with the usual fruitages in the border. The edge of a second cloth is shown at the other side of the painting. We have modelled the painted cloth at the Globe on these examples, both in general style and colouring. The subject matter is Hercules supporting the celestial globe (discussed in the next chapter).

The SCENAE FRONS: *The Second Level*

This level, where the Lords' Rooms are, is more elevated culturally. The Lords' own learning is reflected (and flattered) by inscriptions, mottoes and tags such as HARMONIA MUNDI and CONCORDIA DISCORS lettered on the inside of the rooms, along with fictive panelling representing legendary scenes, pasted prints and the like.

A standard form of domestic decoration (apart from the virtually amateur deployment of rudimentary stencils and plaster-stamps) was the kind of journeyman painted decoration which is extensively treated in Francis Reader's two, still classic, articles of 1937.[46] This often consists of framed texts and mottoes or else repeat-pattern decoration fitted round and over the existing architectural features of a room (let us say for example the kind of infill of plaster found between structural wooden members.) Very often this repeat-pattern painting uses the cheapest pigments, lamp-black, black and iron-oxide red. We have included such texts and repeat-pattern decoration in our design.

There is evidence from the Fortune contract of 'carved proporcions called Satiers' in the decoration of the theatre space. There are surviving examples of such herms, but mostly in that stiff and blockish way now familiar from bedheads, hall screens and house façades. Local colour can be applied to the herms in the manner of ships' figureheads or for example on the Bed of Ware (c.1590) in the V&A,[47] plus gilding or its substitutes (plate 17). The bases of the herms are not quite stone colour as is the case at lower levels, but somewhat richer and stronger. The lozenge frame within the base is gilded, with red marble and a porphyry bullet at the centre, like Knole. The Ionic capitals are also gilded.

The balustrade on this level has turned balusters, since it represents a more polite level than mere stone. We have chosen to have it green, as is the surviving balustrade at the Queen's House (fig. 61), and to marble it, in order to pick it out as a superior element from the surrounding white marble. It could as easily have been rendered as fine hardstone; its place in the hierarchy seems the important thing.

The auditorium

The balustrade colour scheme has been taken right round the rest of the theatre. The degrees, or seating levels, are painted 'russet' following hints in the Works accounts. In the declared Accounts for 1582–3, relating to the Banqueting House at Whitehall we find that the Sergeant Painter, George Gower, was paid 'for layinge all ye windowes, and Joul pillers in white leade, oile, and russet.'[48] There are allusions of 1600 or so in the Works accounts to garden furniture painted russet: 'Leonard Fryer for pryming and laying twenty timber seates in Raunce and Erusset Colloures on the one side and a pryming Colour on the backe syde for the pryuy garden and Orchard & spring garden in the parke being all donne in Oyle Colloures … '.[49]

Rance is another colour (liver-red) frequently cited for external work, and influential in our decisions over colour at the new Globe.[50] There seems to have been a fashion for it outdoors at Court in about 1599. At Richmond in that year the master carpenter William Portington was paid for making six seats in the gardens there 'with backes to them being arched with architrave freese and Cornishe and Taffrells funyalls …', and these were included with some arbours to be painted by Fryer: 'For stopping and woorking iiij Arbors in the prevy garden their types and piramides with Oyle Coloures in Rance …'. In the previous season, at Greenwich, Fryer was paid 'for Woorkinge with ashcolor & Jasperlike raunce in water colour her Majesties seate in the garden xxxs'.[51] Fifteen seats in the garden were 'refreshed & mended', among them an interesting group: 'and for the pryminge Jasperinge in raunce coloures and guildinge of the Perymentes & cuppes with fyne golde of ye vj seates with pilasteres aboue & belowe Cs'. While Fryer painted the great penthouse in the base court in lead colour in oil, he used jasper colour 'lyke to raunce' for the posts and rails under galleries in both the gardens and on the garden doors on both sides. He used 'Raunce in oyle colour' for a mantletree.[52] The interpretation of what these colours actually were is approximate, but taken together a dull dark red does seem to be typical for outdoor furnishings.

The Third Level

The crestings

At the topmost level, the main decorative technique is strapwork, if the framing round the pillar bases is discounted. Generally, the whole area is made out of simulated stone, with the edges enriched by gilding, gold knobs and finials. The inner tablet is a play of white and red marbles, and two different hardstones, while console brackets on the outside of the structure appear as granite. This reliance on strapwork is a conscious reference to the cut-out look of the skylines of contemporary prodigy houses such as Hardwick, a decision which is strengthened by Serlio, who specified that the rooftops and statues of his tragic scene should be cutouts. The cut-out arches at the back of the vistas in the Teatro Olympico in Vicenza are left square-cut, though the best 'profiling' work would be 'feathered' or bevelled back to hide the edge. Domestic dummy board figures, popular from about 1600, are good examples of this technique, which is the one we follow.[53]

Heavens ceiling

The so-called *English Wagner Book* of 1594 describes the ceiling of an Elizabethan stage: 'Now above all was there the gay Clowdes ... adorned with the heavenly firmament, and often spotted with golden teares which men call Stars'.[54] A stage direction in an unpublished manuscript academic play called *The Birth of Hercules* (translated from Plautus and probably from Christ's College, Cambridge), performed possibly between 1597 and about 1610, calls for a special arrangement to be made for a heavens: 'Ad comoediae magnificentiam apprime conferet ut coelum Histrionium sit luna et stellis perspicue distinctum' (it would especially contribute to the splendour of the play if the actors' heavens were clearly set out with a moon and stars). A design with gilded frets, a background of dark blue indigo and a sky fringed by clouds and sprinkled with stars, together with the moon in its four phases, appears on the soffit of an Elizabethan tomb at Ockenden Church, Essex and this guided us in our design for the 1996 temporary heavens (plate 23). A similar design appears at North Mimms.

Since most contemporary ceilings of any size were fretted, large uninterrupted fields were unusual. We have therefore designed a heavens divided into compartments. Velarium cloths were traditional from Roman arenas, and were used at the Teatro Olympico in Vicenza. But a velarium cloth is unlikely at The Globe, since it would billow distractingly, and the 'creaking throne' lowered from above would need to pass through it.

Although a velarium is unlikely at the Globe, examples of overhead cloths at the more illusionistic indoor Court theatre, where no such practical or structural criteria apply, may offer some clues to the possible decorative content of a painted heavens. The 1581 Banqueting House at Whitehall had a canvas ceiling originally bordered with ivy and other vegetation, which is adequately recorded in the Works accounts.[55] We have to turn to Holinshed's *Chronicles*, however, (the 1587 edition) for a description of what the cloths contained: 'great spaces of canvas, which was most cunninglie painted, the clouds with starres, the sunne and sunne beams, with divers other cotes [of arms] of sundrie sorts belonging to the queenes majestie, most richlie garnished with gold'.[56]

We have had good levels of finish to choose from in decorating the heavens at the Globe. The pleasing 1630s sky in Rycote Chapel in Oxfordshire is rather flat, with only a single line of shading to the clouds (plate 22). It does have original playing-card stars, and does agree with the intestinal-looking shape of the clouds shown in the engravings of de Vos and Solis. The Star Chamber at Bolsover also had playing-card stars.

The Greenwich accounts of 1527 speak of lead stars that were gilded and pinned up. The church at Lydiard Tregoze near Swindon has a Tudor chancel ceiling that originally had a central sun smiling down through clouds stuck with gilded stars. This was repainted in 1837 without quite obliterating the Rycote-style clouds. Similarly simple clouds were painted on the curved soffits of Harrison's 1604 'Flemish Arch' and 'Arch of London' (*see* figs 51 and 50, p. 125). The early-seventeenth-century heavens of Cullen House, Banffshire (destroyed by fire in 1984), and Muchelney Abbey, Gloucestershire, are inhabited by personifications of the zodiac and other worthies, not simply by the moon and stars. Our eventual design draws on many of these exemplars without slavishly following any one of them. (*See* plate 21.)

The Gable

Fame is personified on the gable in modelled plaster relief, with gilded enrichments including a trumpet and flying ribbons. The figure of fame in Harrison/Dekker's *Nova Felix Arabia*
arch (fig. 52) provides a good model 'in a Watchet Roabe pale blue, thickly set with open eyes,
and Tongues, a payre of large golden Winges at her backe, a Trumpet in her hand ....'[57] Of
course, this description is of a living actor, who speaks lines from the niche where she (he,
in fact) stands. But the iconography is sound, as probably is the stance, though the eyes and
ears in our representation are transferred to a banner on the trumpet, as in (among others) de
Vos and Solis, who are discussed in the following chapter.

Appendix

Painting Techniques

All of the technical knowledge outlined below has been drawn on in making decisions about the decoration of the Globe. We have not attempted to reproduce Elizabethan techniques or use Elizabethan equipment (a number of reasons militate against this, not least the genuine danger to the actors and public of lead- and arsenic-based paints), but we have tried to gain the effect of what we infer was the original decorative scheme by using modern methods and materials to approximate the original as closely as possible.

Painters

John Smith's *Art of Painting* (1676) describes in detail the tools, materials, and style of traditional trade painting, as opposed to the techniques of fine art painting. More sophisticated treatises of an earlier date are available, and will be referred to here, but since they deal with limning (manuscript illumination), easel-painting and other indoor, small-scale studio arts, they are of less direct relevance.

Painting, like other trades, was well organised in London. John Smith recognised the metropolitan nature of skilled trades when he wrote of 'great Cities where painters usually reside', of 'Colour shops', of books of gold leaf from the 'Gold Beaters', and offered hints on glue-making for those 'not willing to send to London'. The Painter-Stainers Company demanded a seven year apprenticeship, most of which was spent grinding colours. 'Stainers' were the craftsmen who painted onto cloths. The most common job for painters was painting the exterior woodwork of houses and shops, where protection from the weather was as much a priority as decoration in the customers' minds.

Plain painting

Even for plain timber painting, the preparation was long and tedious, because of its protective purpose. First, any cracks in the wood had to be filled with putty, for, according to Smith, 'if these are not secured the wet will insinuate itself into those defects, and make the quicker despatch in rotting the whole Work.' Then followed a thin wash of boiled linseed oil and Spanish Brown, a cheap and plentiful earth colour, which acted as a sealer. After two days this layer would be dry to the touch, although linseed oil actually stays soft for years underneath its surface. Another sealing wash might be applied before two or even three priming coats of thick white lead. Before the colour was applied, this priming could be sanded with 'sharp stone or emery'.

Decorative painting

Working with simple, formalised motifs is essential in trade decoration, where everything must be reduced to a system that can be tackled by a team, without individual style. Examples of this kind of work abound, for example, a late-sixteenth-century balustrade in the lecture hall of the Hôtel Lamoignon, rue Pavée, Paris, painted in a system of light, middle and dark tones. A lack of sophistication is a virtue here; beautifully modulated shadows do not always 'register' from a distance. A 16th-century door in the V&A collection (item W37–1913) shows the same simplicity, decorated as it is with a sort of informal, high-speed strapwork (fig. 57, p. 130).

Drawing and stencilling

For transferring the design to the work itself, pouncing (dusting charcoal through lines of pin holes in a paper drawing) and templates were traditional. Richard Tothill, in his treatise of 1573, suggested a sort of home-made carbon paper (*A very proper treatise wherein is briefly sett forthe the Arte of Limming*). Smith tells us that lead pencils could be bought, but says they are 'made up so deceitfully' that he recommends the reader to buy lead in the lump, and to glue cuttings of it on to a quill. He goes on to list squares, rulers, and brass compasses 'for setting out and proportioning your work'. Stencils were used as a quick way of painting repetitive motifs. A fifteenth-century stencilled panel from West Stow Church, Suffolk is preserved in the V&A, as are some of the seventeenth-century Hill Hall murals (the rest are still *in situ*), which include stencilled borders. Stencilled strapwork appears on the beams of Little Moreton Hall chapel (*c.*1560).

Brushes

In the 17th century, the term *brushes* referred only to the large, coarse type. Smaller ones were called, confusingly, *pencils*. Brushes were always made of bristle, usually hog bristle. They were mostly round, up to 2 inches in diameter, although flat ones were known, and were used for drawing lines and wood-graining. Round brushes were normally held in split wooden handles lashed round with cord. When buying brushes, Smith was wary of 'hairs that sprawl about', and if the hairs were loose he recommended 'driving in thin Wooden Wedges between the Thread with which they are bound round'. Metal stocks were known, and were made of tin; but the stocks or 'tails' for pencils were the quills of feathers. Their sizes were based on the kind of quills used, from the smallest, those of the duck, right up to those of the goose and the swan (the quills of water fowl were preferred on account of their natural resistance to moisture). The feather end of the quill was cut off and replaced by a wooden handle. The hair used for soft brushes was taken from the tails of squirrels, from ermine (which is slightly more resilient for fine work) and possibly from red sable. The first specific mention of sable brushes was in the 18th century, but sable was certainly available in the 17th century.

Pigments

Mixing colours with the unrefined pigments of the 17th century was haphazard, although ready-ground and mixed oil paint, tied up in skin bladders, was beginning to be sold. Pigment names were often generic and unspecific. Sometimes they referred to different treatments of the same material. A few examples of pigments will show the vast range of their sources and the difficulty of their production.

White lead was made, notably in Venice, by corroding sheets of lead over vinegar. Ceruse was the name given to the purest type, sometimes called 'Vennis Cerius'. Another mineral pigment, orpiment, was equally dangerous to make and handle. It is yellow arsenic sulphide, and Smith warns his readers to 'take care the fumes of it don't offend the brain in the time of grinding'.

Various reds were available. All writers on pigments praise the colour vermilion, obtained from quicksilver and brimstone (mercury and sulphur), though it was both dangerous and expensive. Tothill implies another disadvantage when he recommends that the painter 'puts into it three chyves of Saffron' to 'take away the evil sente'. Red lead was unpredictable, since burning it at different rates produced different colours, from orange-red to purple-red, but was cheap. A less spectacular red was made from 'Brasill', or Brazil wood, originally a tropical dye, which is mentioned in many English accounts, though in 1634 John Bate in *The Mysteryes of Nature and Art* explained that an equivalent colour could be produced from a variety of yellow ochre which was dug out of the Shotover Hills near Oxford.

For blue and green shades, the painter had a number of possibilities. They included byze, or bice, known in a blue and green form as was verditer, a nitrate of copper mixed with whiting. Tothill warns that green byze was often mixed with sand by the apothecaries, 'to multiply it to their gain'. Indigo, a tint of vegetable origin, was imported from the tropics, and the term was notoriously corrupted. Tothill, for example, lists it as 'Indebaudias', while the Greenwich Palace accounts speak of 'ynde bavedens'. The best blue, ultramarine, 'so vastly dear', was also, as the name suggests, 'from beyond the seas', and was in fact derived from lapis lazuli. It is almost certainly irrelevant to a building such as the Globe.

Lamp black, as the name suggests, was lamp soot. Large quantities were obtained by burning sappy fir trees. Smith indicates that Norway and Sweden were the main producers and says that 'this colour is usually made up in small boxes and Barrels of Deal, of several sizes and so brought over to us.' The ivory fragments burned to make ivory black were the raspings of the comb-makers.

Different pigments required different handling techniques. Lake pigments such as crimson and madder were liquid before being mixed with a medium. Dry pigment had to be ground with a 'muller' or pebbled on a marble grindstone using a 'voider' or spatula of 'lanthorn horn' to keep the powder from dispersing. The oils and mediums were as hard to obtain as were the pigments. Sir Hugh Platt illustrates a press for extracting oils from herbs and the apparatus for distilling spirits from oils in his *The Jewel House of Art and Nature* (London, 1673).

Gold

In Elizabethan times, gold leaf was sold in books of 24 three-inch-square leaves, as it still is. The leaves are extremely thin and have to be transferred delicately from the book to the work. Smith recommends picking it up with 'Cane Plyers' or a cloth 'Pallat' moistened with the breath, or a foxtail, as mentioned in the Greenwich accounts, which was stroked on the cheek to create static electricity. He suggests that gold, once burnished down, can be shadowed with a transparent solution of burnt umber. Substitutes for pure gold include 'party gold', a sandwich of silver and gold, 'green gold', an alloy of silver and gold, and 'orsedye', an alloy of copper and zinc. Gold paint (that is powdered metal in suspension) was mentioned as early as the 12th century by Theophilus, but was rarely used for large-scale work.

The most common technique for cutting costs, especially outdoors, was to lay a silver, or even a tin foil, and colour it gold 'with a Lacker-Varnish made of Gum-Lake dissolved in spirits of wine.' Models for admiralty ships were lavishly gilded, for example, that of *The Prince* (1670), preserved in the Science Museum, London. In the fully scaled-up ship, however, the gilding was simply represented by yellow paint.

Notes to Chapter Seven

1   This chapter and the following one by Siobhan Keenan and Peter Davidson were originally intended to form a single essay and should be read together. Much implicit cross-reference remains. The chapters were edited and shaped by Jane Stevenson and Ronnie Mulryne at the University of Warwick.

2   *See* the discussion by Simon Blatherwick, above.

3   This chapter was written while the final scheme was still in preparation.

4   Robert Peake's translation of part of this work, based upon Book V, as published in Venice in 1569, appeared in this year.

5   E351/3228. I am grateful to John Orrell for providing me with much chapter and verse from royal Office of Works accounts and other manuscript sources. References here and elsewhere are to Office of Works reference-numbers in the Public Record Office (PRO) unless otherwise stated.

6   E351/3235.

7   E351/3245.

8   A 'pencil' was a fine, long haired brush. *See* Eric Mercer, 'The Decoration of the Royal Palaces 1553–1625', *Archaeological Journal* 110 (1953).

9   In a letter of John Chamberlain to Sir Dudley Carleton, 21 June 1617, PRO SP14/92, no. 70.

10 *See*, e.g., Sebastian Serlio's comments on magnificence in his *Le Deuxcieme livre d'architecture* (Paris, 1545). There is a modern translation in *The Renaissance Stage: Documents of Serlio, Sabbatini and Furttenbach*, ed. Barnard Hewitt and trans. Allardyce Nicoll, John D. McDowell and George R. Kernodle (Coral Gables, MI, 1958), p. 30.

11 Mercer, 'The Decoration', p. 152.

12 Eric Mercer, *English Art 1553–1625* (Oxford, 1962), p. 99.

13 Mercer, 'The Decoration', p. 156.

14 Now at Burghley House, and reproduced on p. 134 of the *Dynasties* catalogue, Tate Gallery, 1995.

15 Illustrated in Timothy Mowl, *Elizabethan and Jacobean Style* (London, 1993), p. 81.

16 *The Works of Henry Vaughan*, ed. by Leonard Cyril Martin (Oxford, 1914), p. 10. Unfortunately, Vaughan does not offer any indication of the tavern's location and we cannot be certain that it was a real place. However, if it did exist, its microcosmic decorative programme could have been informed by the stylistic treatment of the First Globe.

17 E.K. Chambers (*The Elizabethan Stage*, (Oxford, 1923), II, p. 434) cited Malone as the source for his information about the sign but hinted that the account was of suspect veracity; but, in 1988, Richard Dutton argued convincingly that Hercules was represented on the sign of the Globe. He noted how Ernest Schanzer identified Malone's source as being George Steevens, 'the great Shakespeare scholar, who in turn possibly got it from the antiquarian William Oldys'. While this ' does not establish it as fact [...] it at least takes it out of the realm of pure conjecture, where Chambers seemed to imply that it belonged'. In addition he drew attention to a number of apparent references to the sign in Shakespeare's Globe plays, including the debate about the 'war of the theatres' in *Hamlet*, during which the Prince asks 'Do the boyes carry it away?' and Rosencrantz responds , 'Ay, that they do, my lord. Hercules and his load, too' (Richard Dutton, '*Hamlet, An Apology for Actors* and the sign of the Globe', *Shakespeare Survey*, 41 (1988), 35–7).

18 Thomas White, writing in 1577, soon after the construction of the Burbages' Theatre, spoke of 'The sumptuous Theatre houses' as a 'continual monument of London's prodigalitie and folly' (Cited in Chambers, *The Elizabethan Stage* II, p. 358).

19 Shute published *The First and Chief Groundes of Architecture* in 1563. *See* Edward Croft-Murray, *Decorative Painting in England, 1537–1837* (London, 1962).

20 Chambers, *The Elizabethan Stage*, II, pp. 436–39; and *see* below pp. 182–4.

21 The Latin description is cited in Chambers, II, p. 362: 'ligneis suffultum columnis quae ob illitum marmoreum colorem, nasutissimos [?] quoque fallere possent.'

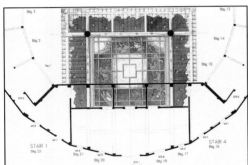

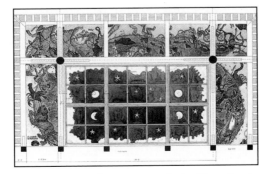

PLATE 21 Drawings from Pentagram Design illustrating the
process of designing the Heavens for the
reconstructed Globe.

PLATE 22 Painted clouds at Rycote Chapel, 1630s.

PLATE 23 The Heavens as executed for the Prologue season, 1996.

22 Stephen Harrison, *Arch's of Triumph* (London, 1604). Victoria and Albert Museum, Department of Prints, Drawings & Paintings, 14005–12. They are reproduced in C. Walter Hodges, *The Globe Restored: A Study of the Elizabethan Theatre* (London, 1953) and elsewhere.

23 Ben Jonson 'devized' the first (Fenchurch St) and the last (Temple Bar), while Dekker was responsible for three of the others. Devizing meant scripting and iconography, not actually designing. Jonson was a Globe playwright, Dekker wrote for the Fortune, and Alleyn, the famous actor there, actually appeared on each of the Jonson arches and – naturally – made speeches from them.

24 Discussed in Lucy Gent ed., *Albion's Classicism: The Visual Arts in Britain* (London and New Haven, 1995).

25 Mercer, 'The Decoration', p. 154.

26 Illustrated in Celestine Dars, *Images of Deception: The Art of Trompe-l'oeil* (London, 1979).

27 Illustrated in Mowl, *Elizabethan & Jacobean Style*, p. 33.

28 Victoria and Albert Museum item W125 – 1890.

29 Jim Murrell, 'John Guillim: A Heraldic Painter's *Vade Mecum*' p. 26, n.29.

30 Masticot is a generic word for varnish; pine sap.

31 Raphael Holinshed, *The Chronicles of England, Scotland and Ireland*, 3 vols (London 1587), III, p. 1315. Quoted by Glynne Wickham, *Early English Stages*, 1300–1600 (London, 1980), II.1, p. 283.

32 From the contract for the Fortune, Chambers, *The Elizabethan Stage*, II, p. 437, and p. 181 *below*.

33 Niccolo Sabbatini, *Pratica di fabricar scene e machine ne' teatri* (Ravenna, 1638).

34 Illustrated in John Harris, *The King's Arcadia: Inigo Jones and the Stuart Court* (London, 1973) p. 48. See also Stephen Orgel and Roy Strong, *Inigo Jones and the Theatre of the Stuart Court*, 2 vols (London, Berkeley and Los Angeles, 1973).

35 E351/3237.

36 *See* Alan Young, *Tudor and Jacobean Tournaments* (London, 1987), pp. 47, 75, 77 (painted as ashlar), 87, 97.

37 *See* Irwin Smith, *Shakespeare's Blackfriars Playhouse* (London, 1966), p. 318: 'The floor of the Blackfriars stage, like the floors of contemporary cottages and palaces all over England, was strewn with rushes. In Elizabethan and Jacobean homes, moist green rushes served primarily to lay the dust; on the stage they served that purpose and others. In outdoor scenes they represented an accustomed item of domestic furnishing, and in both they protected theatrical costumes.'

38 Sir Balthazar Gerbier, *Counsel and Advice to all builders* (London, 1663).

39 E351/3255.

40 Royal Collection, no. 15.

41 E351/3233.

42 *A Short Introduction to the art of painting and varnishing* (London, 1685), thought by the British Library cataloguer to be by Smith, though it is in a coarser and more obscure style of writing.

43 E351/3233.

44 Sir Balthazar Gerbier, *Counsel and Advice to all builders* (London, 1663).

45 National Portrait Gallery No. 665, artist unknown. The anonymous artist of the conference between representatives of England and Spain appears to have depicted a painted cloth, rather than a tapestry hanging on the wall to the (viewer's) left of the picture, with a depiction of the border of a matching cloth to the right of the window. That these are representations of painted cloths rather than of tapestries is suggested by the fact that the artist, who has experienced no problem with the depiction of the folds and fall of a table carpet, deliberately shows the wall-hangings as hanging absolutely stiff, as do the Hardwick cloths, and as, indeed, does sized canvas generally. I am grateful to Anthony Wells-Cole for pointing out how closely the scenes in the Hardwick New Hall painted cloths are modelled on prints, most of which he has identified in his forthcoming book, *Art and Decoration in Elizabethan and Jacobean England: The Influence of Continental Prints, 1558–1625* (New Haven, 1997).

46 In the *Archaeological Journal*, nos. 92 and 97.

47 The Victoria & Albert Museum, London, item W47 – 1931.

48 John Orrell, *The Human Stage: English Theatre Design, 1567–1640* (Cambridge, 1988), p. 107.

49 PRO E351/3235 Whitehall emptions.

50 Rance or raunce is a liver-red marble cited in the OED as appearing on the title page of I. Sylvester's *Du Bartas: his divine weekes, and workes* (London, 1598) describing 'A tomb with Ivory Pillars mixt with jet and rance.'

51 1598-99, PRO E351/3234.

52 All from E351/3234.

53 Serlio, *Le Deuxcieme livre d'architecture* (Paris, 1545). A modern translation is in *The Renaissance Stage* (*see note* 11) p. 30.

54 *English Wagner Book* (1594). For a discussion of the *Book*'s relevance to the staging of Elizabethan plays *see* Chambers, *The Elizabethan Stage*, III, pp. 71–2.

55 E351/3216. This ceiling cloth was repainted in 1584-5 'with Diamondes frutage and other kinde of woorke' (PRO E351/3219); it was repaired and painted again in 1603-4: 'Thomas Breize and Thomas Greene uphol-sters for sewing the Canvas for the Ceiling for the great Banqueting house –xxs. for straining and setting up the same Canvas – xxs and for trashnailes leather and thred – xxiij s iiijd … Leonard ffrier Sergeant Painter for laying upon Canvas in the Ceeling of the great Banqueting house cxxxij yardes square of worke called the Cloudes in distemper, at xd the yard square – [and] for of [sic] lxxij yardes square at the endes [probably of the hall, on the walls rather than the ceiling] being the kinges Armes' (E351/3239). This in turn lasted two or three years until the building was replaced (and the new plaster ceiling, by Dungan, was treated with 'deepe pendauntes and Compartments') (E351/3243). 532 yards is quite an area; so there was a ceiling – albeit short-lived – rather like the one we have installed, done not very long after the Globe's and by a craftsman who doubtless knew the Globe and other public theatres. (Fryer helped to prepare rooms used for plays at Court and may have discussed such matters with the players).

56 *See* n. 31 above.

57 Thomas Dekker, *The Magnificent Entertainment*, 'the Device at Soper-lane end', ll. 572–4 in Fredson Bowers, ed., *The Dramatic Works of Thomas Dekker*, II, p. 276.

❧ 8 ❧

THE ICONOGRAPHY OF THE GLOBE

Siobhan Keenan and Peter Davidson

THE PROBLEM OF REPRESENTING THE PAST

THIS ACCOUNT of the iconography of the Globe may fittingly begin with some considerations which apply to the whole project, not only to the decoration of the interior of the playhouse.

It would be fair to say that the 1590s Globe Theatre, which the present structure seeks to represent, was itself a building which sent forth a double message about the past and the present. To the eye of the late twentieth century, the circular depictions of the playhouses in Hollar's great view of London are unequivocally Elizabethan, but in the eyes of the 1590s, these structures evoked the splendour of the classical world of Roman antiquity. Amongst the very few descriptive notes on the interior of the theatre which survive, there is enough reference to marbling and columns to suggest that the structure was using and combining referentially classical elements in a way designed to signify 'classical Rome' to the spectator. Consequently, the structure encodes the idea that the theatrical performance itself stands in a tradition deriving from the admired poets and dramatists of antiquity.

During the decade that followed the building of the first Globe, an intensification of cultural interchange between England and Italy led to the development of a radically different and lasting set of signifiers for the concept of classical antiquity. From then on, Palladian classicism and archaeological Romanitas came to signify the authentic experience of antiquity. Thus the 'classicism' of the 1590s Globe was changed and redefined even during Shakespeare's career.

The problem of double signification is very much with us now. While nobody involved with the 1990s Globe would claim that it is any more than a shadow, a representation, a laboratory for the player and the theatrical historian, there can be no doubt that many visitors will impose their own notion of reality, their own idea of 'secular pilgrimage' upon it. In the summer of 1996, it has been reported that spectators in Elizabethan costume were turned away from a (modern-dress) production of *The Two Gentlemen of Verona*. Before the structure was even finished, it had been appropriated, theme-parked (by its visitors) and (at the same time) reified, all in direct contradiction to the stated aims of those who have worked for the project and on this book.

This is not the appropriate place to attempt to contextualise the Globe within the history of architectural visualisations of Elizabethan England. Yet if we understand this history we may begin to understand why it is impossible to prevent some people reading as somehow 'really' Shakespeare's Globe a structure dedicated to theatrical experimentation and revaluation, securely grounded in the later twentieth century.

We are aware that the brightly painted decoration and elaborate iconography of the Bankside Globe will be one of the most surprising elements of the structure to the late-twentieth-century audience. In its attempt to escape the 'Shakespearean' cliché of silvery oak and glimmering plaster it represents a rejection of a whole tradition of the visual reading of the Shakespearean past. In its attempt at a consistent iconography and a consistent use of pattern-books in use in the England of the 1590s it makes no claims of exclusive authenticity (although it advances the much more modest claim of *possibility*). Rather, it points to the continuity of the double signal, the way that Shakespeare's Globe was itself a reading of the past and a living theatrical space.

THE PAINTED WORLD: AN ICONOGRAPHY FOR THE THIRD GLOBE

Given the limited direct evidence for the iconographical treatment of the first Globe and the fact that any quest for 'authenticity' is, as noted earlier, inherently problematic, any definitive reconstruction of the decorative scheme is obviously impossible. However, by considering the indirect evidence afforded through contemporary accounts and dramatic allusions, and surveying the world of English Renaissance design more broadly, it has been possible to establish a sense of the conventions and techniques which characterised the visual culture within which the theatre emerged and thus the likely nature of its décor.

While the iconographical programme outlined in the following section therefore represents an adaptation governed by the stage configuration in place and the paucity of hard evidence, it constitutes a symbolic schema *plausible* within the practice and mentality of 1599. Indeed, as far as possible, the current decorative scheme has been modeled upon designs known to have been used, or available to, the craftsmen of 1590s London. Consequently, emblematic material and the Flemish pattern books have been a particularly rich source of analogues.[1] Sources of the early sixteenth or later seventeenth centuries have generally been avoided, for similar reasons: to be plausible analogues it was felt that any designs drawn upon needed to date as closely as possible to the time of the Globe's (re)construction in 1599.[2]

Inside the 'Wooden O': Reading the Globe

The paint work of the reconstructed Globe is colourful and elaborate, combining Northern continental 'classicism' with the grotesques, strapwork, cartouches and feigned architectural patterns of Flemish Mannerism, in keeping with the conventions of Early Modern English design and the likely decoration of the original auditorium. For similar reasons the new Globe (and, we assume, its predecessor), observes a coherent scheme of iconography. As has been indicated, it was conventional for Early Modern decorative schemes to make some statement about their use, purpose or patrons. In the case of the Burbages' theatre, common sense and analogy would suggest that its internal décor also made some reference to their chosen name.

In christening their new playhouse 'the Globe', it may be expected that the Burbages commissioned a decorative scheme intended to foster an emblematic conception of the theatre as a microcosm of the real world. Indeed, arguably, the stage of a playhouse called the Globe, acting out various human fortunes and possibilities under a painted sky, is *de facto* making some claim for itself as a theatre of the world, a space in which can be represented all possible human actions and emotions. Consequently, a simple iconographic message, elaborating upon this conceit, has underpinned the designs prepared for the reconstructed theatre. Through its ornamentation, the theatre is to suggest that its stage is a microcosm of the whole world in all its variety, where, under the starry sky, through the influence of the planetary deities (who stand also for the stages of human life), in the genres of Tragedy and Comedy, guided by Apollo and Mercury (poetry and eloquence) we can perform the mimesis of all human life. How this symbolic 'statement' was translated to the decoration of each stage component is outlined below, as are the scholarly grounds for the chosen designs .

The Heavens

The decoration of the stage cover with a celestial scene resembling a night sky is particularly appropriate in an iconographical scheme which seeks to identify the stage as a microcosm of the world (plate 21). The allusions contained in a number of First Globe plays indicate that the Globe was decorated in this fashion. In *Julius Caesar*, for example, the protagonist describes how the 'skies are painted with unnumb'red sparks,/They are all fire, and every one doth shine'; while in *Hamlet*, the prince remarks upon 'this majestic roof fretted with golden fire'. In both cases, the terminology employed by Shakespeare is that of the artificer and points towards the construction of the artificial 'heavens'. As noted above, gilded stars or 'fiery sparks' *were* nailed or painted upon the ceilings in other chambers decorated with celestial scenes. Likewise, Hamlet's reference to 'fretting' evokes a popular technique amongst contemporary painters.[3]

Other contemporary accounts and dramatic references suggest that it was similarly usual to incorporate representations of the zodiac on some part of the stage (e.g. in *Titus Andronicus*, when firing arrows to the gods, the protagonist jokes with Publius that 'thou hast shot off one of Taurus' horns').[4] Notably, in Heywood's *Apology for Actors*, his description of Julius Caesar's amphitheatre at Campus Martius includes an account of its 'heavens' as incorporating such ornamentation: he refers to the depiction of 'the planets in their degrees [...] and above all these [...] the twelve signes'.[5] He thus demonstrates that Shakespeare's contemporaries were at least familiar with a classical model of celestial depiction which included representations of the zodiac. Furthermore, as his account is believed to conflate a number of features of the Classical and Elizabethan theatres his description of the 'heavens' at Campus Martius may even have been informed by the contemporary examples of theatrical decoration with which he was familiar.[6]

In the current scheme, zoomorphic and anthropomorphic forms of the zodiac circle the central panel of the 'heavens', which is decorated with a supernal light. In addition, a sun and moon have been located at the two foremost corners of the canopy. The Globe's craftsmen would have found fine models for their zodiac in the coloured Planisphere of the Northern Heavens by Augustinus Rhyther ('Angulus'),[7] or upon the Celestial Globe of Emery Molyneux.[8] The present designs certainly draw upon these typical depictions of the celestial bodies. (*See* plate 21.)

The central panel of the stage canopy, painted with its radiating light, completes the celestial hierarchy, suggesting a traditional heavens in which divine force is central. There is, however, a further reason for the incorporation of the central motif in the current iconography of the 'heavens'. Divine descents occur in a number of Elizabethan and Jacobean plays and the relevant stage directions (and contemporary allusions) indicate that 'gods' could be lowered through the 'heavens'. For instance, in *Cymbeline* Jupiter is described as descending from his 'marble mansion' and Sicilius observes how 'the marble pavement clozes' after he re-enters 'His Radiant *Roofe*' (own emphasis). The imagery invites us to visualise the staging of this scene and the role played by the artificial 'heavens'. As a converted trap-door the central panel, with its divine iconography, becomes a symbolically appropriate point from which to stage such descents and ascents.

The Frons Scenae *wall above the Lords' Rooms*

The separating braces in this section of the scenic wall are, in conventional Renaissance fashion, atlantid figures. The planetary deities are figured upon the attic panels to depict the transmission of celestial influence downwards, since these deities were understood in the Renaissance to exercise power over various aspects of human life . At a simple level, the engraver Virgil Solis of Nuremberg relates them to the days of the week, (Sol = Sontag [Sunday]; Luna = Montag [Monday]; Mars = Entas [Tuesday]; Mercuris = Mittwoch [Wednesday]; Iuppiter = Donerstag [Thursday]; Venus = Freitag [Friday]; Saturnus = Samstag [Saturday]). Maarten de Vos, another popular designer, records their association with the stages of human life (1586).[9] Again, the incorporation of the deities into the iconographic scheme is also in keeping with the indirect evidence of the plays and contemporary accounts of the theatre. For example, Heywood's account of the 'heavens' at Campus Martius, already mentioned (which may have been informed by those known to him in the Early Modern theatres), describes the depiction of the 'sky of the moone, and sky of Mercury, Venus, Sol, Mars, Jupiter and Saturne'.[10] Furthermore, there are numerous Early Modern precedents for their incorporation in celestial decorative schemes.

At Stodmarsh Court, for example, a number of *grisaille* panels are painted with the planetary deities (*see* fig. 59, p. 132), based upon the Solis engravings;[11] and an analogous set of planetary gods, derived from Solis, is drawn upon in the *locus memoriae* garden of Edzell Castle, near Brechin (1603). Solis' engravings could have afforded a model for the Globe's designers in similar fashion. Equally, they might have turned to the engravings of Maarten de Vos. Representations of the planetary deities occur in his *Planetarum Affectus.*[12]

Those designs employed in the new Globe have been modeled principally upon the Solis engravings but have been arranged, left to right, following De Vos's ordering of the gods: Venus, Luna, Mars, Iupiter, Saturnus. Drawing upon those associations described by the Dutch designer, this sequence symbolically suggests the ages of human life, in keeping with Shakespeare's own portrait of the ages in *As You Like It*.

The Second Level

Herms and caryatids would have been an obvious ornament for the pillars of the gallery and, typically, such figures were allegorical or emblematic in character. In keeping with the iconographical statement outlined above, personifications of Tragedy and Comedy occupy this area in the new Globe.

Together, the dramatic muses symbolically declare the capacity of drama to represent all

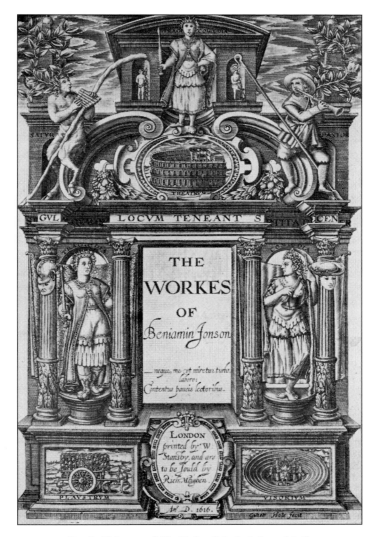

FIG. 62 Title page of *The Workes of Beniamin Jonson* (1616)

things under the heavens, the serious and the comic, human misfortune and human happiness. The inclusion of Melpomene and Thalia, the dramatic muses, representing Tragedy and Comedy respectively, would have been particularly appropriate in a theatre. They are also in keeping with the Induction scene of an early Globe play, *A Warning For Fair Women*. In this scene, Tragedy and Comedy engage in a discussion with History of 'the relative merits of their various kinds of work'. The symbolism of the Induction is noted by Orrell: [13]

> Tragedy comes on through one of the side doors, and then Comedy at the other. 'Enter Comedie at the other end', says the stage direction, emphasising the polarity.

Orrell suggests that the two Muses were present, similarly, as counterpointed 'mute sculptural decoration' on the Globe's *frons scenae*. Certainly, it became conventional to include Tragedy and Comedy at either side of the stage in later theatres, such as the Cockpit-in-

Court, a theatre designed, in part, for use by the King's Men.

We find a relatively contemporary depiction of Tragedy and Comedy (as well as several other dramatic personifications) on the frontispiece of Jonson's 1616 *Folio* (fig. 62). It is a title-page of particular pertinence to the subject of the Elizabethan theatre, for if emblematic title-pages are 'essays on architectural themes', this frontispiece is distinctive as an 'essay' on a theatrical theme.[14] In addition, although it is of a slightly later date than the First Globe, the title-page is conservative in design, and so may give an indication of the form the muses would probably have taken if carved upon the Globe's *frons scenae* in 1599. Consequently, in the current reconstruction the attributes of the muses have been derived primarily from the 1616 frontispiece. However, the form for their herms has been taken from the designs of de Vries.[15]

To complete the dramatic iconography of the Second level, the end panels, flanking the galleries, carry images of Mercury and Apollo. They are the 'speaking out' gods, the gods of poetry and eloquence: their powers, therefore, govern the dramatic genres and contribute to the presentation of the world upon the microcosmic stage. The gods are equipped in traditional Renaissance emblematic fashion. Once more, the engravings of continental craftsmen and the popular emblem books of the period have been the guide for the new depictions of the gods (the prints of Hendrik Goltzius have afforded us contemporary representations of both deities).[16]

Stage Pillars

These pillars have been painted to resemble marble, following the example of the Swan. However, in the light of the Globe's symbolic association with the figure of Hercules (*see above*), their decoration is also intended to invoke the pillars of Hercules. The marbled shafts have been ornamented with *rosso antico* work and surmounted by gilded capitals, mirroring the typical representation of the Pillars of Hercules in the period (as found in Charles V's *impresa* and in a number of Elizabeth's later portraits). Similarly, the treatment of the bases has been modeled upon another contemporary de Vries design.[17]

Painted Cloths / Hangings

Contemporary accounts and dramatic allusions regularly refer to the 'arras' or painted cloths adorning the tiring-house façades of Elizabethan theatres. Florio's 1598 dictionary definition of *scena* suggests that they were regarded as a normal part of stage decoration: '*Scena*, a skaffold, a pavillion, or fore part of a theatre where the players make them readie, being trimmed with hangings'.[18]. Furthermore, many Renaissance plays seem to assume the existence of such hangings. In *Volpone*, the protagonist describes how he will 'get up / Behind the curtain on a stool', and in the Induction to *Cynthia's Revels* another of Jonson's characters exclaims that 'I am none of your fresh Pictures that use to beautifie the decay'd dead Arras, in a publique Theater'.[19] Similarly, as noted above, we know from Henslowe's inventory that the companies at the Rose had the use of at least two painted cloths: 'Tasso's picture' and 'a clothe of the sune and moone'.[20] Early Modern cloths and hangings were typically decorated with biblical, mythological or allegorical scenes, as a number of Shakespearean allusions confirm (*quoted above*, p. 136).

Drawing upon Richard Dutton's evidence that Hercules was featured on the Globe's

FIG. 63 Detail from the hangings made for the new Globe by the New Zealand Shakespeare Association. The central pair, covering the discovery space, show Hercules and Atlas, while the flanking pair in front of the adjacent sections of blank wall show Venus and Adonis.

sign, the painted cloth which covers the central opening of the new *frons scenae* carries an image of the mythological hero bearing the 'load' of the globe (which he took from Atlas as one of his Twelve Labours). By using the cloth's central location for the Herculean motif the audience's first sight on entering the yard is allowed to be one of the theatre's traditional classical 'protectors', bearing 'his load' between his Herculean pillars (plates 25, 26): symbolically, the audience is prepared for a world of drama in which the limits of human knowledge, strength, and ability are open for test, exploration and demonstration. Hercules would have been a familiar character for Elizabethan audiences as contemporary representations of the classical hero were numerous (*see* fig. 63). The design of an overmantel in the house of Sir Paul Pindar of Bishopsgate, London (1600) affords one such depiction. It features Atlas and Hercules with the globe and may even have been influenced by, or informed by, the sign at the Burbages' theatre. As we are basing the cloth's design upon that of the first Globe's sign it seemed equally appropriate that we draw upon the motto traditionally associated with the Globe (and its Herculean motif), *totus mundus agit histrionem* (The Whole World Moves the Actor), an expression of the conceit of the theatre as a microcosmic world.

The Lords' Rooms

The Lords' and Gentlemen's Rooms were privileged areas. According to Thomas Platter's 1599 account, you had to pay three pence to gain entry to the Gentlemen's Rooms, as opposed to the flat rate of a penny charged to gain entry to the yard.[21] The Lords' Rooms, accessed through the Tiring House, cost sixpence or more. Lavish, 'élite' decoration would be conventional, and the current 'Rooms' have accordingly been painted to achieve a more luxurious effect. Similarly, inspired by Jon Greenfield's suggestion that the elite spectators should be reminded 'by the iconography of their surroundings [...] that they are watching the human comedy of the theatre as well as the comedy on the stage',[22] the Lords' Rooms are fitted with an iconographical scheme tailored to the interests of the privileged playgoers traditionally associated with these boxes. For example, an hermetic sun and moon are painted upon the ceiling and a figure of Harmonia (based on the design in Cesare Ripa's *Iconologia*) is to be incorporated upon the back wall of the galleries. In similar fashion, the two rooms feature a pair of emblems upon the wall least visible from the auditorium, accompanied by apposite Latin tags painted over the openings through which the stage is viewed. Thus the spectacle of the 'stage-play world' can be framed by the élite commentary of the emblems.

No final decision has been taken (as we write), but the proposed emblems build upon the systematic identification of the theatre as a microcosm of the world. In the same way, it is likely that the additional Gentlemen's Rooms, four in number, will be decorated using a scheme of the elements. For the first emblem an image from Robert Fludd's *Cosmology* or a contemporary musical treatise might be accompanied by the popular motto, '*Harmonia Mundi Concordia Discors*' (The harmony of the world is the consonance of discords). The second proposed device derives from an emblematic portrait of William Style of Langley in the Tate Gallery, featuring a globe enclosed within a flaming heart and the inscription '*microcosmus microcosmi non impletur megacosmo*' (The heart of the microcosm [man] is not filled even by the great world itself).[23] Such conceits (and their select symbolism) would have appealed to the elite Elizabethan taste for emblems and *imprese*. At the same time, accompanied by explanatory notes (upon wall notices or in programmes) these cryptic messages can remain comprehensible and can afford privileged modern playgoers a source of additional, private entertainment.

Notes to Chapter Eight

1   Emblem collections, such as Geoffrey Whitney's *A Choice of Emblems* (1586), were easily available and could be used by craftsmen, writers and individuals of all sorts (e.g. emblems found in Peacham's *Minerva Britannica* formed the basis of a series of plasterwork designs on the gallery ceiling at Blickling Hall). Mark Girouard emphasises the importance of the emblem culture in his work on Robert Smythson, one of the most important English Renaissance architects: 'In England foreign emblem books were in circulation from early days [...] Emblems and devices are frequently described in Elizabethan romances; they were expressed in bright enamels and made into jewels or were embroidered on bed hangings or decorated like shields in the tourneys at court' (Girouard, *Robert Smythson and the English Country House* (London and New Haven, 1983), p. 241). The Flemish pattern books were similarly accessible and popular sources for Early Modern designers. These collections drew together a range of engraved designs which fellow craftsmen could study and adapt. Especially influential (and, therefore, important for our purpose) were the designs of Hans Vriedeman and Maarten de Vos (e.g. Robert Smythson adapted the designs of de Vries in his decorations for the screen at Wollaton; de Vos's engravings of the Four Ages of Man were the model for a series of paintings at Knole).

2   When looking for analogues for the internal treatment of the new auditorium the key date is the Globe's opening in 1599, as it is unlikely that the Theatre's ornamentation was preserved during its brisk dismantling and removal to the Bankside site. As Peter McCurdy and Jon Greenfield point out, 'Allen claims that Burbage's people started on Boxing Day 1598 and took four days, finishing before he could arange for them to be stopped by power of Attorney [...] Four days is very fast work, even for sixteen men, and it seems that they could only achieve such speed by stripping out all secondary elements' (Jon Greenfield and Peter McCurdy, 'Shakespeare's Globe theatre: The Construction of two Experimental Bays in June 1992', in *The Design of the Globe*, ed. Andrew Gurr, Ronnie Mulryne and Margaret Shewring (University of Warwick, 1993), p. 62).

3   In 1601 'John Cobb was rewarded for 'frettishing' the ceilings of the great chamber and long gallery at St. John's College, Cambridge' (John Orrell, *The Human Stage: English Theatre Design, 1576–1640* (Cambridge, 1988), p. 98).

4   *Titus Andronicus* was first performed at the Rose, rather than the Globe, but the apparent allusion remains pertinent since it may indicate a decoration that was typical in contemporary theatres.

5   Cited in Richard Dutton, '*Hamlet*', *An Apology for Actors* and the sign of the Globe', *Shakespeare Survey*, 41 (1988), p. 40.

6   One conflation identified by Dutton relates to Heywood's description of the way 'an ensigne of silke waved continually' from a louvre or turret above the roof: 'he and his readers knew very well that it was contemporary practice in public houses to fly such an ensign', rather than a convention of the Roman theatre. As Dutton notes, Heywood 'had misread the passage in Ovid [...] from which the quoted Latin tag comes. The phrase should have read 'In those dayes from the marble house did wave/No saile, no silken flagge, or ensigne brave'. The 'mistranslation ' underlines the contemporary dimension Heywood obviously saw in this text' (Dutton, '*Hamlet*', p. 41).

7   Dated 1590. British Library Maps, 184. n.1.

8   London, 1592. British Library Maps, 8 bb.10.b).

9   He linked *Adolescentia amore* with Venus; *Ivventus Labori* with Minerva; *Virilitas Honori* with Diana and *Senectus* with Saturn.

10 Cited in Dutton, '*Hamlet*', p. 40.

11 British Library Prints & Drawings 1871–12–9–517; 1860–4–10–180–184;1871–12–9–519.

12 (Antwerp, 1585); British Library Prints & Drawings 1877–8–11–1306 et. seq. The designs of de Vos were, like those of Virgil Solis, widely used in England at the turn of the seventeenth century as source materials for painted decoration in a wide variety of genres (e.g. the painters and carvers who worked at Bolsover, Knole and Edzell were all familiar with such designs).

13 John Orrell, 'Melpomene and Thalia', privately circulated ts., p. 1.

14 Margery Cobbett and Ronald Lightbown, *The Comely Frontispiece: The Emblematic Title-page in England, 1550–1660* (London, Henley and Boston, 1979), p. 5. Jonson creates a monument to drama, including personifications of the different genres and a condensed visual theatre history. The design also illustrates a Roman amphitheatre (although it has been suggested that the illustration owes some of its details to contemporary playhouses). If Jonson's frontispiece does afford a conflation of Roman and Elizabethan theatres its design might be similarly informed by the interior design of the contemporary playhouses. The figures he incorporates could even have been inspired by similar representations at the Globe.

15 British Museum Prints & Drawings 168 b. 25/b. 26/b. 5.

16 British Museum Prints & Drawings 1852–12–11–115–116.

17 British Museum Prints & Drawings Album 168* b. 25 nos. 119 et seq.

18 Cited in Chambers, *The Elizabethan Stage*, II, p. 539.

19 Ben Jonson, *Volpone*, ed. by Alvin Kernan (New Haven and London, 1962; repr. 1967), Act V, sc. ii, lines 83–5, p. 169. *Cynthia's Revels* cited in Chambers, *The Elizabethan Stage*, II, p. 79.

20 Cited in Wickham, *Early English Stages*, II.1, p. 317.

21 Thomas Platter's account is translated in Jean V. Wilson, *Entertainments for Elizabeth I* (Ipswich and Totowa, NJ, 1980), pp. 62–3.

22 Jon Greenfield, private communication, July 1996.

23 Tate Gallery, no. T.2308.

PART THREE

THE GLOBE
IN PERFORMANCE

❧ 9 ❧

STAGING AT THE GLOBE

Andrew Gurr

THE ENORMOUS labours of the past years, joining so many different kinds of expertise together to design and build the Globe and its related structures, are nothing in comparison with the work that must follow in putting it to best use. Essentially the new Globe is no more than a test-tube, the basis for experiments aimed at getting a better idea of how Shakespeare expected his plays to be staged. The experiments that will follow its completion depend on a new cross-fertilisation of different skills. Now it will lie chiefly between the scholars analysing the original features of Elizabethan staging and the actors who test their ideas in practice in the new playhouse.

It is far too early to say or even to predict with any confidence what this next labour might bring forth. The Workshop season of 1995 and the Prologue season of 1996 both in their different ways showed some of the areas to explore, although both of them produced more questions than answers. What follows here renews a few of those questions, and in the following chapter Mark Rylance, Artistic Director and chief actor of the Globe company, recounts a few of the lessons he learned from the Prologue season, and identifies some of the opportunities he will explore and the constraints he will work under in the coming seasons.

Some distinctive features of staging at the original Globe

The Globe offers the opportunity of making a variety of new measurements, ranging from how long it takes to walk offstage, to the acoustics of a soliloquy directed at only one section of the total surround of audience. One of the largest and most complex measurements is the amount of different information that the original audiences brought to the plays compared with what we know now, and the related difference in the responses to the plays of modern audiences compared with the original audiences. Measurements such as these need to be made as we try to gain information from the experiment of reconstructing Shakespeare's theatre that will help our understanding of his plays.

Even in the theatre, a place where we pay money to let us believe for a transitory moment things that we know cannot be real, the minds of modern audiences are conditioned by the cinematic image. The modern mindset is fixed in the belief that the camera does not lie, and that moving images are the most graphic and immediate form of access we have to reality. We think in cinematic images. If in a supermarket we see an actor from a familiar soap we automatically assume them to be the person they play in front of the camera. The Elizabethan audience had no such training. At the Globe they knew they were in a playhouse because it and its occupants always made their presence felt, all too often uncomfortably so. They could all be seen, sometimes they could be heard, and often they were smelled.

What follows is an account of ten of the more distinctive aspects of the original staging of the plays, where the Globe's features had a positive function. They range from specific structural elements, such as the two massive stage posts upholding the heavens, to the holes that an aside or an in-joke could so often punch through the thin gauze of stage illusion. The original Globe's physical and visible discomforts, inescapably features of the game of illusion-making in broad daylight, made Elizabethans more aware than modern audiences in cinemas have to be that what they are watching is a deception. When Hamlet complained to the groundlings about the Player bringing tears to his own eyes by speaking what was only a fiction, a 'dream of passion', Elizabethans would have understood much more readily than we do that, although Hamlet was making his complaint on the grounds that he was himself real, he too was no more than a fiction.

1. *Stage entrances and stage dimensions*

In the second scene of *Measure for Measure* Mrs. Overdone is hailed on her entry by Lucio, who prompts half a dozen lines of innuendo about venereal disease before his gentleman friend greets her with an enquiry after her own particular venereal disease, sciatica, which has been evident in her comic waddle to join the talkers at front stage (I.ii.56-7). The Folio text runs it like this:

2. GENT.	Yes, that thou hadst; whether thou art tainted,
	or free. *Enter Bawde.*
LUC.	Behold, behold, where Madam *Mitigation* comes.
	I haue purchas'd as many diseases, vnder her Roofe,
	As come to
2 GENT.	To what, I pray?
LUC.	Iudge.
2 GENT.	To three thousand Dollours a yeare.
1. GENT.	I, and more.
LUC.	A French crowne more.
1. GENT.	Thou art alwayes figuring diseases in me; but
	thou art full of errors, I am sound.
LUC.	Nay, not (as one would say) healthy: but so
	sound, as things that are hollow; thy bones are hollow;
	Impiety has made a feast of thee.
1 GENT.	How now, which of your hips hath the most
	profound Ciatica?
BAWD.	Well, well: there's one yonder arrested, and
	carried to prison, was worth fiue thousand of you all.[1]

Her walk, or waddle, was an evident comic turn in its own right, which must have made it worth extending the usual time allowed of two or three lines between a character entering at the *frons* and then joining the speakers at front-stage.

A more complex example is at *Twelfth Night* III.iv. The Folio text places Malvolio's famous entry cross-gartered and wearing his yellow stockings two lines before its placing in

PLATE 24 (*above*) One of Theo Crosby's last versions of the Globe's stage and *frons scenae*, drawn in 1993.

PLATE 25 (*left*) Details of *frons scenae* 'stonework' and research for the Hercules painted cloth.

PLATE 26 Detail of Prologue season stage and Hercules painted cloth.

PLATES 27 The 1996 stage in use.

most modern editions, which supply it only when Olivia greets him saying 'How now, Malvolio?' (III.iv.16). The original text gives him his entry as soon as she says 'Go call him hither'. She then speaks two more lines. They are 'I am as mad as he,/If sad and merry madness equal be,' a claim that she is indeed mad for love. Literal-minded modern editions reposition Malvolio's entry after these two lines, as if to give the person fetching him time to find him offstage. In the original text, though, he arrives just as she asks for him, as if he's been there eagerly waiting to make his colourful entrance. And if he does enter then, and hears her last two lines as he walks forward in his yellow stockings visible to the audience before she catches sight of him, the way he might react to Olivia's words about being mad with love just like 'he himself' has wonderful comic possibilities well beyond the visual shock that his grossly miscoloured dress so famously provides.

In this and many other places, the locations of the entries in the Folio or quarto texts need testing by trying them out on the Globe stage. The stage area was wide and deep, and entrances and exits alike took more time than the instant 'Enter' or 'Exit' of a stage direction allows. The two or three lines of time it took to pace between the *frons* and the front of the stage allowed interplay between characters leaving and others entering, whether in actual encounters, by interrupting the exits, or in the symbolism of characters who manage not to actually cross each other as one enters and the other exits.

When Cleopatra is needling Antony over his Roman cares, in *Antony and Cleopatra* I.ii., for instance, she starts to exit when she sees Antony come in. This is how the first Folio reproduces the lines:

CLEO.	He was dispos'd to mirth, but on the sodaine
	A Romane thought hath strooke him.
	Enobarbus?
ENOB.	Madam.
CLEO.	Seeke him, and bring him hither: wher's Alexias?
ALEX.	Heere at your seruice.
	My Lord approaches.
	Enter Anthony, with a Messenger.
CLEO.	We will not looke vpon him.
	Go with vs. *Exeunt.*

Antony walks in listening to a messenger from Rome, and does not notice Cleopatra and all her entourage, two women and two men, as they walk off by the other door. His concentration on Roman affairs is visibly at the expense of his love. The long stretch of space between the doors in the *frons* at the back of the stage and the front-stage area where most characters walked while they spoke had complex uses, which the last three centuries of two-dimensional proscenium-arch staging have obscured.

2. Uses of the central opening

So far as current thinking about entrances and exits go, the central opening was the doorway used chiefly by authority figures and their parodies, the clowns. The authority signified by using the central opening for formal entries in royal processions was matched by harmonious exits at the close of most comedies and all of the plays where two warring factions have been reconciled. It could function at the ends of plays as the location where the divided loyalties previously marked by entries through the two flanking doors could be visibly re-united. In *A Midsummer Night's Dream*, II.i., Oberon and his train enter at one flanking door, while Titania and her fairies enter '*at another*'. Exits side by side through the central space were the visible signifiers of newly-achieved harmony in *Romeo and Juliet, A Midsummer Night's Dream,* and *The Two Gentlemen of Verona*, where previously the opposing factions had used the flanking doors. The satirical *Love's Labour's Lost* does not end like a romantic comedy, since there the exit with no marriages to celebrate is by the ordinary doors on each side: 'You that way, we this way'.

The central opening was closed off by the stage hangings, or arras. They gave kings the dignity of making an entry heralded by the blue-coated stage hands[2] who held the curtains back to admit the stately procession. The clowns poked their heads through the hangings and pulled faces before entering. The space behind the central hangings was available for 'discoveries', set-pieces or tableaux such as the murder of Duke Humphrey in *2 Henry VI*, the display of Volpone's gold, the shrine he kneels at when the play opens, or the revealing of Ferdinand and Miranda at their game of chess in *The Tempest*.

Covered by the stage hangings, the central space had many functions. In the 'closet' scene in *Hamlet*, the hangings are first drawn back when young Hamlet unveils the corpse of Polonius. The king used the same hangings to spy on Hamlet in company with Polonius when they set Ophelia on him. When Polonius conceals himself in the same authority space it is understandable that Hamlet should at first think he is the king. Furthermore, the stage being Gertrude's chamber for this scene, it is the same opening, with the body visible inside it, that the ghost of the dead King Hamlet uses to enter by. In appearing, he completely ignores the body he has to step over to enter his wife's chamber. He exits similarly 'out at the Portall', as Hamlet exclaims. According to the first Quarto, his visit to Gertrude is in the form of her nightgowned husband, even though she cannot see or hear him. His use of the appropriate authority entrance for all the corpse that blocks it is a powerful image of his single-minded role in the play, there only to rebuke his revenging son.

3. *Uses of the* frons *and balcony*

One of the more spectacular uses of the tiring-house wall was for battle scenes where a town or castle is besieged. Jasper Mayne praised Ben Jonson in the 1630s because in his plays, unlike Shakespeare, he 'laid no sieges to the music room'. The most famous scene of that kind in the Shakespeare plays was in *Henry V*, at the gates of Harfleur, where Henry's soldiers put scaling ladders to the balcony and climbed up them. It might have been more visible to Elizabethan audiences than to modern viewers of the films of *Henry V* that Henry's attempts to penetrate the town by force were unsuccessful. His 'Once more unto the breach, dear friends' speech, and the climb to the balcony with scaling ladders that followed, led only to the other kind of use of the *frons* for sieges. For this the balcony still serves as the town wall, but now the central opening below it becomes the town gates. Henry only captures Harfleur when the Governor, standing on the balcony which the English soldiers have just scaled with their ladders, invites Henry and his men to 'Enter our Gates, dispose of us and ours,/For we no longer are defensible.' The army then '*enter the Towne*' through the opening below the Governor.

The most celebrated use of the *frons* was of course for Juliet's balcony. Besides its function in *Romeo and Juliet* and *Henry V*, its most striking uses were written for *Richard II* and *Julius Caesar*. These two plays had one distinctive feature of the balcony scenes that suggests a distinctive element in the backstage design. In *Julius Caesar* V.iii., as Bernard Beckerman pointed out,[3] it takes only two lines of speech for a descent from the balcony to the stage, and two and a half for an ascent. In *Richard II* III.iii., King Richard is given only two lines for his symbolic descent from the walls of Flint Castle to the 'base court'. There must have been a backstage ladder or staircase conveniently adjacent between the two tiring-house levels, since two lines of verse would normally take barely five seconds to deliver.

4. *The stage hangings*

In Francis Beaumont's *The Knight of the Burning Pestle*, staged at the indoor Blackfriars playhouse by its boy company in 1607, two boys pretending to be a comic citizen and his wife join the gentry sitting on stools on the stage to watch the performance. During one of the Interacts, while a boy fills the pause by dancing to music from the balcony music room, the Citizen and his wife discuss what they can see around them. The stage hangings catch their eye, and they try to work out what scenes are depicted on the tapestry, whether it is 'the Confutation of St. Paul', or 'Rafe and Lucrece'. Wall hangings, woven in Flanders or Arras, or, as a cheaper alternative, cloth painted to look like tapestry-work, were a standard fitting in the great houses of Tudor times. (*See* the discussions pp. 136–7 and 152–4 *above*.) They could conceal draughty doors or mouldy wall-plastering. They helped to keep heat in, and dampened the gloom and the echoes that emanated from bare walls. They were hung in front of alcoves, or niches where funeral statuary might be kept. Many monuments from the time show servants or deities holding back the hangings to display or 'discover' the object of reverence placed behind them. The players used their hangings at the central opening to make similar 'discoveries' on stage. Chettle's *Hoffman*, written for the Globe's neighbour theatre with a similar stage design, the Fortune, includes a whole series of 'discoveries', all of monuments or bodies, sleeping or dead.

The cloth of arras or painted cloth behind which Polonius and Claudius concealed themselves to eavesdrop on Hamlet, and through which in a later scene Hamlet thrust his sword to kill the spying Polonius, is only one of a multitude of uses that Shakespeare found for the stage hangings at the Globe. The same cloth would have been held open by two stage hands for the formal entry of the king in the play's second scene, and was used subsequently when the Players entered to perform their 'Mousetrap' for the watching Court. It was the place for the caskets in *The Merchant of Venice*, and where Hermione's statue stood to be 'discovered' in *The Winter's Tale*. It was the entrance to Prospero's 'cell' in *The Tempest*, where opening the hangings reveals Miranda and Ferdinand playing at nothing more erotic than chess.

5. *The stage posts*

The posts could be used as forest trees, for Orlando's verses in *As You Like It*, for the post which Launce's dog Crab gets tied to, as the orchard where Romeo coming to Juliet's balcony and Benedick in *Much Ado* hide, and as the midnight forest in *A Midsummer Night's Dream*. Modern audiences lose the in-joke in the 1599 play, *As You Like It*, where Orlando echoes an earlier hero called Orlando when he pins his love-verses on the stage posts. That incident parodies a scene in Robert Greene's *Orlando Furioso* in which the maddened hero does just that.[4] Shakespeare may have been mocking Greene, who attacked Shakespeare in 1592 as the player who thought himself the only Shake-scene in the country. The play may have been paying off some old grievances. It also twice quotes Marlowe, who was attacked in Greene's booklet along with Shakespeare, much more reverentially than the Greene echo.

The stage posts figured in the language and images used in the plays more strongly than we now recognise. Julius Caesar's power over the conspirators invites a gesture to the two posts when we are told that he 'doth bestride the narrow world/Like a colossus, and we petty men/Walk under his huge legs'. From that eloquent gesture we might move downwards to the more practical uses, as indicated by Will Kemp's claim that cutpurses when identified at the Globe would be 'tied to a post on our stage, for all people to wonder at.' In general they worked admirably as a place for concealment from other characters on stage while in full view of the surrounding audience. The two sets of eavesdroppings in the orchard in *Much Ado About Nothing*, spying on Malvolio in *Twelfth Night*, and the ambush in *The Two Gentlemen of Verona*, all require characters to hide visibly behind the stage posts.

6. *Reiterated signifiers*

Staging plays at the Globe entailed extensive use of symbolism, which our habit of focusing on the words on the page has tended to obscure. Use of the two opposed entry doors and the central opening was only one of a multitude of ways in which features of the stage were employed to signify different things. The most obvious was the stage platform itself as the earth on which a play's normal events take place, with the heavens literally overhead, and hell down the trapdoor underneath the stage. Marlowe sent two of his heroes, Faustus and Barabas the Jew of Malta, down the trap to symbolic perdition at the end of their stories. In the original staging of *Hamlet* the trap which served as Ophelia's grave at the beginning of Act V had already supplied one highly relevant function. It was the ghost's point of entry for its appearances out of its purgatorial fires in Act I. The point the gravedigger considers, that Ophelia's suicide should make her death 'doubtful' as a matter for Christian burial, and the priest's reluctance to do more than offer the most truncated rites, fits her delivery into hell. It also prompts Hamlet, when he finds out whose grave it is, to repeat the ghost's action by stepping forward to proclaim 'This is I, *Hamlet* the Dane' to the uncomprehending courtiers.

In the next scene, Osric shows his misreading of Hamlet's pose by refusing to put his hat on when he is talking to the prince. Courtiers always held their hats in their hands when talking to their king. Speaking to lesser figures like Hamlet, they should put them back on after the initial greeting. Hamlet's unsuccessful attempt to get Osric to put his hat back on was for Elizabethans much more than just a response to a piece of excessively mannered politeness. Osric was flouting custom by remaining bare-headed because he assumed that Hamlet was mad and thought himself to be his father the king. Hamlet was rightly irritated by the breach of decorum. To Elizabethans hats gave potent service as what are now called 'paralinguistic signifiers'.

The love-beds which become deathbeds in both *Romeo and Juliet* and *Othello* have been familiar symbols for centuries. Less well noted is the throne in *Richard II*. In the opening scene, Richard sits in it to pass judgement on two of his subjects over their quarrel. In the final scene Bullingbrook sits on the same throne. In the middle of the play, when Bullingbrook tries to exercise the same judicial function as Richard, to the same throwing-down of gauntlets in challenge, he cannot occupy the judicial seat. He has to stand amongst the quarrelling peers, because he is not yet king. The throne stands empty, brooding over the quarrels as a visible emblem of the power vacuum, while Richard and Bullingbrook hold the crown between them in a ridiculous tug-of-war. Crowns themselves, a precisely signifying form of royal headgear, become emblems of lost authority, especially in *King Lear*. Lear starts the play crowned, in the presence of two sons-in-law wearing ducal coronets, with a third coronet ready for whoever marries his third daughter. For his second appearance he wears a hunting hat, emblem of the carefree life he now expects to be able to lead. By the middle act of the play, however, he is out in the storm bareheaded, stripped of everything by his two elder daughters. The crown of wildflowers he wears in his madness has its own parodic value as a mark of his loss of role and dignity. The only token of surviving authority in the final scene is Albany's ducal coronet, which he tries to surrender to Edgar. Clothing, especially headgear, was used to mark status, and it changed with changes in status or mind. It was not only Hamlet's funeral black or Malvolio's amorous yellow stockings that put out signals to the Elizabethan audiences.

Other symbolic properties were used for more routine significations. When servants or stage hands came on carrying flaming torches or rushlights, it meant a night scene. Similarly a character entering in a nightgown and nightcap was just roused out of bed. Characters entering in riding boots and cloaks had just completed a journey. A stage direction in a Massinger play, *The Guardian*, written in the 1630s for the Blackfriars has '*a noyse within, as the fall of a Horse*,' followed by the entry of a character in a muddied cloak, who shouts 'Hell take the stumbling Jade.' A boy playing a female character in a wig with unbound hair floating free was mad. These are only the most easily recognisable features of the uses of early costume and properties. The work of identifying the visual elements in staging that carried significances that we have forgotten is a major task for modern actors and scholars.

7. *Girls for boys for girls*

Having a boy play a girl who then has to cross-dress as a boy, who then pretends to be a boy playing a girl, is one of the more delicate pleasures of *As You Like It*. That play took the practice of girls dressing as boy pages, long familiar in Tudor literature and on its stages, to its jokey extreme. Since all girls' parts were played by boys in the original productions, it had an extra dimension for Elizabethans that the restoration in 1661 of women to play the girls' parts has lost for us. Shakespeare used the trick of doubly cross-dressing the boys to play girls playing boys in his comedies from *The Two Gentlemen of Verona*, via *As You Like It* and *Twelfth Night*, to *Cymbeline*. The boy who played Rosalind playing Ganymede playing Rosalind took the game one step further.

Much has been made both of the erotic sexual politics of this cross-dressing, and of the broader sexual policies which forbade women to perform on public stages through this period in England and other northern countries, while it was possible in Italy, Spain, and France. These, however, are dimensions that will not concern the Globe company directly. The artificiality of using boys to play the women's parts creates some odd problems in modern society, none of them particularly relevant to the work of negotiating between the early habits of mind and the modern. The boys apprenticed to the adult players were generally aged between nine and fifteen in Tudor times. They lost their value for women's parts when their voices broke. Quite apart from the lack of boys who have undergone the years of training that the Tudor boys had, modern employment laws and the need to give modern children a standard education make this aspect of the original staging impossible to replicate. We have to accept the relatively small loss of the cross-dressing games by using women to play the women's parts. We can live with the loss of the other sexual politics.

8. *Descents*

Shakespeare did not use the descent machinery which allowed small gods to be lowered sitting on a throne hung by ropes from the heavens in any of his plays until his last. Few gods ever appeared in his plays, even in dreams, and even then mostly on foot and on stage. Oberon and Titania with their fairies in *A Midsummer Night's Dream*, and Hymen at the end of *As You like It* walked onstage from the *frons*.[5] Only Jupiter, mounted on his eagle, made a descent from the heavens to speak in Posthumus's dream in *Cymbeline*. Prospero's staging of his masque for Ferdinand and Miranda in *The Tempest*, an equally dream-like feat of magic, called for Juno to make a slow descent.

Other writers were much more lavish in their use of this heavenly property. The boy companies' writers in particular liked to use it. Their plays made more use of gods than did Shakespeare's company, but they also had the advantage of a smaller weight on the 'throne'. So far as we can tell, almost all the 'descents' were made by boys. Jupiter on his eagle throwing fireworks as thunderbolts may have been almost the only exception. Juno would certainly have been played by a boy. Shakespeare seems to have avoided using descents at least partly out of his own reluctance to exploit the Globe for static 'spectacles'. While his Juno descends the other boys speak almost thirty lines of verse.

Shakespeare made Hamlet scorn spectacles in his advice to the Players, along with clowns who speak more than is set down for them and Polonius's taste for jigs and tales of bawdry. *Hamlet* may in fact have marked a turning-point in Shakespeare's attitude to his audiences. Up to then he had called them 'auditors', people who came to a play to listen to the words. In the advice to the Players and in every reference in the later plays he called them 'spectators', a word that his friend Ben Jonson used contemptuously of people who could learn only through their eyes, not their ears.[6] Other writers were less conservative in this aspect of staging than Shakespeare, though how far the players went in trying to enact what they demanded in their scripts we cannot be sure.

9. *Rushes on stage*

The evidence from the plays about what covered the boards of the stage floor is important, but regrettably contradictory. Bare boards make a different sound from rush or matting-covered surfaces, and knowing what the players were used to makes a difference to several aspects of staging. In his famous 'degree' speech in Act I Scene iii of *Troilus and Cressida*, Ulysses speaks scornfully of the player who likes to make the echoes of his stamping resound through the galleries: 'the strutting Player, whose conceit/Lies in his Ham-string, and doth think it rich/To heare the woodden Dialogue and sound/'Twixt his stretcht footing, and the Scaffolage.' Similar references by other writers to a 'stalking-stamping Player'[7] argue that the boards were bare. But the Tudors routinely strewed rushes over their floors, and other evidence suggests that matting and green rushes might have covered the Globe's stage. Unfortunately, it is not really possible to claim that statements such as Bullingbrook's in *Richard II* III.iii. that he will walk on 'the Grassie Carpet of this plaine', or the references in *The Tempest*'s masque to 'this short gras'd Greene' and 'this green-Land' actually demand green rushes on the stage, since the references might equally mean that the stage floor really was green or that you had to be told that it was because it wasn't.

Some other references, however, are more positive. Dekker's fashion-conscious gull is told that when visiting a playhouse one of his tricks might be to take up a rush and tickle the ear of the person in front of him.[8] For that, rushes had to be routinely available on stage. In George Chapman's *The Gentleman Usher* the stage is prepared for a masque to be given for the king and his courtiers. In his preparations, the fussy chamberlain insists that the floor be covered with a carpet for the king, and everywhere else rushes be set down 'in threaves', or bundles.

> lay me 'em thus,
> In fine smooth threaves, look you, sir, thus in threaves.
> Perhaps some tender lady will squat here,
> And if some standing rush should chance to prick her,
> She'd squeak and spoil the songs that must be sung.

This invites some comic by-play. Unfortunately, though, it leaves unclear whether rushes were laid on the stage routinely for every play, or whether they were strewn only for special occasions, when some dialogue to cover the strewing would be expected. Sir Henry Wotton's famous letter about the burning of the Globe in 1613 says that the stage was matted. (*See* p. 189 *below*.) That would have made the regular use of rushes rather less necessary.

10. *Piece out our imperfections*

Probably the greatest single difference between the mindsets of the audiences Shakespeare wrote for and those of today is realism. Tudor playgoers were much more aware than we are of the dangers that the illusion of reality as conveyed by stage realism posed to susceptible minds. English pulpits in the Reformation insisted that any attempt to deceive through illusion was devilish. William Perkins, a contemporary of Shakespeare and the sharpest of the intellectual reasoners of the late Elizabethan church, put the case against any form of deception: 'An illusion is the work of Satan, whereby he deludeth or deceiveth man. And it is two-fold: either of the outward senses, or of the minde.'[9] All play-acting was compre-hended in Perkins's insistence that the work or rather 'play' of illusion is Satanic. Eliza-bethans were trained to be more sceptical of realism than we are. This is probably the greatest of the shifts in audience expectation that the Globe will have to work on.

Roofed theatres equipped with electric light, the many uses of which can enhance any illusion, have done more even than the supply of comfortable seating to turn modern audi-ences towards passive acceptance of stage realism. To be told at the beginning of *Hamlet* at the Globe, old or new, that it is past midnight and bitter cold calls for a distinctly active intervention from the audience's imagination. Even being told just by words or the sight of torches that it was not supposed to be daytime any longer but night requires something more than the modern expectation of suspending disbelief. For long periods of dream-time in night scenes, like in the central three Acts of *A Midsummer Night's Dream*, the audience has to turn into a version of what Theseus derides as the lunatic, the lover and the poet. Relearning more energetic habits, taking a more positive role in the act of playgoing, is a prerequisite for audiences at the new Globe. It will mean not sitting passively but sharing the play in performance with the actors. From such experiences we hope will grow a new sense of what Shakespeare wanted from his performances.[10]

Notes to Chapter Nine

1   All quotations are taken from the first Folio or the first Quarto printing of each play.

2   Stage hands, used for transporting properties like the chair of state on its dais, and to hold open the hangings for entrances, as well as sword-carrying in battle scenes, normally wore a blue livery. Their presence in court scenes ready to run their master's errands on demand would, in a society thoroughly accustomed to the presence of silent house-servants, have been an easily assimilated feature of the staging.

3   *Shakespeare at the Globe 1599–1609*, New York, 1962, p. 230.

4   Shakespeare's relations with Greene, who attacked him as an 'upstart crow' in a pamphlet written shortly before he died in 1592, make the joke plausible. *As You Like It* also has two explicit references to Marlowe, whom Greene attacked in the same pamphlet.

5   This is really only an inference, although since Hymen enters accompanied by Rosalind and Celia it would have been almost impossible for the three of them to share a descent. *A Midsummer Night's Dream* was written to be staged at the Theatre, before the Globe was dreamed of, but Shakespeare's same self-imposed statute of limitation on the use of extravagant staging facilities seems to have prevailed then too.

6   *See* Jonson's Prologue to *The Staple of News*, 1626, and Gurr, *Playgoing in Shakespeare's London*, second ed., Cambridge, 1996, pp. 86–98.

7   *The Puritan*, 1607, III.iv. A boy company play, it reflects the youths' rejection of one of the more exuberant styles of playing by adult players.

8   *The Gull's Hornbook*, 1610, Chapter 6.

9   Quoted by Kurt Tetzeli von Rosador, *Yearbook of English Studies* 23, 1993, p. 32.

10 For a discussion of the Prologue Season, *see* Gurr, 'The First Plays at the New Globe', *Theatre Notebook*, LI (1997) 4–7.

～ IO ～

PLAYING THE GLOBE
ARTISTIC POLICY AND PRACTICE

Mark Rylance

SAM WANAMAKER used to emphasise to me the wide spectrum of people interested in Shakespeare whom he was able to involve in the Globe project. I now think how wise it was of him, as a matter of policy, not to appoint just one particular person from one particular field of Shakespearean work to run things. Instead, he brought together the Artistic Directorate, a group who would give him guidance and feedback on artistic matters.

I was invited to join the Artistic Directorate in 1991, when Sam and I met to talk about the group called Phoebus Cart and our production of *The Tempest*, a project which my wife and I had mortgaged our flat to complete. Sam said we could use the Globe site, which was dormant at the time, a big, wet, hole in the ground, so long as it cost him nothing. Curiously, the *Tempest* project was, like the Globe, an attempt to draw a community into a very old structure, in this case the Rollright Stone Circle in Warwickshire. For our London performances, we didn't want an indoor space, but an outdoor circular space of similar dimensions to those of the Stone Circle. Here was the site of such a space, with the same near-one-hundred-foot dimensions and north-eastern orientation. Sam and I shared a similar desire to explore old structures for new theatre, but I did not then foresee that I would be invited to join the Artistic Directorate or subsequently be chosen as Artistic Director. When Sam died we lost the leadership of a man who guided the Globe from many different perspectives, but for the Artistic Directorate especially from the perspective of an actor.

Though born in England, I was brought up about a hundred miles north of Chicago, where Sam lived, and shared for this reason perhaps some of his interests and convictions. I returned to England in 1978 to train as a theatre actor. After my first season with the RSC in 1984 I found myself eager to explore other ways of communicating Shakespeare, and thought a good place to start was with the fundamental company structure of theatre. Seven actors came together to form the parent company of Phoebus Cart, called the London Theatre of Imagination, the aim of which was to explore working without a director. We produced *Othello* on tour, and looking for a space in London found the Bear Gardens theatre, part of what became the International Shakespeare Globe Centre. That was my first introduction to the Globe site, and the first time I met Sam, though only briefly.

I realise now that a democratically-run theatre company of seven profit-sharing actors was unknowingly close to Burbage's original Globe company. We were looking for different management structures, and different ways of creative working between actors, because in the early eighties there was a great lack of actors' artistic involvement in productions. We hoped that shared responsibility for the whole production would inspire more committed involvement from actors. Not all actors desire, or flourish with, greater responsibility. But the role modern directors were shouldering seemed unfairly heavy. Too often they were expected to be fathers, teachers, therapists, patrons, gurus, and many actors had become passive or cynical. The old channels of communication and mutual inspiration between actors had broken down. Work on scenes was too often done only by the director, who frequently had to leave, for financial reasons, as soon as the show opened. One would find oneself acting to the director's notes rather than through sharing with the other actors and the audience. Good Shakespeare productions, I have always found, grow enormously once they are playing. The greatest discoveries are made, if room is left for inspiration, between the actors and the audience, not in the rehearsal room.

In the eighties, these discoveries did not always come about, due to the working relationships and practices that had developed. Today, one can see many actors leading companies. Perhaps the most notable of these are Kenneth Branagh, who formed the Renaissance Company in 1985, also after acting with the RSC, and Barrie Rutter who founded Northern Broadsides. In the London Theatre of Imagination we asked ourselves whether our new ways of working had made any substantial difference to our productions. In working with the Globe, I am as interested in exploring the structure and working practices of the original Globe company as I am in exploring the theatre space itself.

Many believe that Shakespeare's scripts grew from the experience of playing in the Globe, and the other Elizabethan theatre-spaces, responding to both the actors' and audiences' reactions. How the plays were directed, if they were directed, is not known. But every circle needs a centre, even if that centre is still – which is indeed the most difficult kind of director to be. At its best, my experience of working without directors has shown me that it is possible for different members of a company to lead at different times, and in different situations. Some have given good direction in working on scenes, some have been very patient and fair when there have been personal differences, and some have been very good with money and practical matters. No doubt the situation was similar at the first Globe. One wonders who was the centre of the circle in that company. Burbage perhaps, or Shakespeare. Hamlet's instructions to the players suggest they were not altogether unused to taking direction from outside their ranks, a situation that may not have been all that uncommon, as patrons sought to influence the players to express, for instance, reformation ideas. Yet Hamlet's instructions concern not only what to act but how, suggesting the actors also had experience of direction from fellow players.

This does not mean that I do not wish to work with directors at the Globe. My experience of working *without* directors, and more recently of directing from the leading actor's position, has mightily confirmed my understanding of the need for directors and the difficulty of that role. We do not however want tyrants. Fortunately in the theatre climate of the nineties it feels as if there has been a swing in the conception of the director's role. Many more directors are now interested in freedom of communication between actors and audience. For a director to control this communication at the Globe will be, in any case, impossible. There is minimal scenery, no lights, and so many random variables – the weather, planes flying over, and most importantly the direct and much more equal interplay between audience and actors – all of which demand constant adjustment from the actor outside the director's control.

At the Globe, it is the audience who have been recognised and empowered in their creative role as imaginers of the drama. They have been, you might say, allowed into the Bullring. I recently met an Irish story-teller who said that only in story-telling events had he previously experienced the kind of narrative co-creation he had witnessed during the 1996 Prologue season at the Globe. Never before in a theatre. From my early experience in working on *The Two Gentlemen of Verona*, (fig. 64) and from talking to the company of *Damon and Pythias* and to Northern Broadsides (who performed *A Midsummer Night's Dream*), I am certain that the relationship between actor and audience at the Globe is genuinely unique and awakening. The same is true of the relationship between audience and audience. At a football match some time ago a perfect stranger turned to me during play and gave me his full opinion of the quality of the game and what should be done about it. I experienced the same easy communication between strangers while watching *A Midsummer Night's Dream* at the Globe. I would make no claims yet for the quality of the communication, but the possibilities are refreshing, and suggest that it may be possible at the Globe to celebrate in a particular way the simple social pleasures of going to live theatre.

When I played Hamlet for the Royal Shakespeare Company in the early nineties I was inspired by the acting work of Mike Alfreds and the Shared Experience company. Drawing in a discriminating way on the scholars' Satan, Stanislavsky, Mike's work was always directed at enhancing the quality of *play* between the actors and audience. He tried to achieve a harnessing of intentions and desires as against presenting the *idea* of a character, a process which at its best creates very lively and flexible play, involving and responding to an audience. The contrast between presentation and play, between showing something and playing it, is another feature that attracts me to experimental work at the Globe. It will be very difficult to 'present' a play there, to present a 'solution' to a play. An audience responds to the playing. The idea of the word 'playing', and a space that demands play, could be very beneficial to the theatre profession. Cinema and television, which pay many actors their livelihood, are in essence mediums of 'presentation'. They cannot respond to their audiences. To create a space like the Globe, where playing is all, will I hope benefit and refresh theatre performance generally.

When I first acted I would prepare a soliloquy so that I could *present* it, almost like an internal gymnastic display. Later I found that this kind of formal preparation could easily destroy the subtle drama of discovering together with an audience the mental and emotional life of the character. With discovery, words are found and heard again as if for the first time. Hamlet offers a good instance. Even a speech as well known as 'To be or not to be …' can be heard afresh if the actor does not present it as something prepared off-stage, but on the contrary comes on with a need, and discovers with the audience the words for his unspeakable situation. If, that is to say, he almost literally 'cooks' it in front of the audience. The Globe, a big, open cauldron of a theatre, is ideal for this kind of 'cooking'.

Hamlet's advice to the players is one of the strongest pieces of evidence we have as to the nature of acting at the Globe, especially in its insistence on mirroring nature. It is Shakespeare's infinite observance of human nature that shakes us so. Yet perhaps we forget that while the presented dumb show has no effect on the guilty King, *words* make him stand and cry for light. Seeing and hearing the truth seem to produce different effects for Shakespeare. The eye has usually been associated with the mind, and the ear with the heart.

Shakespeare's Globe, with its attachment to the word, may therefore place more emphasis on emotional experience than intellectual. The Ghost in *Hamlet* has little effect on the men who merely *see* him, but when Hamlet *hears* his words, as he later confesses, it drives him mad. 'This distracted Globe' he names his mind, an allusion that will have added meaning for an audience hearing him in the galleries of the Globe itself. For the actor, it may suggest that where in film he might *turn in* to speak to himself, in the Globe he might *turn out* to speak to himself. 'This wide and universal theatre presents more woeful pageants/Than the scene wherein we play in', says the exiled Duke in *As You Like It*. The scene wherein we play will have particular and moving reference for actors and audiences in the rebuilt Globe.

'Sit still my soul, foul deeds will rise/Though all the earth o'erwhelm them to men's eyes', I used to say as Hamlet to the audience, giving them a clear instruction on their role as my 'soul' in the drama ahead. Involving the audience emotionally as one's soul, one's conscience, is a skill I was taught at the Royal Shakespeare Company, but the space at the Globe facilitates this kind of relationship enormously. The audience can see that I am looking directly at them, speaking with them, inciting them to guide me in the drama.

I have been told that in Greek temples all initiates had to pass between pillars of Hercules, representing the polarised qualities of Mars and Venus, judgement and love (or desire, as Adonis puts it). In Virgil, the pillars of Hercules stand at the entrance to the Mysteries. Acting between the pillars on the Globe stage, with its sign of Hercules, it is as if one is playing a drama which draws an audience towards the mysterious, veiled *frons scenae*, and behind that Prospero's cell perhaps, or Rosalind's forest glade. 'So, bring us to our palace, where we'll show/What's yet behind that's meet you all should know', as the Duke says to close *Measure for Measure*. *Much Ado About Nothing* is set in Messina, a location that may serve to draw attention to the Straits of Messina, another of the entrances to Virgil's Mysteries, penetrated only by the deathly experience of passing between Scylla, the brain-devouring Harpy on the cliff, and the monstrous whirlpool, Charybdis. It could be that the architecture of Shakespeare's Globe has an intimate connection with the themes of his plays. For instance, the struggle between learning and loving, so brilliantly described in *Love's Labour's Lost*, may at the Globe set actors and audiences playing like Ulysses as he sails between these potent forces of human nature.

The theatre is a place where ideas are floated on emotional energy. The skill of generating emotional energy without it imploding or exploding is the actor's alchemy. Even with a generally light-hearted play such as *The Two Gentlemen of Verona*, I felt the round space of the Globe very conducive to the generation of emotional energy (plate 30). Audibility proved not to be a question of volume or even diction, but the movement in the speech. The lack of intervals and time-consuming scenery changes evoked respect for the rhythms of the drama.

We know from Alberti and Vitruvius writing about the Roman amphitheatres, as well as our own experience from the reconstructed Globe, that round or polygonal theatres were designed in this way for their acoustic qualities. At the same time, with minimal or no settings, as at the Globe, the presence of the actor's physical being, how he is seen, remains very important. The De Witt sketch of the Swan gives a clear impression of the actors' physical presence on and around a bench. Indeed, it might be said that the actors' expressive gestures are the real focus of a drawing so often used only to given controversial information about the structures of a theatre interior.

In *The Two Gentlemen of Verona*, the director, Jack Shepherd, wanted to create different locations in the audience's imagination. Given that we were using a minimal number of stage properties, he tried to evoke the locations by drawing on the devices used by the actors to bring the situation to life. There were problems here, sometimes, for the actors. In one scene, which we imagined as being set at cafe tables on an Italian piazza, I became concerned that our physical realisation of the scene was excluding the audience. I started therefore to move around the tables in order to create more visual inroads for the audience. Jack pointed out that my movements were motivated by concern for the audience and not by the reality of the scene or the needs of my character. It is helpful to respond to the audience, as I explained above, in creating a character, or developing a speech, but a commitment to the reality of the scene has to take precedence over any attempt to provide the audience with a pleasing or significant visual rendering of location.

Live theatre is always a mixture of either going out to an audience, or drawing them in, and ideally the actor needs flexibility to adjust to an audience's imaginative temperament. At the Globe, one's choices may be more limited than in more recent spaces because of the added narrative responsibility borne by the body. The Japanese are masters of this kind of physical scene-setting, creating whole worlds by behaving as if in a wood or a cell or a palace. For all the Elizabethan love and understanding of the power in words, it is evident from the records of costume expenses alone how important to the players of Shakespeare's day the visual signals and visual delights of theatre were.

Costuming in the reconstructed Globe presents an interesting paradox. On the one hand it is obvious that Elizabethan actors could not have dressed themselves in the modern clothes of today. On the other hand it is equally true that they usually dressed in the clothes worn by members of their audiences. One of the intentions I intuit in Shakespeare's work is that he wanted to ground historical narratives and archetypal stories in contemporary human nature – Cleopatra becomes a recognisable woman – and to employ the mundane details of life within mythical structures. In both of these modes he was commenting directly on present day issues from behind the mask of history and myth. Does the use of Elizabethan costume aid Shakespeare's intentions today? It is a question every production has to ask itself. The drawing of *Titus Andronicus* showing a cast partly dressed in historical Roman clothing and partly in Elizabethan clothing suggests the presence of layers of reality within the world of a play.

Apart from period costume running the risk of distancing modern audiences in a way that cannot have been intended, if even imagined, by Shakespeare, my fundamental problem with such costume is that it can become so obviously costume rather than clothing. When you wear it as an actor it may not feel like clothes. This can have a subliminal effect, and the actor may then not feel the need to be real either. The King's Men, I believe, employed on the stage what they considered to be real clothing. We shall certainly, each season, play some productions in Elizabethan or Jacobean costume, but we shall make it, by hand where possible, as *clothing*, out of materials in use at the time. The rigour of the oak, lime plaster and thatch used in the reconstructed Globe demands this kind of authenticity. Authentic clothing of this kind, rather than theatrical costuming, will encourage the true and detailed playing of human nature that Hamlet demands, and that report seems to suggest vitalised the original Globe.

FIG. 64 Mark Rylance and Stephanie Roth as Proteus and Julia in the Prologue Season production of *The Two Gentlmen of Verona*

For me, *The Tempest* stands at the beginning of the First Folio like an index and introduction to all of Shakespeare's work. It is a drama which draws heavily on Virgil and on the Hermetic thinking that had thrived in Florence when Ficino worked on the ancient texts of Plato and Plotinus, and which subsequently exercised an influence on a great deal of writing in Elizabeth's England. The play describes the initiation of the characters through imaginary experience. The remorse necessary to bring about forgiveness is generated in the powerful. The young lover develops visionary wisdom. The sensual servants learn humility. The murderous fish-man Caliban 'will be wise hereafter,/And seek for grace'. The spirit, Ariel, is released into nature. The Magus gives up his control. I find myself asking whether this initiation through the imagination is what Shakespeare thought of his plays as effecting in the Globe. Or was he inspired by money and the prospect of fame? He doesn't seem to give money and fame much credence in his plays.

The alchemy-like transformation of lead into gold, as in Romeo's character, and the cabalistic tree of life which, it may be argued, forms the spine of plays such as *The Two Gentlemen of Verona* and *Much Ado About Nothing*, were all masks and games of transformation in society and within ourselves. Our world view today forms a very different picture from the Elizabethan. Many now scorn any suggestion of the influence of the heavens on human activity. Modern psychology has tried, with no more than limited success, to interpret and cure the soul. As a classical actor, I naturally have enormous faith in classical drama as an enriching and beneficial force in the individual and society.

I am excited to see such a profound force of theatre revived in our day and age. Yet we must not forget that theatrical tools and theatrical form, no matter how authentic and wonderful, are not an end in themselves, and neither is the Globe. The historical architecture and practices of Shakespeare's original theatre, which we are striving to revive, are tools towards an end, tools of communication. As an actor it is not enough to know how a character speaks. To be authentic one must also know *why*. Is the desire at any particular moment to stir, soothe, illumine, ridicule? Of course *how* and *why* are intrinsically linked in the hand of a great artist such as Shakespeare, and one can illuminate the other. This is the heart of our argument for the Globe. Yet in concentrating on how they did it, we must not forget why.

The architecture of the Globe has much to teach us about *how* Shakespeare's plays spoke to their audiences, and the research of the education and exhibition teams on London culture and society will help to guide us as to *why*. But all the discoveries about authentic playing practices, at the Globe and the Inigo Jones theatres, however revealing and enabling, will really only bear fruit when they discover not means alone but *meaning*. My firm belief is that Shakespeare intended that meaning to be found in the imaginary space between audience and actor, hence the absolute necessity to explore the architecture that Shakespeare chose to define that space. I am certain that the space he chose, especially one with a name like the Globe, will help to reveal much meaning through the authentic relationship between plays and audiences.

As the first Artistic Director of Shakespeare's Globe, I hope we can provide theatrical experiences that reflect and enrich human nature in its many physical, psychological, spiritual and divine forms. The wide spectrum of the Elizabethan world picture may have assisted Shakespeare in creating drama that has proved universal in application, while remaining firmly rooted in Nature. The geometric forms of the Globe's architecture, and the emblematic language of its decorative schemes, have much to reveal about these matters. More generally, I hope we shall empower people, especially young people, by providing them with a language for the unspoken, stories that enrich and encourage change in our lives, and truthful experience of the effects of justice and mercy in human situations.

My own belief is that drama can initiate us into a deeper awareness and more fruitful use of our desire, thought and action. Dr John Dee, the great scholar who taught Lord Leicester, the first patron of a professional playing company in Elizabethan England, described the worlds of desire, thought and action by employing a sun or circle, a moon or triangle, and a cross or square: his famous *Monas Hieroglyphica*. The Globe, this roughly circular theatre, with its roughly square stage, two thirds revealed and one third hidden behind the *frons scenae*, and its huge triangular gable supported on the pillars of Hercules, may help us to tap into the meaning of Shakespeare in new and powerful ways. This reconstructed stage and auditorium may demonstrate, through lively representation, that loving desires can lead to illumined thoughts, and that the marriage of love and understanding within our psyche creates actions that are beneficial to life. This marriage of love and understanding I would call *intuition*, the development of which is, for me, the goal and fruit of all Shakespearean work, academic and theatrical.

PLATE 28 Exterior of the Globe, 1996.

PLATE 29 Exterior from the Thames, 1996.

PLATE 30 *The Two Gentlemen of Verona* in performance.

PLATE 31 *The Two Gentlemen of Verona,* with Mark Rylance as Proteus, Anastasia Hille as Sylvia.

PART FOUR

DOCUMENTS OF THE ELIZABETHAN PLAYHOUSE

THESE DOCUMENTS have been selected to represent those surviving accounts, from legal contracts to informal letters, that provide the historian and the builder with some of the information on which he or she can draw in attempting to reconstruct Shakespeare's Globe. The written accounts gathered here must be supplemented by visual evidence (such as the comprehensive collection drawn together in R.A. Foakes, *Illustrations of the English Stage, 1580–1642*, London, 1985 or in the selection reproduced in this book) and by evidence derived from hints in the surviving play-texts. Much can be learned also, as chapters in the present book show, from studying building types of the period, and contemporary styles of decoration. But the documents, even if they are frequently more tantalising than helpful, nevertheless give the reader a keener sense of the circumstances within which the builders of the Globe must have worked, economic, practical, artistic and social. For this reason, I have tried to give the documents in as complete a form as possible, and even when they are offered in extract, have tried to retain as far as practicable their original spelling and expression.

The documents are grouped under four headings, the last of which, the list of plays thought to have been designed for original performance at the Globe, scarcely qualifies as a document, but may be found informative in relation to the documents in the other groups. The categories of Legal Contracts, Theatre Business and Visitors' Accounts refer directly to the Globe only in a minority of cases, and are chosen for the light they cast by implication. At the same time, it is one of the themes of this book that theatres and their personnel differ from each other as much in the seventeenth century as they do now, and it must not be assumed that what is true for the Rose or the Swan is true also for the Globe. The Fortune contract, for example, is at pains to distinguish the new playhouse in certain respects from the Globe, even while in other respects it seeks to mimic it. Like all the other evidence, therefore, the documents must be used with discrimination, and generalisation from what has fortuitously survived has to be resisted.

R.M.

A. LEGAL CONTRACTS

I

THE ROSE PLAYHOUSE AGREEMENT

THE AGREEMENT between Philip Henslowe the theatrical impressario and John Cholmley 'cittizen and grocer' deals with the financial arrangements that were to obtain in the erection of the Rose playhouse. Henslowe had acquired the lease of the Rose site in March 1584 (modern dating 1585), the deed is dated 10 January 1586 (1587 in modern dating), and the playhouse, the first on the South side of the river Thames, was open by the autumn of that year. The deed does not detail occupancy of the playhouse by a particular company or companies of players, nor does it give the arrangements for splitting the take between owners and players. It does however afford some glimpses into the business side of playhouse ownership, with Cholmley's victualling business clearly important as a peripheral but financially significant part of the enterprise (twentieth century theatres still have to take serious account of their catering contracts). The stucture of the playhouse is not discussed, so that the document offers little assistance to the builder of a reconstructed Globe, but it is salutary for the study of the Globe as a business to note the responsibilities Henslowe carried in having to 'repaire and amende all the brigges [bridges] and wharffes belonginge to the saide parcell of grounde'. The Burbages had similar responsibilities at the Globe. A nice touch provides, even in a formal document of this nature, for Henslowe and Cholmley 'to suffer theire frendes to go in for nothing'.

The text printed here derives from Carol Rutter's transcription of the Henslowe documents (Carol Rutter, ed., *Documents of the Rose Playhouse*, The Revels Plays Companions Library, Manchester, 1984, pp. 37–39). Abbreviations in the original have been silently expanded.

This Indenture made the Tenthe daye of Januarye Anno domini 1586 … Betwene Phillippe Hinshley cittizen and Dyer of London one thonne partye and John Cholmley cittizen and grocer of London one thother partye … for the great zeale and good will that is betwene them and tothentente that they maye better increase theire substance are entrid into partner shippe … in the … posessinge … of all that parcell of grownde or garden plotte contayninge in leng[t]he and bredthe sqare every waye ffoorescore and fourteene foote of assize little more or lesse As allso … of all the beniffytte somes of moneye proffitte and Advauntage of a playe howse now in framinge and shortly to be ereckted and sett vppe vpone the same grounde or garden plotte from the Daye of the Date of these presentes for and duringe and vntill the ende and terme of Eighte yeares And three monthes from thence nexte ensuinge … if the saide partyes doe so long Lyve Whereuppone yt is … agreed … That yt shall and maye be lawfull to and for the saide John cholmeley … To have … The moytie or one halfe of All suche some and somes of moneye gaynes profytt and comodytye which shall arysse growe be colectted gathered or become due for the saide parcell of grounde and playe howse when and after yt shalbe ereckted and sett vpe by reasonne of any playe or playes that shalbe showen or played there or otherwysse howsoever And … the saide Phillippe Hinshley … To have … The other moytie … And further That he the sayde John cholmley … shall … have … All that small tenemente or dwellinge howsse scittuate and standinge at the sowthe ende or syde of the saide parcell of grownde or garden plotte to keepe victualinge in or to putt to any other vse or vsses whatsoever … with the whole beniffyte … which he … shall … make … by the same howse neare adioyninge vnto a lane there comonly called mayden Lane now in the tenure of the saide John Cholmley or his assignes with free … passage … as well in by and throughe the Alleye there called Rosse Alleye leadinge from the Ryver of thames into the saide parcell of grownde As allso in and by and throughe the waye leadinge into the saide mayden Lane …

And likewyse That he the saide Phyllipe ... shall ... at his ... owne proper coste and chargis with as muche expedicion as may be ereckte fynishe and sett vpp or cause to be erected finished and sett vpe by John Grygges Carpenter his servantes or assignes the saide play house with all furniture therevnto belonginge ... All which premisses ... ar scittuate ... on the bancke syde in the paryshe of St Savoyes in Sovthworke in the County of Surrey In consideracion whereof the saide John Cholmley ... dothe covenant ... with the saide Phillippe Hinshley ... well and truly to paye ... for a yerlye anuyttie the some of Eighte hundreth and Sixteene Poundes of lawfull moneye of Englande in manner and forme followinge that is to saye One the feaste Daye of the Nativitie of St John Baptiste ... Twentie five Poundes and Tenne shillinges ... And so further after that from feaste daye to feaste Daye quarter to quarter and yeare vnto yeare ... vntill all the saide somme of Eighte hundreth and Sixteen Poundes be so truly contented and payde ... And yf yt shall happen the saide ... quarterly payments ... to be bhinde and vnpayde in parte or in all by the space of Twentye and one dayes ... after any feaste daye ... then and from thencforthe the saide copartner shippe ... shalbe voyde ... And that yt shall and maye be lawfull to and for the saide Phillipe Hinshley ... to renter And the saide John Cholmley ... vtterly to expell ... And further ... yf yt happen eyther of the saide partyes ... dye or decease this mortall lyffe before thende of the saide terme ... yt shall ... be lawfull ... for thexecutors ... to have ... the parte ... of him so deceasinge as copartner with the surviver ... And further the saide partyes doe ... graunte eyther with the other by these presentes that yt shall and may be lawfull to and for the saide Phillype Hinshleye and John Cholmley ... joyntly to appoynte and permitte suche personne and personnes players to vse exersyse & playe in the saide playe howse at theire wills and pleas-ures beinge for the profytt and Comodytie of them bothe And likewaye that the saide Phillype Hinshley and John Cholmley when any playe or playes shall be played or showen in the saide playe howse ... shall and wilbe there present them selves or appoynte theire sufficiente debutyes or assignes with them selves or otherwysse at their Choyse to Coleckte gather and receave all such some and somes of moneye of every personne & personnes resortinge and Cominge to the saide playe howse to vew see and heare any playe or enterlude at any tyme or tymes to be showed and playde duringe the saide terme of Eighte yeares and three monethes excepte yt please any of the said partyes to suffer theire frendes to go in for nothinge And that all suche some and somes ... so colected ... shall ymediately that nighte after accompte made by them selves theire debutyes or assignes be equally devided ... whereof the saide Phillipe Hinshleye ... to have the one halfe ... And ... John Cholmley ... to have the other ... And further the saide Phillipe Hinshleye ... shall ... paye ... All and all manner of quitte rentes and other rente Chargis due and payable to the Lorde or Lordes of the premisses ... And likewayes shall ... repaire and amende all the brigges and wharffes belonginge to the saide parcell of grounde ... at or before the xxixth daye of September nexte cominge ... And likewayes the saide John Cholmleye and Phillipe Hinshleye ... doe ... graunte eyther with the other ... That they ... shall ... after the saide xxixth daye of September nexte Cominge ... repare amende sustayne mantayne and vpholde the saide play howse brigges wharffes and all other the wayes and brygges now leadinge ... into onto and from the saide parcell of grownde ... when and as often as neede shall require ... And further the saide Phillipe Hinshley ... dothe ... graunte to and with the saide John Cholmleye ... That he ... will not permitte or suffer any personne or personnes other then the saide John Cholmley ... to vtter sell or putt to sale in or aboute the saide parcell of grownde ... any breade or drinke other then suche as shalbe solde to and for the vse and behoofe of the saide John Cholmley ... In Witness Whereof the saide partyes to theis presente Indentures Interchaungeably haue sett their Seales the day and yeres firste aboue Written

Sigillatur et deliberatur in
presentia mei

Cut: Jones Scriviener
Edward Pryce

(*On Verso*) By me John Cholmley grocer

II

THE FORTUNE CONTRACT

MUNIMENT number 22 among the Henslowe papers contains the contract between Peter Streete 'Cittizen and Carpenter of London' and Philip Henslowe and Edward Alleyn 'gentlemen' for the erection of the Fortune playhouse. The contract is dated 8 January 1599 (8 January 1600 in modern dating), and covers the detailed construction of the playhouse, requiring Streete to 'make, erect, sett upp and fully finishe' the building, with the exception of the paintwork and the provision of certain finishes. The dimensions stated for the frame and 'jutties' or jetties offer useful clues for the designer of the reconstructed Globe, though the square shape of the building and the evident wish to make advances on the Globe require caution in applying the details to the earlier playhouse. It is also disappointing that, when it comes to specifics of the staircases and the stage and tiring house, the contract is content to refer to 'a Plott thereof drawn' (an attached drawing now lost) or similarities with 'the late erected Plaiehowse On the Banck[side] in the saide parishe of St Saviors Called the Globe'. Evidently Henslowe intended a building in some respects even grander than the Burbages' theatre, since he provides for timbers 'lardger and bigger in assize Then the Scantlinges' of the Timber for the existing house. The building cost £440, and the first performances at the new theatre probably took place in November or December, 1600.

The transcription given here is based on that in R.A. Foakes and R.T. Rickert, eds., *Henslowe's Diary* (Cambridge, 1961) pp. 307–10. Abbreviations have been expanded and some spellings have been regularised for the sake of clarity, though even when this has been done an attempt has been made to preserve the characteristic spelling of the document.

This Indenture made the Eighte daie of Januarye 1599 And in the Twoe and ffortyth yeare of the Reigne of our sovereigne Ladie Elizabeth by the grace of God Queene of England ffraunce and Irelande defender of the ffaythe &c. Betwene Phillipp Henslowe and Edwarde Allen of the parishe of Ste Savior in Southwark in the Countie of Surrey gentlemen on thone parte And Peeter Streete Cittizen and Carpenter of London on thother parte witnesseth That whereas the saide Phillipp Henslowe & Edward Allen the daie of the date hereof Haue bargayned Compounded & agreed wth the saide Peter Streete ffor the erectinge buildinge & settinge upp of a newe howse and Stadge, for a Plaiehowse in and vppon a certeine plott or parcell of grounde appoynted oute for that purpose Scytuate and beinge nere Goldinge lane in the parishe of Ste Giles wthoute Cripplegate of London To be by him the saide Peeter Streete or some other sufficyent woorkmen of his provideinge and appoyntemente and att his propper Costes & Chardges for the consideracon hereafter in theis presentes expressed Made erected, builded and sett upp In manner & forme followeinge (that is to saie) The frame of the saide howse to be sett square and to conteine ffowerscore foote of lawfull assize everye waie square wthoute and fiftie fiue foote of like assize square everye waie wthin, wth a good suer and stronge foundacion of pyles brick lyme and sand, both wthoute & wthin, to be wroughte one foote of assize att the leiste aboue the grounde And the saide fframe to conteine Three Stories in heighth The first or lower Storie to Conteine Twelue foote of lawfull assize in heighth The second Storie Eleuen foote of lawfull assize in heighth And the Third or vpper Storie to conteine Nyne foote of lawfull assize in height All which Stories shall conteine Twelue foote and a half of lawfull assize in breadth througheoute besides a Juttey forwardes in eyther of the saide Two vpper Stories of Tenne ynches of lawfull assize, wth ffower convenient divisions for gentlemens roomes and other sufficient and convenient divisions for Twoe pennie roomes wth necessarie Seates to be placed and sett Aswell in those roomes as througheoute all the rest of the galleries of the saide howse and wth suche like steares Conveyances & divisions wthoute & wthin as are made & Contryved in and to the late erected Plaiehowse On the Banck in the saide parishe of St Saviors Called the Globe Wth a Stadge and Tyreinge howse to be made erected & settupp wthin the saide fframe, wth a shadowe or cover over the saide Stadge, wch Stadge shalbe placed & sett As alsoe the stearecases of the saide fframe in suche sorte as is prefigured in a Plott thereof drawen And wch Stadge shall conteine in length ffortie and Three foote of lawfull assize and in breadth to extende to the middle of the yarde of the saide howse, The same Stadge to be paled in belowe wth good stronge and sufficyent newe oken bourdes And likewise the lower Storie of the saide fframe wthinside, and the same lower storie to be alsoe laide over and fenced wth stronge yron pykes And the saide Stadge to be in all other proporcions Contryved and fashioned like vnto the Stadge of the saide Plaiehowse Called the Globe, Wth convenient windowes and lights glazed to the saide Tyreinge howse And the saide fframe Stadge and Stearecases to be covered wth Tyle, and to haue a sufficient gutter of lead to Carrie & convey the water frome the Coveringe of the saide Stadge to fall backwardes And alsoe all the saide fframe and the Stairecases thereof to be sufficyently enclosed wthoute wth lathe lyme & haire and the gentlemens roomes and Twoe pennie roomes to be seeled wth lathe lyme & haire and all the fflowers of the saide Galleries Stories and Stadge to be bourded wth good & sufficyent newe deale bourdes of the whole thicknes wheare neede shalbe And the saide howse and other thinges beforemencioned to be made & doen To be in all other Contrivitions Conveyances fashions thinge and thinges effected finished and doen according to the manner and fashion of the saide howse Called the Globe Saveinge only that all the princypall and maine postes of the saide fframe and Stadge forwarde shalbe square and wroughte palasterwise wth carved proporcions Called Satiers to be placed & sett on the Topp of every of the same postes And saveinge alsoe that the said Peeter Streete shall not be chardged wth anie manner of pay(ntin)ge in or aboute the saide fframe howse or Stadge or anie parte thereof nor Rendringe the walls wthin Nor seelinge anie more or other roomes then the gentlemens roomes Twoe pennie roomes and Stadge before remembred nowe theiruppon the saide Peeter Streete dothe covenannte promise and graunte ffor himself his executors and administrators to and wth the saide Phillipp Henslowe and Edward Allen and either of them and thexecutors and administrator of them and either of them by theis presentes In manner & forme followeinge (that is to saie) That he the saide Peeter Streete his executors or assignes shall & will att his or their owne propper costes & Chardges well woorkmanlike & substancyallie make erect, sett upp and fully finishe In and by all thinges accordinge to the true meaninge of theis presentes wth good stronge and substancyall newe Tymber and other necessarie stuff All the saide fframe and other woorkes whatsoever In and vppon the saide plott or parcell of grounde (beinge not by anie aucthoretie Restrayned, and haveinge ingres egres & regres to doe the same) before the ffyue & Twentith daie of Julie next Comeinge after the date hereof And shall alsoe at his or theire like costes and Chardges Provide and finde All manner of woorkemen Tymber Joystes Rafters boordes dores boltes hinges brick Tyle lathe lyme haire sande nailes leede Iron Glasse woorkmanshipp and other thinges whatsoever wch shalbe needefull Convenyent & necessarie for the saide fframe & woorkes & eurie parte thereof And shall alsoe make all the saide fframe in every poynte for Scantlinges lardger and bigger in assize Then the Scantlinges of the Timber of the saide newe erected howse, Called the Globe And alsoe that he the saide Peeter Streete shall furthwth aswell by himself As by suche other and soemanie woorkmen as shalbe Convenient & necessarie enter into and vppon the saide buildinges and woorkes And shall in reasonable manner proceede therein wthoute anie wilfull detraccion vntil the same shalbe fully effected and finished In consideracion of all wch buildinges and of all stuff & woorkemanshipp thereto belonginge The saide Phillipp Henslowe & Edwarde Allen and either of them ffor themselues theire and either of theire executors & administrators doe Joynctlle & seurallie Covenante & graunte to & wth the saide Peeter Streete his executors & administrators by theis presentes That they the saide Phillipp Henslowe & Edward Allen or one of them Or the executors administrators or assignes of them or one of them Shall & will well & truelie paie or Cawse to be paide vnto the saide Peeter Streete his executors or assignes Att the place aforesaid appoynted for the erectinge of the saide fframe The full some of ffower hundred & ffortie Poundes of lawfull money of Englande in manner & forme followeinge (that is to saie) Att suche tyme And when as the Tymberwoork of the saide fframe shalbe rayzed & sett upp by the saide Peeter Streete his executors or assignes, Or wthin Seaven daies then next followeinge Twoe hundred & Twentie poundes And att suche time and when as the saide fframe & woorkes shalbe fullie effected & finished as is aforesaide Or wthin Seaven daies then next followeinge, thother Twoe hundred and Twentie poundes wthoute fraude or Coven Prouided allwaies and it is agreed betwene the saide parties That whatsoever some or somes of money the saide Phillipp Henslowe & Edward Allen or either of them or thexecutors or assignes of them or either of them shall lend or deliver vnto the saide Peter Streete his executors or assignes or anie other by his appoyntement or consent ffor or concerninge the saide Woorke or anie parte thereof or anie stuff thereto belonginge before the raizeinge & settinge upp of the saide fframe, shalbe reputed accepted taken & accoumpted in parte of the firste payment aforesaid of the saide some of ffower hundred & ffortie poundes And all suche some & somes of money as they or anie of them shall as aforesaid lend or deliver betwene the razeinge of the saide fframe & finishinge thereof and of all the rest of the saide woorkes Shalbe reputed accepted taken & accoumpted in parte of the laste payment aforesaid of the same some of ffower hundred & ffortie poundes Anie thinge abouesaid to the contrary notwthstandinge In witnes whereof the parties abouesaid to theis presente Indentures Interchaungeably haue sett theire handes and Seales Yeoven the daie and yeare ffirste abouewritten

PS

Sealed and deliured by the saide Peter Streete in the presence of me william Harris Public Scrivener And me frauncis Smyth apprentice to the said Scrivener

[endorsed:]
Peater Streat ffor The Building of the ffortune

III

THE HOPE CONTRACT

THE CONTRACT by Gilbert Katherens with Philip Henslowe and Jacob Meade, dated 29 August 1613, for the demolition and rebuilding of the Hope playhouse provides useful information on building practices. The relevance of this information to the Globe is limited by its late date (1613), by the fact that it refers to a dual-purpose theatre (for animal baiting as well as playing) and by the fact that it belongs to a line of theatre buildings that bypasses the Globe – its model is the Swan, in contrast to the Theatre, Globe I, Fortune, Globe II line. Nevertheless, the detailing of structural arrangements, the use of materials and the dimensions of various joists and posts provide useful analogues for the builder of the reconstructed Globe. The contract's specification that the workmen 'shall also builde the Heavens all over the saide stage' has in addition been influential on scholars studying the extent of the Globe's stage cover.

The transcription here derives from W.W. Greg, ed., *The Henslowe Papers* (London, 1907) I, pp. 19-22. Abbreviations have been expanded and a small number of spellings regularised for the sake of clarity.

Articles Covenauntes grauntes and agreementes Concluded and agreed vppon this Nyne and Twenteithe daie of Auguste Anno Domini 1613 Betwene Phillipe Henslowe of the parishe of St Savior in sowthworke wthin the countye of Surrey Esquire, and Jacobe Maide of the parishe of St Olaves in sowthwork aforesaide waterman of thone partie, And Gilbert Katherens of the saide parishe of St Saviour in sowthworke Carpenter on thother partie, As followeth That is to saie the saide Gilbert Katherens for him, his executors administrators and assignes dothe convenaunt promise and graunt to and wth the saide Phillipe Henslowe and Jacobe Maide and either of them, thexecutors administrators & assigns of them and either of them by theise presentes in manner and forme followinge That he the saied Gilbert Katherens his executors administrators or assignes shall and will at his or theire owne proper costes and charges vppon or before the last daie of November next ensuinge the daie of the date of theise presentes above written, not onlie take downe or pull downe all that Same place or house wherin Beares and Bulls haue been heretofore vsuallie bayted, And also one other house or stable wherin Bulls and horeses did vsuallie stande, Sett lyinge and beinge vppon or neere the Bankesyde in the saide parishe of St Saviour in sowthworke Comonlie Called or knowne by the name of the Beare garden But shall also at his or theire owne proper costes and Charges vppon or before the saide laste daie of November newly erect, builde and sett vpp one other Same place or Plaiehouse fitt & convenient in all thinges, bothe for players to playe Jn, And for the game of Beares and Bulls to be bayted in the same, And also A fitt and convenient Tyre house and a stage to be carryed or taken awaie, and to stande vppon tressells good substanciall and sufficient for the carryinge and bearinge of suche a stage, And shall new builde erect and sett vp againe the saide plaie house or game place neere or vppon the saide place, where the saide game place did heretofore stande, And to builde the same of suche large compasse, fforme, widenes, and height as the Plaie house Called the Swan in the libertie of Parris garden in the saide parishe of St Saviour now is And shall also builde two stearecasses wthout and adioyninge to the saide Playe house in suche convenient places as shalbe moste fitt and convenient for the same to stande vppon, and of such largnes and height as the stearecasses of the saide playehouse called the Swan, nowe are or bee And shall also builde the Heavens all over the saide stage to be borne or carryed wthout any postes or supporters to be fixed or sett vppon the saide stage, And all gutters of leade needfull for the carryage of all suche Raine water as shall fall vppon the same, And shall also make Two Boxes in the lowermost storie fitt and decent for gentlemen to sitt in And shall make the particions betwene the Rommes as they are at the saide Plaie house called the Swan And to make Turned Cullumes vppon and over the stage And shall make the Principalls and fore fronte of the saide Plaie house of good and sufficient oken Tymber, And no furr tymber to be putt or vsed in the lower most, or midell stories, excepte the vpright postes on the backparte of the saide stories (All the Byndinge Joystes to be of oken tymber) The Jnner principall postes of the first storie to be Twelve footes in height and Tenn ynches square, the Jnner principall postes in the midell storie to be Eight ynches square The Jnner most postes in the vpper storie to be seaven ynches square The Prick postes in the first storie to be eight ynches square, in the seconde storie seaven ynches square, and in the vpper most storie six ynches square Also the Brest sommers in the lower moste storie to be nyne ynches depe, and seaven ynches in thicknes and in the midell storie to be eight ynches depe and six ynches in thicknes The Byndinge joistes of the firste storie to be nyne and Eight ynches in depthe and thicknes and in the midell storie to be viij and vij ynches in depthe and thicknes Item to make a good, sure, and sufficient foundacion of Brickes for the saide Play house or game place and to make it xiijteene ynches at the leaste above the grounde Item to new builde, erect, and sett vpp the saide Bull house and stable wth good and sufficient scantlinge tymber plankes and bordes and particions of that largnes and fittnes as shalbe sufficient to kepe and holde six bulls and Three horsses or geldinges wth Rackes and mangers to the same, And also a lofte or storie over the saide house as nowe it is And shall also at his & theire owne proper costes and charges new tyle wth Englishe tyles all the vpper Rooffe of the saide Plaie house game place and Bull house or stable, And shall fynde and paie for at his like proper costes and charges for all the lyme, heare, sande, Brickes, tyles, lathes, nayles, workemanshipe and all other thinges needfull and necessarie for the full finishinge of the saide Plaie house Bull house and stable And the saide Plaiehouse or game place to be made in althinges and in suche forme and fashion, as the saide plaie house called the swan (the scantling of the tymbers, tyles, and foundacion as ys aforesaide wthout fraude br coven) And the saide Phillipe Henslow and Jacobe maide and either of them for them, thexecutors administrators and assignes of them and either of them doe covenant and graunt to and wth the saide Gilbert Katherens his executors administrators and assignes in manner and forme followinge (That is to saie) That he the saide Gilbert or his assignes shall or maie haue, and take to his or theire vse and behoofe not onlie all the tymber benches seates, slates, tyles Brickes and all other thinges belonginge to the saide Game place & Bull house or stable, And also all suche olde tymber whiche the saide Phillipe Henslow hathe latelie bought beinge of an old house in Thames street, London, whereof moste parte is now lyinge in the Yarde or Backsyde of the saide Bearegarden And also to satisfie and paie vnto the saide Gilbert Katherens his executors administrators or assignes for the doinge and finishinge of the Workes and buildinges aforesaid the somme of Three Hundered and three score poundes of good and lawffull monie of England in mannr and forme followinge (That is to saie) jn hande at thensealinge and deliuery hereof Three score pounds wch the saide Gilbert acknowlegeth him selfe by theise presentes to haue Receaued, And more over to paie every Weeke weeklie duringe the firste Six weekes vnto the saide Gilbert or his assignes when he shall sett workemen to worke vppon or about the buildinge of the premisses the somme of Tenne poundes of lawffull monie of Englande to paie them there Wages (yf theire wages dothe amount vnto somuche monie,) And when the saide plaie house Bull house and stable are Reared then to make vpp the saide Wages one hundred poundes of lawffull monie of England, and to be paide to the saide Gilbert or his assignes, And when the saide Plaie house Bull house and stable are Reared tyled [and] walled, then to paie vnto the saide Gilbert Katherens or his assignes, One other hundred poundes of lawffull monie of England And when the saide Plaie house, Bull house and stable are fullie finished builded and done in mannr and forme aforesaide, Then to paie vnto the saide Gilbert Katherens or his assignes, One other hundred Poundes of lawffull monie of England in full satisfacion and payment of the saide somme of £CCClx And to all and singuler the Covenantes grauntes Articles and agreementes above in theise presentes Contayned whiche on the parte and behalfe of the saide Gilbert Katherens his executors administrators or assignes are ought to be observed performed fulfilled and done, the saide Gilbert Katherens byndeth himselfe his executors administrator[s] and assignes, vnto the saide Phillipe Henslowe and Jacob Maide and to either of them, thexecutors administrator[s] and assignes of them or either of them by theise presentes In wittnes whereof the saide Gilbert Katherens hath herevnto sett his hande and seale the daie and yere firste above written

the mark G K of Gilbert Katherens

Sealed and Deliuered in the presence of
witnes Moyses Bowler
Edwarde Griffin

B. THEATRE BUSINESS

PETITION OF BURBAGES TO THE LORD CHAMBERLAIN (1635)

A series of documents reprinted by the Malone Society from the papers of the Lord Chamberlain's office (L.C. 5/133) traces the petitions made by Robert Benfield, Heliard (or Eliard) Swanston and Thomas Pollard to the Lord Chamberlain, the Earl of Pembroke, asking for what they regarded as a more equitable share in the proceeds of the Globe (and the Blackfriars). The petitioners complain that the actors are given insufficient recompense (Benfield and Swanston were members of the King's Men), arguing that while the 'housekeepers' (or investors) share among themselves 'the full moyety of all the Galleries & Boxes in both Houses & of the tireing house dore at ye Globe', the actors, while they 'haue the other moyety with the outer dores', there are more of them (nine) among whom to divide their earnings, and furthermore they are required to defray the costs of the playhouse, including the wages of the hired men and boys, the music expenses and lighting. Among replies to the actors is the answer of the Burbage family, as printed below, which offers a potted history of the business affairs of the Globe and Blackfriars, from their own perspective. The Lord Chamberlain was inclined to require a re-distribution of the shares, and instructed his officers to arrange for this to be done on a fair and sound financial footing.

This transcript is based on that in the Malone Society *Collections* vol. II Part III (Oxford, 1931) pp. 370–72. Abbreviations have been expanded, superscripts regularised and the modern £ sign substituted for the seventeenth century form.

To ye Right Honorable Philip Earle of Pembroke & Montgomery Lord Chamberlaine of his Majestes Houshold.
Right Honorable & our singular good Lord. Wee your humble suppliantes Cutbert Burbage & Winifrid his Brothers wife & wm his sonne doe tender to your honorable consideration for what respectes & good reasons wee ought not in all charity to bee disabled of our liuelyhoodes by men soe soone shott vp, since it hath beene the custome that they should come to it by farre more antiquity and desert, then those can iustly attribute to them selues.
And first humbly shewing to your honor the infinite Charges, the manifold law suites, the leases expiration by the restraintes in sicknes times & other accidentes that did cutt from them the best part of the gaines that yr honor is informed they haue receaued.
The father of vs Cutbert & Richd Burbage was the first builder of Playhowses & was himselfe in his younger yeeres a Player. The Theater hee built wth many Hundred poundes taken vp at interest. The Players that liued in those first times had onely the profitts arising from the dores, but now the players receaue all the comings in at the dores to them selues & halfe the Galleries from the Houskeepers. Hee built this house vpon leased ground, by wch meanes the Landlord & Hee had a great suite in law & by his death, the like troubles fell on vs, his sonnes; wee then bethought vs of altering from thence, & at like expence built the Globe wth more summes of money taken vp at interest, which lay heauy on vs many yeeres, & to our selues wee ioyned those deseruing men, Shakspere Hemings, Condall, Philips and others partners in ye profittes of that they call the House, but makeing the Leases for 21 yeares hath beene the destruction of our selues & others, for they dyeing at the expiration of 3 or 4 yeeres of their lease, the subsequent yeeres became dissolued to strangers as by marrying wth their widdowes & the like by their Children.
Thus Right Honorable, as concerning the Globe, where wee our selues are but Lessees. Now for the Blackfriers that is our inheritance, our father purchased it at extreame rates & made it into a play house wth great charge & trouble, which after was leased out to one Euans that first sett vp the Boyes comonly called the

Queenes Majestes Children of the Chappell. In processe of time the boyes growing vp to bee men which were Vnderwood, Field, Ostler, & were taken to strengthen the Kings service, & the more to strengthen the service, the boyes dayly wearing out, it was considered that house would bee as fitt for our selues, & soe purchased the lease remaining from Evans wth our money & placed men Players, which were Hemings, Condall Shakspeare &c. And Richard Burbage, who for 35 yeeres paines, cost, and Labour made meanes to leaue his wife and Children, some estate (& out of whose estates, soe many of other Players and their families haue beene mayntained) these new men that were neuer bred from Children in the kings service, would take away wth Oathes & menaces that wee shall bee forced, & that they will not thanke vs for it, soe that it seemes they would not pay vs for what they would haue or wee can spare which, more to satisfie your honor then their threatning pride, wee are for our selues willing to part wth a part betweene vs, they paying according as euer hath beene ye custome & ye number of yeeres the lease is made for.

Then, to shew your Honor against these sayinges that wee eat the fruit of their Labours. Wee referre it to your honors iudgement to consider their profittes, which wee may safely maintaine, for it appeareth by their owne Accomptes for one whole yeere last past begining from Whitson-Munday 1634 to Whitson Munday 1635 each of these complainantes gained seuerally as hee was a Player and noe Howskeeper £180, Besides Mr Swanston hath receaued from the Blackfriers this yeere as hee is there a Houskeeper aboue £30, all which beeing accompted together may very well keepe him from starving.

Wherfore your honors most humble suppliantes intreates [sic] they may not further bee trampled vpon then their estates can beare seeing, how deerly it hath beene purchased by the infinite cost & paynes of the family of the Burbages, & the great desert of Richd Burbage for his quality of playing that his wife should not sterue in hir old age, submitting our selues to part wth one part to them for valuable consideration & let them seeke further satisfaccion else where (that is) of the Heires or assignes of Mr Hemings & Mr Condall who had theirs of the blackfriers of vs for nothing, it is onely wee that suffer continually.

Therefore humbly relyeing vpon your honorable Charity in discussing their clamor against vs wee shall, as wee are in duty bound still pray for the dayly increase of your honors health & happines.

II
THE GLOBE BURNS DOWN, 29 JUNE 1613

The burning down of the Globe on 29 June, 1613, was a news event that attracted the attention of a number of commentators, from letter-writers to composers of ballads. I give below a small selection of contemporary descriptions, drawn from E.K. Chambers, *The Elizabethan Stage*, II, pp. 419–23. All agree that the disaster came about as the result of an accident involving a cannon or 'chamber' (the firing-chamber of a cannon) employed in the performance of Shakespeare's *Henry VIII*, and all note the fierce blaze that consumed the playhouse in a relatively short time. The nice touch in Wotton's letter that picks out the single casualty as the spectator's ill-fated breeches nevertheless serves to remind us of the remarkable fire-resistance of the building, a feature on which the modern rebuilding relied, to the eventual satisfaction of the fire authorities.

Howes' continuation of Stowe's Annales, *p. 926*
Upon S. Peters day last, the play-house or Theater, called the Globe, upon the Banck-side near London, by negligent discharging of a peal of ordinance, close to the south-side thereof, the thatch took fire, and the wind sodainly disperst the flame round about, and in a very short space the whole building was quite consumed, and no man hurt; the house being filled with people to behold the play, viz. of Henry the Eighth. And the next spring it was new builded in far fairer manner than before.'

Thomas Larkin to Sir Thomas Puckering, 30 June, 1613
No longer since than yesterday, while Burbage's company were acting at the Globe the play of Henry VIII, and there shooting off certain chambers in way of triumph, the fire catched and fastened upon the thatch of the house, and there burned so furiously, as it consumed the whole house, all in less than two hours, the people having enough to do to save themselves.

Sir Henry Wotton to Sir Edmund Bacon, 2 July, 1613
Now, to let matters of state sleep, I will entertain you at the present with what has happened this week at the Bank's side. The King's players had a new play, called *All is True*, representing some principal pieces of the reign of Henry VIII, which was set forth with many extraordinary circumstances of pomp and majesty, even to the matting of the stage; the Knights of the Order with their Georges and garters, the Guards with their embroidered coats, and the like: sufficient in truth within a while to make greatness very familiar, if not ridiculous. Now, King Henry making a masque at the Cardinal Wolsey's house, and certain chambers being shot off at his entry, some of the paper, or other stuff, wherewith one of them was stopped, did light on the thatch, where being thought at first but an idle smoke, and their eyes more attentive to the show, it kindled inwardly, and ran round like a train, consuming within less than an hour the whole house to the very grounds. This was the fatal period of that virtuous fabric, wherein yet nothing did perish but wood and straw, and a few forsaken cloaks; only one man had his breeches set on fire, that would perhaps have broiled him, if he had not by the benefit of a provident wit put it out with bottle ale.

John Chamberlain to Sir Ralph Winwood, 8 July, 1613
The burning of the Globe, or play-house, on the Bankside, on St. Peter's day, cannot escape you; which fell out by a peal of chambers (that I know not upon what occasion were to be used in the play), the tamplin or stopple of one of them lighting in the thatch that covered the house, burn'd it down to the ground in less than two hours, with a dwelling-house adjoining, and it was a great marvaile and fair grace of God, that the people had so little harm, having but two narrow doors to get out.

A Sonnett upon the pittiful burneing of the Globe playhowse in London

Now sitt the downe, Melpomene,
Wrapt in a sea-cole robe,
And tell the dolefull tragedie,
That late was playd at Globe;
For noe man that can singe and saye
[But?] was scard on St. Peters daye.
Oh sorrow, pittifull sorrow, and yett all this is true.

All yow that please to understand,
Come listen to my storye,
To see Death with his rakeing brand
Mongst such an auditorye;
Regarding neither Cardinalls might,
Nor yett the rugged face of Henry the Eight.
Oh sorrow, &c.

This fearfull fire beganne above,
A wonder strange and true,
And to the stage-howse did remove,
As round as taylors clewe;
And burnt downe both beame and snagg,
And did not spare the silken flagg.
Oh sorrow, &c.

Out runne the knightes, out runne the lordes,
And there was great adoe;
Some lost their hattes, and some their swordes
Then out runne Burbidge too;
The reprobates, though druncke on Munday,
Prayd for the Foole and Henry Condye.
Oh sorrow, &c.

The perrywigges and drumme-heades frye,
Like to a butter firkin;
A wofull burneing did betide
To many a good buffe jerkin.
Then with swolne eyes, like druncken Flemminges,
Distressed stood old stuttering Heminges.
Oh sorrow, &c.

No shower his raine did there downe force
In all that Sunn-shine weather,
To save that great renowned howse;
Nor thou, O ale-howse, neither.
Had itt begunne belowe, sans doubte,
Their wives for feare had pissed itt out.
Oh sorrow, &c.

Bee warned, yow stage-strutters all,
Least yow againe be catched,
And such a burneing doe befall,
As to them whose howse was thatched;
Forbeare your whoreing, breeding biles,
And laye up that expence for tiles.
Oh sorrow, &c.

Goe drawe yow a petition,
And doe yow not abhorr itt,
And gett, with low submission,
A licence to begg for itt
In churches, sans churchwardens checkes,
In Surrey and in Midlesex.
Oh sorrow, pittifull sorrow, and yett all this is true.

Attrib. *William Parrat*

Ben Jonson, in his *Execration upon Vulcan* is another commentator on the burning of the Globe and may have been a spectator of the fire. He refers to the Globe 'Flanked with a ditch, and forced out of a marish', of which nothing was left by the fire but the piles on which it stood. He also mentions that the re-builders had 'wit since to cover it with tiles'.

C. VISITORS' ACCOUNTS

I

REMARKS ON THE LONDON THEATRES BY JOHANNES DE WITT

JOHANNES DE WITT, a Dutch traveller whose European journeys included a visit to London probably in 1596, wrote a series of observations under the title *Observationes Londinenses*. His former fellow-student in Utrecht, Aernout (or Arend) van Buchel copied into his commonplace book an excerpt from the *Observationes*. De Witt's manuscript is now lost, but van Buchel's transcript is extant in Utrecht, and was discovered there in the 1880s by Karl Gaedertz.

The following is an excerpt from van Buchel's transcript, based on E.K. Chambers, *The Elizabethan Stage*, II, pp. 361–2. De Witt offers a description of (old) St Paul's, and refers to tombs in Westminster Abbey, before commenting in this extract on four London theatres, the Theatre and the Curtain north of the river and the Rose and the Swan on Bankside to the south. He also comments on the Bearbaiting arena. He is especially impressed by the newest of these four theatres, the Swan, and attaches to his written comments a sketch of its interior, now famous in reproductions of van Buchel's copy. (*see* fig. 5, p. 29, *above*.) De Witt's remarks are given in their original Latin and in a literal translation.

Amphiteatra Londinij sunt iv visendae pulchritudinis quae a diuersis intersigniis diuersa nomina sortiuntur: in iis varia quotidie scaena populo exhibetur. Horum duo excellentiora vltra Tamisim ad meridiam sita sunt, a suspensis signis ROSA et Cygnus nominata: Alia duo extra vrbem ad septentrionem sunt, viâ quâ itur per Episcopalem portam vulgariter Biscopgat nuncupatam. Est etiam quintum, sed dispari [vsu?] et structura, bestiarum concertationi destinatum, in quo multi vrsi, tauri, et stupendae magnitudinis canes, discretis caueis & septis aluntur, qui [drawing occupies rest of page] ad pugnam adseruantur, iocundissimum hominibus spectaculum praebentes. Theatrorum autem omnium prestantissimum est et amplissimum id cuius intersignum est cygnus (vulgo te theatre off te cijn [off te swan]), quippe quod tres mille homines in sedilibus admittat, constructum ex coaceruato lapide pyrritide (quorum ingens in Britannia copia est) ligneis suffultum columnis quae ob illitum marmoreum colorem, nasutissimos quoque fallere possent. Cuius quidem formam quod Romani operis vmbram videatur exprimere supra adpinxi.

[There are four amphitheatres in London of notable beauty which from their different signs are given different names. In these each day a different play is performed for the people. The two more splendid of them are situated across the Thames to the south, and from the signs hanging before them are called the Rose and the Swan. There are two others outside the city to the north, on the road going through the Bishop's gate, called in the vernacular 'Biscopgat'. There is also a fifth, but of a different [use?] and structure, being given over to animal contests, in which many bears, bulls and dogs of huge size are reared in various dens and cages and kept for fighting, so providing a most entertaining spectacle for the people. The grandest and largest of all the theatres, however, is that whose sign is the Swan (in the vernacular 'the Swan theatre'), which in fact accommodates three thousand people in its seats. It is built of compacted flint stones (of which there is a huge supply in Britain) and furnished with wooden columns which are so painted as to deceive even the most prying. I have drawn it above since it appears to imitate in its shape the form of a Roman structure [theatre]].

II

THOMAS PLATTER VISITS LONDON THEATRES, 1599

THOMAS PLATTER was a young Swiss from Basle, who visited London from 18 September to 20 October, 1599. This is fortunate dating, since the Globe was first erected in 1599, and Platter visited it to see Shakespeare's *Julius Caesar*. Unfortunately he gives us only a glimpse of the performance, but he does provide some interesting details of the Globe and two other theatres, one of which seems to have been the Curtain. Platter's discussion of performance practices, the collection of entrance money and the costuming of the actors is of great interest, even though, as with most documentary evidence of the period, it has to be treated with caution.

The transcription of the original German given here is taken from E.K. Chambers, *The Elizabethan Stage*, II, pp. 364–5. A less literal translation than the one offered here may be found in Peter Razzell, *The Journals of Two Travellers in Elizabethan and Early Stuart England: Thomas Platter and Horatio Busino* (London, 1995), pp. 166–7.

Den 21 Septembris nach dem Imbissessen, etwan umb zwey vhren, bin ich mitt meiner geselschaft über dz wasser gefahren, haben in dem streüwinen Dachhaus die Tragedy vom ersten Keyser Julio Caesare mitt ohngefahr 15 personen sehen gar artlich agieren; zu endt der Comedien dantzeten sie ihrem gebrauch nach gar yberausz zierlich, ye zwen in mannes vndt 2 in weiber kleideren angethan, wunderbahrlich mitt einanderen.

Auf ein andere Zeitt hab ich nicht weit von unserem wirdtshaus in der Vors[t]adt, meines behaltens an der Bischofsgeet, auch nach essens ein Comoedien gesehen, da presentierten sie aterhandt nationen, mit welchen yeder zeit ein Engellender vmb ein tochter kempfete, vndt vberwandt er sie alle, aussgenommen den teütschen, der gewan die tochter mitt kempfen, satzet sich neben sie, trank ihme deszwegen mit seinem diener ein starken rausch, also dasz sie beyde beweinet wurden, vndt warfe der diener seinem Herren den schu an kopf, vnndt entschliefen beyde. Hiezwischen stige der engellender in die Zelten, vnndt entfuhret dem teütschen sein gewin, also vberlistet er den teütschen auch. Zu endt dantzeten sie auch auf Englisch vnndt Irlendisch gar zierlich vnndt werden also alle tag vmb 2 vhren nach mittag in der stadt London zwo biszweilen auch drey Comedien an vnderscheidenen örteren gehalten, damitt einer den anderen lustig mache, dann welche sich am besten verhalten, die haben auch zum meisten Zuhörer. Die örter sindt dergestalt erbauwen, dasz sie auf einer erhöchten brüge spilen, vnndt yederman alles woll sehen kan. Yedoch sindt vnderscheidene gäng vnndt ständt da man lustiger vnndt basz sitzet, bezahlet auch deszwegen mehr. Dann welcher vnden gleich stehn beleibt, bezahlt nur I Englischen pfenning, soer aber sitzen will, lasset man ihn noch zu einer thür hinein, da gibt er noch 1d, begeret er aber am lustigesten ort auf kissen ze sitzen, da er nicht allein alles woll sihet, sondern auch gesehen kan werden, so gibt er bey einer anderen thüren noch I Englischen pfenning. Vnndt tragt man in wehrender Comedy zu essen vndt zu trinken vnder den Leüten herumb, mag einer vmb sein gelt sich also auch erlaben.

Die Comedienspiler sindt beim allerkostlichsten vnndt zierlichsten bekleidet, dann der brauch in Engellandt, dasz wann fürnemme herren oder Ritter absterben, sie ihren dieneren vast die schönesten kleider verehren vndt vergaben, welche, weil es ihnen nicht gezimpt, solche kleider nicht tragen, sondern nachmahlen, den Comoedienspileren vmb ein ringen pfenning ze kaufen geben.

Was für zeit sie also in dem Comoedien lustig alle tag können zubringen, weisset yeglicher woll, der sie etwan hatt sehen agieren oder spilen.

[On the 21st of September, after the mid-day meal, about two o'clock, I and my company went over the water [i.e. across the Thames] and saw in the house with the thatched roof [in dem streüwinen Dachhaus] the tragedy of the first Emperor Julius Caesar quite aptly performed. At the end of the play according to their custom they danced quite exceedingly finely, two got up in men's clothing and two in women's [dancing] wonderfully together.

At another time, not far from our inn in the suburbs, at Bishopsgate according to my memory, again after lunch, I saw a play where they presented different nations with which each time an Englishman struggled over a young woman, and overcame them all, with the exception of the German who won the girl in a struggle, sat down beside her, and drank himself tipsy with his servant, so that the two were both drunk, and the servant threw a shoe at his master's head, and both fell asleep. In the meantime the Englishman crept into the tent, and carried off the German's prize, and thus outwitted the German in turn. In conclusion they danced in English and Irish fashion quite skilfully. And so every day at two o'clock in the afternoon in the city of London sometimes two sometimes three plays are given in different places, which compete with each other and those which perform best have the largest number of listeners. The [playing] places are so constructed that [the actors] play on a raised scaffold, and everyone can see everything. However there are different areas and galleries where one can sit more comfortably and better, and where one accordingly pays more. Thus whoever wants to stand below pays only one English penny, but if he wishes to sit, he enters through another door where he gives a further penny, but if he wants to sit in the most comfortable place on a cushion, where he will not only see everything but also be seen, he gives at another door a further English penny. And during each play things to eat and drink are brought round among the people, of which one may partake for whatever one cares to pay.

The actors are dressed in a very expensive and splendid fashion, since it is the custom in England when notable lords or knights die they bequeath and leave their servants almost the finest of their clothes which, because it is not fitting for them to wear such clothes, they offer [them] for purchase to the actors for a small sum of money.

How much time they can happily spend each day at the play, everyone knows who has seen them act or perform.]

D. PLAYS DESIGNED FOR ORIGINAL PERFORMANCE BY THE CHAMBERLAIN'S-KING'S MEN AT THE FIRST GLOBE, 1599–1608

Richard Hosley (*The Revels History of Drama in English*, vol. III 1576–1613, ed J. Leeds Barroll et al., London, 1975, pp. 181–82) lists twenty-nine plays which he takes to have been designed for original performance at the Globe in the years 1599 to 1608. (The reason for the cut-off date is that the King's Men began to use both the Globe and the indoor Blackfriars from 1609.) These are:

1. Shakespeare, *As You Like It*
2. Jonson, *Every Man out of his Humour*
3. Shakespeare, *Henry V*
4. Shakespeare, *Julius Caesar*
5. Anon., *A Larum for London*
6. Shakespeare, *Hamlet*
7. Shakespeare, *Twelfth Night*
8. Shakespeare, *The Merry Wives of Windsor*
9. Dekker, *Satiromastix*
10. Anon., *Thomas Lord Cromwell*
11. Shakespeare, *Troilus and Cressida*
12. Shakespeare, *All's Well That Ends Well*
13. Jonson, *Sejanus*
14. Anon., *The Merry Devil of Edmonton*
15. Anon., *The London Prodigal*
16. Anon., *The Fair Maid of Bristol*
17. Shakespeare, *Measure for Measure*
18. Shakespeare, *Othello*
19. Shakespeare, *King Lear*
20. Jonson, *Volpone*
21. Shakespeare, *Macbeth*
22. Anon., *A Yorkshire Tragedy*
23. Tourneur (?Middleton), *The Revenger's Tragedy*
24. Barnes, *The Devil's Charter*
25. Shakespeare, *Antony and Cleopatra*
26. Wilkins, *The Miseries of Enforced Marriage*
27. Shakespeare, *Coriolanus*
28. Shakespeare, *Timon of Athens*
29. Shakespeare, *Pericles*